George Crabbe

A Reappraisal

George Crabbe

A Reappraisal

Frank Whitehead

SUP

Selinsgrove: Susquehanna University Press
London: Associated University Presses

Associated University Presses
440 Forsgate Drive
Cranbury, NJ 08512

Associated University Presses
25 Sicilian Avenue
London WC1A 2QH, England

Associated University Presses
P.O. Box 338, Port Credit
Mississauga, Ontario
Canada L5G 4L8

The paper used in this publication meets the requirements
of the American National Standard for Permanence of Paper
for Printed Library Materials Z39.48–1984.

Library of Congress Cataloging-in-Publication Data

Whitehead, Frank S.
    George Crabbe : a reappraisal / Frank Whitehead.
        p. cm.
    Includes bibliographical references and index.
    ISBN 0-945636-70-9 (alk. paper)
    1. Crabbe, George, 1754–1832—Criticism and interpretation.
I. Title.
PR4514.W48   1995
821'.7—dc20   94-38039
                                                                 CIP

PRINTED IN THE UNITED STATES OF AMERICA

Contents

Preface

Much recent writing about the Romantic period in English literature has been marked by a desire to refocus attention outside the traditional canon of "the six great male poets," but as yet this reorientation has not greatly benefited the Reverend George Crabbe. The book that follows is centered on my belief that Crabbe, in his verse-tales in particular, is an important—indeed, a major—poet whose work has been, and still is, seriously undervalued.

After an introductory chapter there follow five chapters that offer a straightforward account of the changes in Crabbe's poetry up to its summit of achievement in 1812. They trace its development from the generalized discursive poetical essays of the 1780s, through the particularized character sketches and anecdotes of *The Parish Register* and much of *The Borough*, to the full-length "verse-tales" that appear first in the later letters of *The Borough* and reach their full maturity in *Tales* (1812). The most important factors leading to this striking change in his poetic practice are outlined, and an attempt is made to specify, as concisely as possible, the characteristics of the mature tales that give them their enduring value and appeal. A further chapter records the gradual decline of his powers as manifested in his two final volumes, *Tales of the Hall* and *Posthumous Tales*.

The second section of the book reopens its subject matter from a set of "slightly altered perspectives" that aim to exemplify what Jerome McGann has extolled as "the critical virtue of certain disciplined discontinuities in literary work."[1] The perspectives embraced in these five chapters cover Crabbe's relationship to the Romantic movement, the question of genre, the concept of "realism," the claim that Crabbe's determinate meanings (often thought to be peculiarly translucent) can be reduced to indeterminacy by a deconstructive approach, and the extent to which "ideology" governed Crabbe's social and poetic outlook. A further, concluding chapter has as its perspective the attempt to set Crabbe's total oeuvre in the context of what we know about his life and personality. The resulting impression that, concealed beneath (yet lending energy to) the calmly controlled surface of his poetic world, there may lie a condition of internal conflict and strain seems to me to make a worthwhile addition to the attractiveness of this fine and still-neglected poet.

Acknowledgments

It was F. R. Leavis's half-dozen pages on Crabbe in *Revaluation* (1936) that first awakened my interest in his poetry. Subsequently I owe a great debt to Denys Thompson for encouraging me to edit in 1955, in a series of which he was general editor, a volume entitled *Selections from Crabbe's Poetry*, which was reprinted four times up to 1968. Later, when I was engaged on my doctoral thesis at University College, London, I also received much valuable suggestion and advice from Professor James Sutherland and from Dr. Lilian Haddakin.

George Crabbe

A Reappraisal

Part I

1

The Last Augustan?

The poetry of George Crabbe has never lacked appreciation from the discerning minority who have actually read it; but as the American critic Walter E. Broman justifiably complained in 1953, for many decades literary historians "read almost nothing except *The Village*, describe[d] Crabbe as an obscure eighteenth-century realist, and abruptly dismiss[ed] him."[1] In reality, of course, this view of Crabbe as a survivor from the Augustan tradition who chanced to live on, out of his element, into the Romantic period leaves out of account all that is most important in Crabbe's life and work.[2] It is true that the non-narrative poetical essays that he published as a young man gained him, in the 1780s, the approval of Dr. Johnson and the patronage of Burke, and that they were followed by a period of twenty-two years during which he lived as a country clergyman in either Leicestershire or Suffolk and published nothing. But throughout these years he was writing incessantly, even though he destroyed almost everything he wrote. And in 1807, in his fifty-third year, he launched into a new writing career with a volume entitled *Poems* that showed clearly (if still in embryonic form) the realistic narrative bent that was to become the dominant feature of a further four substantial volumes of poetry. Unquestionably it is this predominantly narrative poetry of his mature years that must be at the center of any critical consideration of Crabbe. To put it in crudely quantitative terms, the poems that he published during the eighteenth century occupy, in his collected works, little more than a ninth as much space as those that were written after 1800 and published from 1807 on. Qualitatively the preeminence of the nineteenth-century output is even more striking. Clearly it is above all the tales in verse (so highly esteemed by the reading public during the later years of the Napoleonic Wars) on which must rest Crabbe's claim to our attention today.

Since the 1950s some such judgment as this has become almost a commonplace as a result of the publication of some half-dozen books of useful criticism[3] and a similar number of influential articles, all of which concern themselves primarily with the poetry of Crabbe's maturity. To some extent this flurry of critical activity must be attributed to the delayed effect of the seminal few pages on Crabbe in F. R. Leavis's 1936 volume *Revaluation*, with their unequivocal assertion that "it is in the later work, the Tales of the various collections that he [Crabbe] is (or ought to be—for who reads him?) a living classic. . . ." Nevertheless, the Augustan links cannot be shrugged off and should not be underestimated. Leavis himself saw Crabbe's "peculiarly eighteenth-century strength" as "that of a novelist and of an eighteenth-century poet who is positively in sympathy with the Augustan tradition"; and while he described his art as "that of the short-story writer" he commented also that "the Augustan form, *as he adapts it* [my italics], is perfectly suited to his matter and to his outlook." There are, then, certain senses in which we may properly term Crabbe "the Last Augustan" (as Ian Gregor did in 1955 in his titling of an interesting and sensitive essay far removed from the simplicities of the literary historians); yet it should be realized that his poetry has always obstinately resisted easy categorization, being essentially *sui generis*. The fact is that although he had his roots deep in the eighteenth century, his best work must be seen as a strikingly original achievement in a wholly new art form; and the rest of this chapter will be devoted to exploring further the complexities and anomalies implicit in this formulation.

II.

The obvious starting point is, of course, Crabbe's very special stylistic relationship (even in his mature work) to the central Augustan poetic tradition of Dryden, Pope, and Johnson. What could be more Popeian, for instance, than the opening lines of "Arabella," Tale 9 in *Tales* (1812):

> Of a fair town where Doctor *Rack* was guide,
> His only daughter was the boast and pride;
> His *Arabella*, yet not wise alone,
> She like a bright and polish'd brilliant shone;
> Her father own'd her for his prop and stay,
> Able to guide yet willing to obey;
> Pleas'd with her learning while discourse could please,
> And with her love in languor and disease:

(1–8)

Immediately noticeable here are the careful parallelism between line and line, and couplet and couplet; the rhetorical balancing of word against word and idea against idea; the neat and tellingly functional antitheses; and a certain elaborate formality of diction. Clearly, however, the Augustan affinities of the verse go deeper than these surface characteristics and extend indeed to the underlying principle of organization that determines the poetic texture itself. What is evident, in fact, is that the poet's feelings, perceptions, and intuitions are at all times controlled and ordered by his reasoning conscious mind, so that the effect is one of precise measured statement, a sober judicious marshalling of ideas and experience in which each word, each phrase, each element in the formal pattern, can be seen to play its due considered part. This principle of organization extends also to the poet's use of imagery. Thus it is not at all difficult to reason out exactly why the comparison of Arabella to "a bright and polish'd brilliant" is an apt one. It makes clear that her wisdom and learning, far from being heavy or dull, has a sparkling or scintillating quality; it adds a suggestion of personal attractiveness; and it hints also that her accomplishments have been carefully and deliberately cultivated ("polish'd"), and that they are intended for public display. The image may almost be said to invite us to give our conscious attention to just these considerations. What is more, when we have done so, we feel reasonably certain that all these points of resemblance were fully present to the conscious mind of the poet himself. What we have to reckon with is that even when the subject matter, the feeling, or the vocabulary in Crabbe's mature poetry belong to the nineteenth century, the principle that guides and controls his use of words is always Augustan rather than Romantic. In short, the poetic sensibility in question is one that (to quote from Crabbe's own preface to *Tales* [1812]) appeals "to the plain sense and sober judgment" of its readers "rather than to their fancy and imagination."

It can plausibly be argued, however, that Crabbe's relationship to the Augustan age goes even deeper than has so far been brought out. It is fairly common ground that the Augustan tradition in poetry owed its origin to a body of assumptions that were held to be obviously acceptable to all civilized, reasonable human beings. These assumptions were concerned not merely, or even primarily, with questions of literary "good form," but rather with such fundamental issues as the nature and purpose of the universe, and man's duties and obligations to society, to his fellow human beings, and to his Creator. The general tenor of these assumptions is revealed in the unwavering deference paid to such terms as Sense, Reason, Truth, and Nature; and these Augustan "positives" have long been recognized as the common foundation that gave strength to such very different literary achievements as Addison's and Steele's essays, Pope's satires, Gray's "Elegy," and

Dr. Johnson's criticism. In a similar way, Crabbe was able to utilize the Augustan literary tradition as a living force in his poetry only because Augustanism represented for him a living presence in the realm of everyday human behavior. His whole outlook is based on a firm belief in the characteristically Augustan values of sense, judgment, balance and moderation. In religion he upholds "the Faith that Reason finds, confirms, avows"; he suspects zeal and enthusiasm, and regards feeling by itself as an insecure foundation for Christian belief. His morality stresses particularly the virtues of moderation and self-control, and he lays a considerable (but not exclusive) emphasis upon prudence and self-interest as motives for virtuous conduct, though always in a tone that takes for granted that a temperate restrained happiness is the most that man can hope for in his present existence. When he writes of Robert and Susan (in part 1 of *The Parish Register*),

> Blest in each other, but to no excess;
> Health, quiet, comfort, form'd their happiness;
> Love all made up of torture and delight
> Was but mere madness in this Couple's sight

(407–10)

the sedate movement of the verse is in itself enough to tell us that the poet implicitly endorses the attitude he is describing. Even if we met the passage out of its context, we could scarcely fail to realize that "excess" is for Crabbe almost as much a term of reproof as the even more frequently used word "folly." Unmistakably, Crabbe's firm attachment to rational values links him with the Augustan tradition in far more than a purely literary sense.

It should be mentioned at this point that in recent decades the whole concept of eighteenth-century Augustanism has been called into question, particularly by American scholars and critics. In the first place, it has been argued that the term *Augustan* itself, with its implicit invocation of the glories of the golden age of Roman culture under the Emperor Augustus, ignores the fact that Augustus was seen by many English writers in the early eighteenth century as a bloodstained tyrant who had destroyed the balanced constitution of the Roman Republic and established an empire "whose slavery and fall were inherent in its creation."[4] This line of comment had its usefulness in focusing attention upon complexities in the Augustan analogy that earlier critics had tended to gloss over; but these complexities were quite fully explored in the 1960s by both Howard Erskine-Hill and Ian Watt, and their treatment of the issue seems to leave undiminished the value of the term *Augustan* in the contexts we are concerned with. Not only was it used in the period itself by a number of writers from Nicholas Rowe (1706) to Goldsmith (1759), but it also carries within itself some relevant positive connotations that are absent from alternative terms such as *neoclassical*.[5] In the second place it is claimed that *Augustan* had come to be used by literary critics not descriptively but prescriptively, in ways that downgrade non-Augustan eighteenth-century writers as "less interesting and suspiciously aberrant." Concurrently, increasing attention has been paid in recent years (and not only by politically minded or feminist critics) to poets who had previously been somewhat neglected. Thus Roger Lonsdale in his 1984 *New Oxford Book of Eighteenth-Century Verse* unearthed a considerable number of seldom or never previously reprinted poems from the first half of the century, some of them rather feeble, others of real interest, but all decidedly un-Augustan in manner and content. Yet none of this can disturb our recognition of the fact that all the finest poetry of the period belonged to a tradition that can sensibly be described as Augustan. This recognition has quite recently been reaffirmed by Northrop Frye in terms that merit quotation:

> The aspect of the eighteenth century that we associate with Goldsmith's term Augustan is an intensely social aspect: one immediately thinks of the coffee-houses and the various literary circles in what was then, at that social level, the small and gossipy town of London. . . . . Being a trend within a culture, even though a dominant one for much of the period, the Augustan age kept creating, in true Hegelian style, its own opposites, a cultural climate concerned with solitude, melancholy, the pleasures of the imagination, meditations on death and the like. In an early essay I tried to characterise a part of this trend as an "age of sensibility," though the word "age" should not be taken too narrowly. The counter-Augustan trend gradually increases as the century goes on, but such categories are liquid, not solid. Augustans survive to the end of the century. . . .[6]

This clearly gives due credit to the centrality of Augustanism, while at the same time making room for the coexistence with it of other more variegated trends.

Nevertheless it remains true that *Augustan* is a markedly elastic term that can do with rather more specification. As Ian Watt has commented: "The term 'The Augustans,' without any qualifier, makes us think first of the writers who came to prominence after the death of Dryden in 1700—of Addison, Swift, Pope, and their friends."[7] But this, as he went on to point out, is a retrospective application of the term, dating essentially from the late 1750s; and *Augustan* is also frequently used at the other extreme of chronological reference to cover the whole period from the Restoration to the end of the eighteenth century. In recent years the full background to the evocative associations underlying the ambition to recreate in Britain the glories of Augustan Rome has been authoritatively expounded by Howard Erskine-Hill in his book *The Augustan Idea in English Literature* (1983); and there is room here for only a brief recapitulation of some of the aspects relevant to an understanding of Crabbe. In this context only a marginal significance can be attached to that use of the Augustan parallel in which a newly established ruler could be hailed hopefully as an Augustus whose reign might end a period of civil conflict and establish an era of peace in which learning and the arts would be encouraged to flourish. Nevertheless, there can be little doubt that the Augustan period's "consistent collective concern to codify society's positive standards" (Ian Watt's phrase) must be seen as a closing of the ranks after the disturbing upheavals of the seventeenth century and its civil war. Clearly the desire for "Discord" to be succeeded by "Felicity" and "Tranquillity" supplied a strong motive for all men of sense to unite together around an agreed norm—a norm that took as its watchword the slogans of "Reason" and "Nature." Watt has suggested that the values that gave cohesion to the Augustan tradition over such an extended period were essentially those of the landed interest—"the 160 or so temporal peers and the much larger class of gentry, baronets, knights, squires and gentlemen comprising perhaps some 20,000 families"; and this seems plausible, provided at the same time due weight is given to the interpenetration between the landowning elite and the metropolitan center at a time when London, the largest city in Europe, was at the hub of an English culture that was becoming increasing urbanized. Even so, Watt is undoubtedly right in saying that some of the period's most characteristic poetic forms, as well as many of its finest poems, "presuppose an ideal of human civilisation in a rural setting." Thus Pope's "Epistle to Burlington" is, among other things, a supreme celebration of a paternalistic and patrician value system founded on the ideals of social responsibility, benevolence, and philanthropy, a social order in which the owner of an estate, whether large or small, had obligations and duties towards his tenants, his neighborhood and "the poor."[8] And it should not be forgotten that for Pope and his contemporaries these ideals were deeply rooted in sincerely held Christian belief. Reason, Nature, and the "golden mean" were undoubtedly hierarchical and undemocratic in the social forms they enshrined and upheld, but for the early Augustans they had the weight of a strongly felt religious sanction.

It cannot of course be denied that, as the century advanced, the inherent limitations of the Augustan tradition in poetry became more and more evident. Moreover the century's most far-reaching literary innovation, the development of the novel, took place either on the outermost fringe of

Augustanism or actually outside it. The long-continuing dominance of the Augustan tradition, despite these limitations, may most plausibly be attributed to the exceptional stability of eighteenth-century English society and its slow pace of change. Such changes as did take place were destined, however, to have a significant bearing upon the development of Crabbe's writing. Throughout the century the landed interest exerted its political dominance in alliance with the growing power of trade and industry, but in its later decades there was an increasing shift in the balance between the two partners in this alliance, a shift that had as one of its correlates the steady growth of a middle-class public for serious literature. This new miscellaneous reading public, mediated through booksellers and publishers, and no longer confined to the aristocracy or the learned, certainly expanded considerably from the midcentury onward. At the same time it broadened its social base, aided in this by the development of provincial newspapers, the rise in the number of books issued in weekly parts, and the establishment of circulating libraries.[9] The resulting sense of a change in the social composition of the audience for poetry undoubtedly had its influence not only on the selection of personae and subject matter in Crabbe's mature poetry but also upon the values informing their treatment. In the High Augustan period it had been easy for Sir Roger de Coverley to identify as inseparable "the dictates of reason, of religion, of good breeding," but the last-named of the trio must have counted more in the *Spectator's* eyes than it could for Crabbe a century later. Certainly one can hardly imagine Crabbe acquiescing wholeheartedly in Steele's crisply confident reply to a correspondent in search of "the chief qualification of a good poet": "To be a very well-bred man." Crabbe was undoubtedly at one with the *Spectator* writers in their belief that poetry and literature owe an obligation to sustain a whole complex of social and cultural values; but for him these values had become both more plebeian and more democratic. It is noticeable that the most fully Christian characters in *The Parish Register* belong neither to the professional nor to the landowning classes but are quite simply the noble peasant Isaac Ashford and the humble and self-abnegatory village schoolmistress.

With this broadening of the reading public, less significance came to attach to another feature of the high Augustan period that had linked it, in popular belief, with its Roman counterpart—namely, the importance for literature and the arts of aristocratic patronage. Traditionally the cultural achievements of Rome under the Emperor Augustus had been attributed in great measure to his policies of enlightened patronage, executed largely through the agency of his friend Maecenas; and at midcentury Goldsmith, in his essay "An Account of the Augustan Age in England,"[10] had been influenced in his choice of "the reign of Queen Anne, or some years before that period" as England's golden age by his belief that under the ministries of Somers and later Harley (that is, from 1697 to 1714) "patronage was fashionable among our nobility." At that time, he believed, there had "seemed to be a just balance between patronage and the press."

In the past half-century or so, ever since the publication of Namier's pioneering studies of political relationships, it has, of course, often been held that patronage, broadening downwards from the king, from his ministers, and from the nobility, was the key determining factor in English life during the eighteenth century. Certainly aristocratic patronage for literature continued to a surprisingly late date to be of the utmost importance to an aspiring poet, as Crabbe found during his year of hardship in London in 1780–81. His poem *The Candidate*, published anonymously early in 1780, was an appeal (unheeded) for the favorable attention of the *Monthly Review*, but it was not until Edmund Burke had generously taken him under his wing that he began to enjoy any success. His next poem, *The Library* (1781), ends with a tribute to the Duke of Rutland, who the following year appointed the poet as his domestic chaplain at Belvoir Castle; while almost half of book 2 of *The Village* (1783) consists of a rather fulsome eulogy of Rutland's lately deceased younger brother. Again, the final line of *The Newspaper* (1785) contains a complimentary reference to Lord Thurlow, who had given Crabbe two small livings in Dorset in 1783, and to whom the poem is dedicated. Thus at this stage in his career it was the patronage, first of Burke and subsequently of two noblemen, that was decisive in securing Crabbe not only a comfortably assured mode of life as a country clergyman but also a modestly satisfying acclaim as an established poet. But in 1807, when his next volume of poetry appeared, matters were very different. It is true that *Poems* (1807) is prefaced by a dedication to Lord Holland, but the volume's immediate and sweeping success (far above anything his earlier recognition could have led him to expect) was due on this occasion to the uniformly commendatory notices from the critics. Among these, the praise of Jeffrey in the *Edinburgh Review* was decisive, since within two days of the appearance of Jeffrey's enthusiastic notice the whole of the first edition was sold out. Clearly the power to make or break a poet's reputation had now swung away from "patronage" to "the press."

III.

Whatever the weight given to their respective bids for aristocratic patronage, the three poems that Crabbe published under his own name in the 1780s fit in comfortably enough with the prevailing pattern of late Augustan poetic trends. They are extended discursive essays in heroic couplets, mainly didactic in tone, using a diction that is some way removed from that of everyday speech, and for the most part reiterating commonly received opinions, though at the same time adding just enough originality of viewpoint to suggest the emergence of a new poetic voice. In *The Library* the more unexpected touches occur in the lengthy opening preamble that presents books as "the soul's best cure in all her cares." Unfortunately, the discussion is carried on in such elaborately abstract terms that a singular effort of concentration is necessary if the reader is to follow the twists and turns of the argument. After this the poem becomes merely a conducted tour of a library (probably, one has to guess, a wealthy nobleman's family inheritance) progressing through half-a-dozen different sections, starting with Divinity and ending with Criticism. While *The Library* attempts an almost Johnsonian weight of utterance, *The Newspaper* aims at a racy satirical stance in the manner of Pope; it is readable enough, but the targets at which it aims its shafts are too predictable, so that its vivacity of manner comes to seem a little superficial. By contrast with these two poems, *The Village* is seen to have its genuine strengths, most notably in its proclaimed antipastoral determination to "paint the Cot / As Truth will paint it and as Bards will not." However the "Truth" in question is an abstract personification, just as the "Village" has no specific geographic location but is a composite portrayal combining impressions of the barren coastal landscape where "Nature's niggard hand" gives "a spare portion to the famish'd land"; of other more favored scenes, where the laborer's hardships are nevertheless equally severe; and of the sordid workhouse, which may or may not belong to one of the parishes previously mentioned. In fact, the much-quoted passage describing the coastal heath and the description of the workhouse building itself are the only parts of the poem that are at all specific in their detail.

On the other hand, this is the only one of Crabbe's early poems to give any sign of the direction that the poet's talent was later to make peculiarly its own. But even here, in portraying the perfunctory and heartless apothecary or the sporting and negligent parish priest, Crabbe is satisfied at this stage in his development to offer the merest outline-sketch of a type-figure, a mere hint toward a depiction of a figure that is readily subsumed within the generalizing framework of the poem's discursive argument. During the twenty-two years of his poetic silence (from 1785 to 1807) these two sketches were regularly included in the annually revised and widely circulated *Elegant Extracts*, edited by Vicesimus Knox, and along with the description of the parish poorhouse were almost certainly the verses by which Crabbe was then most generally known—a point of some interest, since they do point forward, in however rudimentary a form, to the more rounded-out character sketches of *The Parish Register*.

Nevertheless, it is the wholly unspecific portrayal of "the hoary swain, whose age / Can with no cares except his own engage" that typifies most characteristically the appeal that *The Village* had for the late Augustan taste of its period. (It was indeed with these fifty-odd lines that Edmund Burke opened his 274-line extract from *The Village* in the poetry section of the *Annual Register* for 1783.) Here is a representative extract:

> For yonder see that hoary swain, whose age
> Can with no cares except its own engage;
> Who, propt on that rude staff, looks up to see
> The bare arms broken from the withering tree;
> On which, a boy, he climb'd the loftiest bough,
> Then his first joy, but his sad emblem now.
>
> He once was chief in all the rustic trade;
> His steady hand the straitest furrow made;
> Full many a prize he won, and still is proud
> To find the triumphs of his youth allow'd;
> A transient pleasure sparkles in his eyes,
> He hears and smiles, then thinks again and sighs:
> For now he journeys to his grave in pain;
> The rich disdain him; nay, the poor disdain;
> Alternate masters now their slave command,
> Urge the weak efforts of his feeble hand;
> And, when his age attempts its task in vain,
> With ruthless taunts, of lazy poor complain.
> Oft may you see him, when he tends the sheep,
> His winter-charge, beneath the hillock weep;
> Oft hear him murmur to the winds that blow
> O'er his white locks and bury them in snow,
> When, rous'd by rage and muttering in the morn,
> He mends the broken hedge with icy thorn:
> "Why do I live, when I desire to be
> At once from life and life's long labour free?"

> (1.182–207)

In *Rasselas*, through the voice of Imlac, Johnson had defined the business of a poet as "to examine not the individual but the species"; and it would be hard to imagine a more faithful adherence to this prescription than Crabbe's handling of his unnamed "hoary swain."

It is a far cry from these generalities to the detailed particularization

with which Crabbe introduces (for example) the character of Catharine
Lloyd in *The Parish Register*:

> Down by the Church-way-Walk and where the Brook
> Winds round the Chancel like a Shepherd's Crook:
> In that small House, with those green Pales before,
> Where Jasmine trails on either side the Door;
> Where those dark Shrubs that now grow wild at will,
> Were clipt in form and tantaliz'd with skill;
> Where Cockles blanch'd and Pebbles neatly spread,
> Form'd shining Borders for the Larkspurs' Bed;—
> There liv'd a *Lady*, wise, austere and nice,
> Who shew'd her Virtue by her Scorn of Vice;
> In the dear Fashions of her Youth she dress'd,
> A pea-green *Joseph* was her favourite Vest;
> Erect she stood, she walk'd with stately Mien,
> Tight was her length of Stays and she was tall and lean.
>
> (3.312–25)

Here the specific details have been skilfully chosen to create a highly individualized portrait in a mode very different from that of the earlier poem.
As a further representative example of this particularized mode of character drawing we may quote the opening lines of tale 7 ("The Widow's Tale")
from *Tales* (1812):

> To Farmer *Moss* in Langar Vale came down
> His only Daughter, from her school in town;
> A tender, timid maid! who knew not how
> To pass a pig-sty, or to face a cow:
> Smiling she came, with petty talents grac'd,
> A fair complexion, and a slender waist.
>   Us'd to spare meals, dispos'd in manner pure,
> Her Father's kitchen she could ill endure;
> Where by the steaming beef he hungry sat,
> And laid at once a pound upon his plate;
> Hot from the field, her eager Brother seiz'd
> An equal part, and hunger's rage appeas'd;
> The air surcharg'd with moisture, flagg'd around,
> And the offended damsel sigh'd and frown'd. . . .
>
> (1–14)

In this case the detail renders for us with great economy an individual in a
concrete and vividly realized setting. Moreover, as a further development in

the poet's command of his craft, the situation so deftly evoked of the "school-bred miss" no longer comfortable in her unrefined farmhouse home carries within itself the promise of a story; the implicit conflict of values leads us to wonder immediately (in E. M. Forster's phrase): "What next? What next?"

Even from these limited examples it should be clear that in his mature work, at once narrative, realistic, and particularized, Crabbe has moved some way beyond what could be unquestioningly described as "Augustan." After all, narrative poetry, except in the form of translations, was not gener-ally speaking one of the accepted Augustan modes; even more to the point, realistic narrative verse was virtually nonexistent throughout almost the whole of the eighteenth century. The narrative preoccupation of Crabbe's mature poetry is therefore innovatory in itself. Equally innovatory is his insistence on rendering with a profusion of minutely observed detail both the settings in which the action of his tales takes place and the appearance and clothing of his characters. In the age of Pope and Johnson, as James Sutherland has put it, "the critics were never tired of repeating that it was the poet's duty to avoid the minute and particular and concentrate on the general." By contrast Crabbe now lingers lovingly on "minute particulars" in his descriptions, and his characterization at its best is highly particular-ized, both emotionally and psychologically. Moreover these individualized characters are far from occupying the exalted station in society that would have qualified them, in earlier Augustan eyes, to figure as the central perso-nae in a poem. In *The Borough* Jachin, Ellen Orford, and Peter Grimes, for instance, are among the "poor and humble" who could have been accorded poetic attention by the snobbishly patrician Augustan world of letters only in the guise of a "Bumkin" in a Burlesque. In *Tales* (1812) the protagonists are most typically drawn from the "middle rank" of society (shopkeepers, merchants, sons or daughters of farmers or vicars); but essentially they are ordinary people who could never have gained acceptance as the subject of a serious poem during the first three-quarters of the eighteenth century.

What Crabbe has created, then, in his mature tales is a wholly new art form in which, although the poetic texture remains almost wholly Augustan, the subject matter belongs to the art of the novel and the underlying values display important modifications to their largely Augustan essence. It will help therefore towards a fuller appreciation of the unique flavor of these fine poems if they can be placed more firmly in their literary-historical context, and in particular if some further understanding can be gained of the factors that produced the marked change in Crabbe's poetic practice between 1780–85 and 1807–12.

2

Transitional Influences

The unifying strand that held together almost all eighteenth-century critical theory was the endeavor to reconcile the poet's obligation to imitate nature with his equal obligation to please and instruct his audience. Crabbe never wavered in his attachment to this characteristically Augustan objective, and he seems, in fact, to have been relatively untroubled by any possible contradiction between its twin aspects. Whereas Dr. Johnson in his *Rambler* essay held that great care needs to be taken, on moral grounds, to "distinguish between those parts of nature that are most proper for imitation," Crabbe's position can be fairly represented by the well-known couplet from *The Parish Register*:

> And could I well th'instructive truth convey
> 'Twould warn the Giddy and awake the Gay.
>
> (1.281–82)

This conviction that recording the unvarnished truth will necessarily be "instructive" clearly underlies Crabbe's uncompromising lack of squeamishness in portraying sordid or distasteful aspects of human behavior. Another representative statement is the somewhat laconic description, in the preface to *Poems* (1807), of *The Parish Register* as "an endeavour once more to describe village-manners, not by adopting the notion of pastoral simplicity or assuming ideas of rustic barbarity, but by more natural views of the peasantry, considered as a mixed body of persons, sober or profligate, and hence in a great measure, contented or miserable." While it is unmistakably Crabbe's view that sobriety produces contentment, and profligacy leads to misery, it would be unduly limiting to see his poetic vision in terms merely of a prudential morality. The qualificatory phrase "in a great measure" points to his ability to admit within his conception of human life that which is arbitrary, inexplicable, or seemingly unjust. In the final analysis these baffling inequities would no doubt have to be accepted as constituting a spiritual preparation for "that brighter better world . . . / That souls with souls, when purified, shall share" (*Tales of the Hall*, VII, 785–86); more typically the Christian justification that Crabbe might have recourse to, if pressed, is tacit rather than overt. But here there is surely an important clue to one of his strengths as a poet, in that it absolves him from feeling any need to force his material to fit into a preconceived pattern of rewards and punishments. Secure in his acceptance of the human lot as God in his wisdom has ordained it, he can allow the moral lesson to emerge naturally and organically out of the inner logic implicit in the character or incident he is describing and can explore to the full, in his best work, the complexity of the moral issues raised.

However, as already noted, in the main body of his work Crabbe deals above all with themes, characters, and incidents drawn from ordinary life, and features protagonists who are seldom drawn from anything but the middle or lower ranks of society. In this respect he has clearly come to deviate from the tenets of Augustan critical theory, which found such topics and characters inadmissible in serious poetry. Insofar as they were admitted at all, the critics took the same view as Reynolds did of their introduction into paintings by, for instance, Hogarth—namely, that since "the painters who have applied themselves more particularly to low and vulgar characters" have employed their genius on "low and confined subjects, the praise that we give them must be as limited as its object."[1] It seems likely that Crabbe would have deferred to this view in the 1780s and might indeed have shared it. If so, what were the later changes in poetic practice that may have helped to change his mind?

The earliest would have been the example of Cowper's long meditative-conversational poem *The Task* (1785). Interspersed among the natural scenery that forms the main topic of Cowper's discursive musings, there are some descriptive sketches of the human occupants of the countryside—in book 1 the gypsies, in book 4 the bearer of the postbag and the waggoner, in book 5 the woodman—that strike a new note of homely realism, influential in its assumption that the ordinary and mundane aspects of rural life could form an appropriate subject matter for serious poetry.[2] In the next decade and a half, poor or unexalted characters and ordinary commonplace incidents figured in the verse published by a number of minor poets.[3] Later, and more importantly, there was the impact of *Lyrical Ballads*, and in particular of those poems in it by Wordsworth in which (to use Coleridge's well-known *Biographia Literaria* account)

> subjects were to be chosen from ordinary life; the characters and incidents were to be such as will be found in every village and its vicinity where there

is a meditative and feeling mind to seek after them, or to notice them, when they present themselves.

Modern scholarship has, of course, tended to undermine the traditional view of *Lyrical Ballads* as "a revolution in poetry . . . completely new.." A significant contribution has been that of Robert Mayo, who showed from a study of the poetry of the magazines between approximately 1788 and 1798 that Wordsworth's ballads were not completely different from contemporary taste in subject or form, but that they embraced the heterogeneous types of poem fashionably new in the 1790s. For the present purpose, Mayo's main point is that

> most of the objects of sympathy in the volume belong to an order of beings familiar to every reader of magazine poetry—namely, bereaved mothers and deserted females, mad women and distracted creatures, beggars, convicts, and prisoners, and old people of the depressed classes, particularly peasants.[4]

Some of these typical "magazine poetry" figures appear in Crabbe as well as Wordsworth, so that it will be worth touching briefly on two examples.

Wordsworth's "Convict" first appeared in the *Morning Post* for 14 December 1796; and Mary Jacobus has shown that whereas an earlier unpublished version set "the prisoner's despair against an ironic account of the war-crimes that are not only tolerated, but endorsed, by society," these Godwinian protests against political injustice were omitted in the *Morning Post* version to leave only a philanthropic plea for transportation.[5] Analogues for this tamer version, Jacobus comments, abound in contemporary "magazine poetry," offering a somewhat complacent picture of the operation of British justice. A very early example of the stereotype can be traced back as far as Henry Mackenzie's widely read novel *The Man of the World* (1773), where in chapter 19 the younger Annesley is sentenced to death for a robbery in a nighttime street, in which he had clapped a pistol to the breast of his victim and threatened him with instant death. The judge, after investigation of Annesley's previously blameless history, exercises a clemency that the novelist commends unreservedly and gives him a pardon "on the condition of his suffering transportation for the term of fourteen years." Crabbe's version occurs in letter 23 of *The Borough* (lines 227–332) and the seriousness of the crime—a highway robbery with, again, threats of violent death—does not allow Crabbe to accept the possibility of mercy for the criminal; however, the vivid imaginative insight with which he enters into the consciousness of a man condemned to death does seem to suggest a powerful, if suppressed, emotional protest against the horror of the convict's situation.

Interestingly, Mackenzie's first novel, *The Man of Feeling* (1771), provides a very early version of another recurrent type-figure—that of the young woman thwarted in love who loses her reason as a result. Unfortunately, Mackenzie's picturesque Bedlam inmate is portrayed with (to borrow Jacobus's phraseology) "modish Shakespearean poignancy" and "pretty pathos." A more restrained truthfulness can be felt in Cowper's vignette of "craz'd Kate' in book 1 of *The Task*, where the victim has started out from a lower rung in the social ladder:

> There often wanders one, whom better days
> Saw better clad, in cloak of satin trimm'd
> With lace, and hat with splendid ribband bound.
> A serving maid was she and fell in love
> With one who left her, went to sea and died.

(543–47)

This "Crazy Kate" passage was frequently excerpted as an independent poem, and may have played an important role as forerunner of Wordsworth's Margaret in "The Ruined Cottage." Though written in 1797–98, this was not published until 1814 as part of book 1 of *The Excursion*, and was not therefore available to serve as a model for Crabbe's poetic development; it is relevant, however, as an indicator of the shift in attitude during the 1790s toward the admissibility of constructing stories in verse about the lives of ordinary people. A further variant (which Crabbe may well have known) was Southey's "Hannah, A Plaintive Tale," the magazine version of which, after first appearing in the *Monthly Magazine* for September 1797, was subsequently widely reprinted in other magazines. In this version Hannah

> bore unhusbanded a mother's name
> And he who should have cherish'd her, far off
> Sail'd on the seas, self-exiled from his home;
> For he was poor . . .[6]

The predominant effect is one of pathos, Southey having accurately gauged just that blending of sentimental feeling and limited narrative development that could be relied upon to appeal to the taste of his audience. When Crabbe later took up a closely similar theme in his portrayal of Lucy the Miller's daughter (*The Parish Register*, 1.277–402) his treatment of it comes near, in its own way, to matching Wordsworth's Margaret in its fidelity and restraint as well as in its accumulation of convincing detail.

The drift of these two instances, then, is to illustrate the fact that by the 1790s character sketches, narrative fragments, and verse anecdotes—sometimes melodramatic, often humanitarian in their sentiment, often dealing with humble characters in an increasingly realistic way—formed a significant minority tradition in the verse published in the magazines. Wordsworth's experiments in the same genre, so much more powerful as poetry than their precursors, must have done something to make acceptable in verse such treatment of ordinary people and everyday incident; though it is uncertain when, and to what extent, Crabbe gained awareness of this.

However, in addition to these changes in the literary climate, some influence must clearly be attributed to Crabbe's pastoral experience of human behavior in a succession of country parishes (Stathern, Muston, Parham, Glemham, and Rendham) over twenty-odd years. Indeed, we cannot ignore (even though we cannot take it quite at its face value) the poet's own explicit testimony that firsthand observation had always been the main (almost, he even seems to suggest, the sole) source of his inspiration. In a letter to Mrs. Leadbeater dated "Trowbridge, 1st of 12th month, 1816" he wrote:

> But your motive for writing to me was your desire of knowing whether my men and women were really existing creatures, or beings of my own imagination . . . . Yes, I will tell you readily about my creatures, whom I endeavoured to paint as nearly as I could and dared; for, in some cases, I dared not. This you will readily admit: besides, charity bade me be cautious. Thus far you are correct: there is not one of whom I had not in my mind the original; but I was obliged, in some cases, to take them from their real situations, in one or two instances to change even the sex, and, in many, the circumstances. (*Life*, 221)

Besides this generalized statement we have information about the provenance of Crabbe's characters from the poet's son, who asserted and identified real-life counterparts for some twenty-five of them. As will emerge later, what cannot be swallowed whole in this connection is Crabbe's (indubitably honest) conviction that "he seldom takes anything from books but all from what he sees and hears,"[7] since it can be shown that in a number of cases the real-life "original" has in the poem been fused with traits or details drawn from literature, particularly from eighteenth-century novels. Nevertheless, there can be no doubt that Crabbe's pastoral experience gave him a vast store of impressions that he drew upon to good purpose in his later writings; and although the twenty-five "originals" occupied quite varied stations in life, the majority of them were of unexalted rank, confirming our expectation that, given Crabbe's circumstances as country clergyman, the practice of "drawing from life" would inevitably lead him towards what Reynolds would have called "low and confined subjects."

The second aspect of Crabbe's changed poetic practice that needs discussion here is his markedly increased use of particularized detail, both in his descriptions and in his characterization. There can be no doubt that this proliferation of descriptive detail, whether drawn from firsthand observation or from sources in literature, has to be seen as a departure from the main body of Augustan critical theory. If we take Dr. Johnson as the key representative of mid-eighteenth-century opinion, we shall probably think first of his addiction in his own poetry to "the grandeur of generality" (surely more pronounced than that of any other important poet), and then of such dicta as his oft-quoted generalization that "Nothing can please many and please long but just representation of general nature." In the original context this is coupled with the further line of reasoning (skilfully combining the mimetic criterion with the pragmatic criterion of effect upon the audience) that "Particular manners are known to few and therefore few only can judge how nearly they are copied." Fairness to Johnson demands a more inclusive view than this, however, and the following summing-up by Abrams seems to be as balanced a judgment as we are likely to find:

> Read completely rather than in selected passages, then, Johnson may be said to locate the highest and rarest excellence in the representation of the individualised type, the circumstantially general, and the novel-familiar. Nevertheless, Johnson, and still more Reynolds, Hurd, and other advocates of what A. O. Lovejoy calls "uniformitarian" aesthetics give the more prominent place to the second term in each of these pairs of contraries; the norms that loom largest, as we read through his applied criticism, are the typical, the general, and the familiar.[8]

Nor in his later years was there any weakening of his bias in favor of generality. We need only quote from his *Life of Cowley* (1777) the unhesitating assertion that "Great thoughts are always general, and consist in positions not limited by exceptions, and in descriptions not descending to minuteness." It seems clear that in regard to the portrayal of character, Johnson would to the end of his life have assigned to the poet the same duty as his friend Reynolds assigned to the painter, namely, that of aiming at "the common idea and central form which is the abstract of the various individual forms belonging to a class."[9]

Was there, nevertheless, in the closing decades of the century any increased critical tolerance of "particularity" in characterization that may be thought to have had an influence on Crabbe's practice? It has to be remembered, of course, that in eighteenth-century literature the art of particularized characterization grew up largely outside the borders of neoclassicism. It grew up in the new form of the novel, which was pioneered above all by two writers, Defoe and Richardson, with singularly little interest in any form of critical theory, and in regard to which serious critical discussion was slow to develop. However, one critic has made out a case for detecting in the later years of the century a tendency in critics (in Kames, in Blair, in a letter written by Horace Walpole in 1784) to look with increasing favor upon particularized character drawing, even though what is most usually desiderated is a fusion of the particular with the general, or of the individual with the class.[10] Even Reynolds, for all his attachment to "the general and invariable ideas of nature" was "ready to allow that some circumstances of minuteness and particularity frequently tend to give an air of truth to a piece, and . . . therefore cannot wholly be neglected"; in one of the later Discourses he actually went so far as to say that "he that does not at all express particulars, expresses nothing."[11]

Now, Crabbe's characterization, from *The Parish Register* onwards, does for the most part fit quite closely this prescription for a fusion of the particular and the general. The details, though sometimes rather too numerous, are accurate in themselves and at the same time tellingly chosen in such a way as to create a character that we recognize as at once highly individual, typical of a given social class or group at a given point in time, and also typical in a more general way of some universal aspect of human nature. There is, in fact, to borrow Reynolds's words, a "peculiar nicety of discernment" in "the disposition of these minute circumstantial parts." Nevertheless, Crabbe's character portrayal, in *The Parish Register* and later, attracted even from critics who were generally favorable a considerable weight of adverse comment on the grounds of excessive minuteness. Thus Jeffrey's unsigned notice in *Edinburgh Review*, April 1808, while highly appreciative in general tone, writes as follows of "the series of portraits" in *The Parish Register*:

> They are selected, we think, with great judgment, and drawn with inimitable accuracy and strength of coloring. They are finished with much more minuteness and detail, indeed, than the more general pictures in *The Village*, and, on this account, may appear occasionally deficient in comprehension or in dignity. They are, no doubt, executed in some instances with a Chinese accuracy; and enter into details that many readers may pronounce tedious and unnecessary.

The complaint about excessive detail was picked up and echoed by subsequent reviewers with monotonous insistence in such phrases as "Dutch minuteness," "useless particulars," and "feeble minutiae." It is fair to say that in general these reviewers' dissatisfaction related to what they regarded as Crabbe's failure to subordinate his fondness for minute detail to the over-riding main intention of his poem, an objection that is acceptable enough in principle. However, Jeffrey's use of the word "dignity" in the extract quoted above may suggest that there was also at work a feeling that a degree of particularity that would be acceptable in a novel ought not to be tolerated in the medium of poetry. In any event, the persisting weight of conservative critical opinion on this issue seems to show us Crabbe forging his highly particularized mature style in opposition to prevailing critical theory—and customary practice—rather than in concurrence with changes in it.

A third innovative feature of Crabbe's later poetic practice is his development of a predilection for narrative, of which there had been virtually no sign in his published writings as a young man. Apart from translations there had, of course, been little place for narrative verse in the Augustan tradition. It is true that the "metrical tale" had maintained a sporadic existence somewhere on the fringe of the literary scene, but it was never mentioned by the critics and was not accorded the status of a poetic "kind." One can search through the works of some poet of the period, forgotten or otherwise, and find commonly one or two narrative pieces, often quite short, buried among a considerable volume of non-narrative writing. Moreover, apart from the "progress piece" (to be returned to later in connection with *The Borough*), such narrative pieces as were written were too disparate to be fitted into any consistent scheme of classification. Yet during the eighteenth century there had been developing a vastly increased appetite for prose narrative; this included on the one hand biography, ranging from translations of Plutarch to newly written lives of criminals, politicians, and men of letters, and on the other the self-proclaimed fictions of the newly emergent novel. It might be expected that this interest would have spilled over into the sphere of poetry; but such development seems to have been slow to take place. Admittedly, there were from the 1780s onward some signs of a new trend in which high-flown sentiment and highly melodramatic incident had been imported into tales in verse from the more sensational prose fiction of the period;[13] but these do not have much relevance to the path taken by Crabbe. Nevertheless, there were a few forerunners to Crabbe's narratives, notably a poem by Langhorne published in the 1770s and a number of poems published by Wordsworth, Southey, and Robert Bloomfield around the turn of the century. Because of their importance, discussion of these will be reserved to the next chapter.

The extent to which Crabbe himself was influenced by, and has built upon, prose fiction remains a little uncertain. He was unquestionably an extremely widely read man with an extensive and varied library in his rectory at Trowbridge; and the prefatory quotations to his poems testify to a wide knowledge of Latin and English classical authors, as well as to an intimate acquaintance with Shakespeare's plays. According to his son he was also an inveterate reader of fiction, and in the boxes of books from the circulating library out of which he regularly read aloud to his family it seems that nineteen out of twenty were novels. This acquaintance with the more ephemeral novelists of his own day—not merely those whose names are still remembered, such as Maria Edgeworth, Charlotte Smith, and Mrs. Radcliffe, but also those now completely forgotten, such as Mrs. Elizabeth Bonhote and Mrs. Helme—is displayed in letters 15 and 20 of *The Borough*, though in a tone quizzically critical of their excesses. We may accept Crabbe's son's comment that "even from the most trite of these fictions he could sometimes catch a train of ideas that was turned to excellent use"; but note at the same time that the novels he thought worth purchasing for his own library were those of Richardson, Fielding, and Smollett. Clearly it must have been the "formal realism" (Ian Watt's term) of this first generation of English novelists that played a part in making possible Crabbe's own brand of realistic narrative, and not the gothic or sentimental miasma in which the novel lost itself during the last quarter of the eighteenth century.

This chapter has attempted to trace some of the changing circumstances that facilitated Crabbe's adoption in his middle age of a poetic style and content strikingly different from that of his early manhood. His extensive encounters with ordinary people, the enhanced understanding of their problems and joys gained in his contacts with them as parish priest; his wide reading in the novel, as well as in poetry and the classics; the relaxation of critical theory in relation to the "poetic kinds"; the increasing tendency to present in poetry ordinary and even quite humble personages, to describe them with an increasing particularization of detail, and to present them in some sort of narrative frame—such strands seem likely to have given support to him in his gropings towards a radically new poetic mode, making thinkable in his fifties things that would have been unthinkable in his twenties and thirties. Even so, it would be misleading to give the impression that in his poetic development he was in any sense merely swimming with the tide of cultural change, for there can be no doubt that a very considerable creative effort must have been needed in order to forge this new poetic form.

3

Immediate Precursors

Unfortunately, there is no firm evidence that Crabbe had actually read the poems to be considered in this chapter, though in some cases the probability seems fairly strong. John Langhorne's *Country Justice*, for instance, was both widely read and widely available for several decades after its first publication in 1774, having been reprinted as part of the author's *Poetical Works* in 1776 and again in 1804, as well as having been included in 1793 in vol. 11 of Anderson's *Complete Edition of the Poets of Great Britain*. Wordsworth wrote of it in a letter of 15 January 1837: "As far as I know it is the first Poem . . . that fairly brought the Muse into the Company of Common Life. . . ." Moreover, it has been thought by several commentators to have had some influence on Crabbe's writing, particularly in *The Village*.[1]

Langhorne was, like Crabbe, a country clergyman as well as a poet, and the greater part of his poetic output is typically of the eighteenth century in its static, generalizing and "literary" mode. In *The Country Justice*, however, he seems to have felt a strong involvement in the poem's concern to offer a country magistrate sound advice as to his duties, and this enabled him to achieve a unity and consistency in his poetic rhetoric that was considerably above his customary level. In addition to the natural yet pointed use of the heroic couplet, and the general tone (reasonable, humane, morally serious), which often puts one in mind of Crabbe, there are in this long discursive poem two narrative episodes that in their length, shape, and detailed realization seem to be pointing forward to *The Parish Register*. Thus in the episode in part 1 about the fortune-telling gypsy there is certainly a flavor suggestive of Crabbe in the concision of Langhorne's warning couplet:

> But ah! ye Maids, beware the Gypsy's Lures!
> She opens not the Womb of Time, but yours.

The incident develops, moreover, with an amount of particularized detail that suggests the Crabbe of 1807 rather than the Crabbe of 1783. The two willing victims of the gypsy's predictions are Marian, the parson's maid, and Villaria, the parson's daughter, who has long

> sigh'd to know
> What Vellum's sprucy Clerk, the Valley's Beau,
> Meant by those Glances which at Church he stole,
> Her father nodding to the Psalm's slow Drawl. . . .

> (1.207–10)

The episode continues with an élan that merits quotation:

> Where, in the darkling Shed, the Moon's dim Rays
> Beam'd on the Ruins of a One-Horse Chaise,
> Villaria sat, while faithful Marian brought
> The wayward Prophet of the Woe she sought.
> Twice did her Hands, the Income of the Week,
> On either side, the crooked Sixpence seek;
> Twice were those Hands, withdrawn from either side,
> To stop the titt'ring laugh, the Blush to hide.
> The wayward Prophet made no long Delay,
> No novice she in Fortune's Devious way!
> "Ere yet," she cried, "ten rolling months are o'er,
> Must ye be Mothers; Maids at least, no more . . ."
> Smote to the heart, the Maidens marvell'd more,
> That Ten short Months had such Events in store;
> But holding firm what Village-Maids believe,
> That Strife with Fate is milking in a Sieve;
> To prove their Prophet true, though to their Cost,
> They justly thought no Time was to be lost.

> (1.215–36)

The other narrative element embodies Langhorne's attack on "the sly, pilfering, cruel Overseer," and has as its high point a contrast between the "Ruffian Officer" (i.e., the Overseer), who turned away from the parish-bounds a vagrant and starving mother, and the Felon who saw the same mother lying dead with her baby barely alive on her breast and sacrificed his own chance of escape from the law to the human duty of saving the infant's life by taking it to the nearest cottage for succor. The narrative manner here is less closely akin to anything in Crabbe, but the underlying humanitarian feeling is one to which Crabbe would have responded without reserve. Taken as a whole, *The Country Justice* is a transitional poem, rooted mainly in the poetic practice of the Augustan era, yet containing within it elements of narrative realism, of particularization, and of humanitarian concern for the poor and humble that look forward to later developments.

We shall not dwell on the cameos in the magazine poetry of the 1790s that served as a nursery for the narrative or seminarrative poems of ordinary life in *Lyrical Ballads*, since Wordsworth's own contribution is so outstandingly important as to need discussion at some length. The originality with which he handled the narrative form was in part a matter of his refusal to remain outside the personae (as Southey remains outside his Hannah) and his insistence on trying to achieve an identification with them through the adoption of "the real language of men." As he put it in the 1802 version of *The Preface*:

> [I]t will be the wish of the Poet to bring his feelings near to those of the persons whose feelings he describes, nay, for short spaces of time perhaps, to let himself slip into an entire delusion, and even confound and identify his own feelings with theirs. . . .

We may think Wordsworth has achieved this aspect of his innovatory ambition in, say, "The Last of the Flock" (probably written in 1798); perhaps elsewhere, however, the approach does sometimes become vulnerable to the aspersion of "ventriloquism," a hazard that Coleridge came later to feel his collaborator had not entirely escaped.

It is important to understand that elsewhere also it became part of Wordsworth's experimentalism to question the very nature of narrative, a challenge to "our own pre-established modes of decision" that becomes explicit towards the end of "Simon Lee" (also probably written in 1798) when the poet turns to the reader and bids him reexamine the expectations aroused by the use of a ballad idiom:

> My gentle reader, I perceive
> How patiently you've waited,
> And I'm afraid that you expect
> Some tale will be related.
>
> O reader! had you in your mind
> Such stores as silent thought can bring,
> O gentle reader! you would find
> A tale in every thing.
>
> What more I have to say is short,
> I hope you'll kindly take it;

> It is no tale; but should you think
> Perhaps a tale you'll make it.
>
> (69–80)

In this case the incident, small in itself, is indeed one of those that Wordsworth uses, in Hazlitt's words, "merely as pegs or loops to hang thought and feeling on"; and we are reminded inevitably of the assertion in the 1800 *Preface* that one circumstance distinguishing *Lyrical Ballads* from "the popular Poetry of the day . . . is that the feeling therein developed gives importance to the action and situation and not the action and situation to the feeling." Wordsworth himself cites "Poor Susan" and "The Childless Father" as examples of his meaning here. From our position of hindsight we might perhaps feel that the ultimate in this subversion of the established narrative is achieved in "Strange fits of passion." In any event, it seems clear that in many of the poems in *Lyrical Ballads* (1798), and even more so perhaps in the second volume of 1800, Wordsworth was engaged in turning the conventionally established relationship between incident and feeling virtually on its head.

One example of a poem in which this procedure is evidently at work, but less evidently successful, is "The Thorn," Wordsworth's reworking in his own highly individualistic terms of a theme we have already noted to be common enough from Cowper onward—that of the incautious maiden betrayed and deserted, and possibly losing her reason. From the rambling soliloquy of the "loquacious narrator," all we learn with certainty is that twenty-two years earlier Martha Ray was betrothed to Stephen Hill and the wedding day was fixed,

> But Stephen to another maid
> Had sworn another oath
> And with this other maid to church
> Unthinking Stephen went. . . .

It is established for us also that Martha now regularly visits in all weathers an aged, stunted thorn high on a mountain ridge, and sits there beside it. Adjoining it is a small muddy pond and a mossy mound. Everything else—whether she bore a child, if so what happened to it, whether the mound is an infant's grave, even whether she is actually insane—remains a series of questions, rumors, speculations, superstitious gossip. The subversion of the established narrative mode has been so thoroughgoing that the poet himself seems to have taken fright and added as a defensive rationalization of his procedure a prose character sketch of the alleged narrator that only confuses the issues further. On the whole, "The Thorn" seems to be one of those poems in which Wordsworth's control of tone is too uncertain to justify fully his poetic experiment; but it does indicate how far he was prepared to go in his subordination of "action and situation" to "feeling." A further example of the direction in which he was moving as a poet appears in the three different versions of "Old Man Travelling." In 1798 the closing lines of this sketch read:

> I asked him whither he was bound, and what
> The object of his journey; he replied
> "Sir! I am going many miles to take
> A last leave of my son, a mariner
> Who from a sea-fight has been brought to Falmouth
> And there is dying in an hospital."

In the 1800 edition these last four lines were distanced in their effect by turning them into indirect speech, and the title of the poem was changed into what had formerly been its subtitle: "Animal Tranquillity and Decay; A Sketch." In 1815 the final six lines were omitted entirely, thus leaving the "feeling" wholly detached from its original fragmentary narrative context.

Narrative then, for Wordsworth, came less and less to hold a place anywhere near the center of his poetry; rather, it was made use of to focus attention on a moral sentiment or to induce a feeling in the reader. Out of twenty-three poems in *Lyrical Ballads* (1798) there were twelve by Wordsworth that were in some sense narrative; the 1800 volume (volume 2) included among its thirty-seven poems fifteen that may be said to have some narrative element; while in *Poems in Two Volumes* (1807), a further seven such poems were included. By this time the impulse toward narrative had spent itself, and after 1807 Wordsworth wrote virtually no more realistic narratives. Similarly, Wordsworth's attachment to the real language of men had begun to weaken, so that in two important respects Wordsworth's movement over this period was in precisely the opposite direction to that which Crabbe was following. It would be a mistake, nevertheless, to underestimate the importance of Wordsworth's narrative experiments, even though he rapidly moved beyond them. In their immediate impact they puzzled many readers; but as Mayo points out, some of them were widely reprinted in the magazines. As their poetic qualities began to gain recognition, they must have had a profound influence in further accustoming the reading public to an acceptance of everyday life and ordinary incident as a possible subject matter for poetic treatment.

Points of contact with Crabbe's own early narrative experiments are observable in the two "Pastoral Poems" in volume 2 of *Lyrical Ballads*, namely "The Brother" and "Michael" (both comparatively fully developed narratives). In its form (almost entirely that of a dialogue between the priest of Ennerdale and Leonard, the mariner who has returned home after twenty years at sea) "The Brothers" seems to owe something to Southey's *Botany Bay Eclogues;* the feeling, however, is wholly Wordsworthian, with its accentuation of the intimate relationship between the development of character and the natural environment that fosters it. But an uneasy artificiality of tone is introduced into the dialogue by Leonard's decision to withhold the disclosure of his identity, and while the leisurely and expansive exposition of past events that results goes some way to counteract the reader's uneasiness, the culminating incident (the death, revealed retrospectively, of Leonard's brother James, and the manner of his death) is not untinged with melodrama. The "tale" within the poem does deal nevertheless with material that Crabbe was to use more than once (most notably in "The Parting Hour," tale 2 of *Tales* [1812]); and although it could not be claimed that Wordsworth's *central* purpose was to "tell a story," the narrative element has importance for its own sake as well as for the feelings evoked by it. "Michael" at first sight seems more unequivocally narrative in character; and indeed Wordsworth proclaims at the outset his intention to relate a "story" or a "Tale," saying of it,

> this Tale, while I was yet a boy
> Careless of books, yet having felt the power
> Of Nature, by the gentle agency
> Of natural objects led me on to feel
> For passions that were not my own, and think
> (At random and imperfectly indeed)
> On man, the heart of man and human life.
>
> (27–33)

The greater part of the poem does indeed move forward in a straightforwardly sequential and detailed narrative style, portraying Michael's earlier life, the thrift and industry of his household, his love for his son Luke, the misfortune that fell upon them, the reasoning that led to the decision to send Luke out into the world, and the symbolic compact between Luke and his father when Luke lays the first stone of the sheepfold. At this point, however, we are reminded of the poet's initial designation of the story as one "ungarnish'd with events"; for what one might expect to be the climactic incident of the poem is, by contrast, huddled into a brief five-and-a-half lines, and allowed to happen "offstage," as it were, and with a singular lack of specificity:

> Meantime Luke began
> To slacken in his duty, and at length
> He in the dissolute city gave himself
> To evil courses: ignominy and shame
> Fell on him, so that he was driven at last
> To seek a hiding-place beyond the seas.
>
> (451–56)

It now becomes clear that the function of the lengthy narrative has in fact been to highlight for us, and to enable us to empathize with, the feelings of Michael after this catastrophe—an empathy brought to a focus in the pity excited "in every heart" by the belief that "many and many a day" he went to the still unfinished sheepfold "And never lifted up a single stone" (475) .

The narrative in the poem is thus seen to be only an unusually long and extended "peg or loop" (in Hazlitt's phrase) to hang thought and feelings on. It must be said, however, that it is often read as a story existing in its own right, and that the exceptionally full and detailed realism of the earlier part (almost more copious than is called for by the requirements of the poem, one might feel at times) could well have been seen by Crabbe as a precedent justifying his own tendency to an accumulation of detail in his description of domestic scenes from ordinary life.

There is one other poem in *Lyrical Ballads* (1798) that Crabbe, if he read it, would be likely to have found congenial to his temperament. This is "The Female Vagrant," a sequence of thirty Spenserian stanzas that was written in 1793–94 as part of the long poem ultimately published in 1842 as "Guilt and Sorrow." (It was extracted in spring 1798, probably in slightly revised form, for publication in *Lyrical Ballads*.) The vagrant tells her story in language that is still bestrewn with phrases drawn from the formal poetic diction of the late eighteenth century; and although here the main emphasis falls on the human misery consequent on the ravages of war, the general ambience is quite similar to that of Crabbe's "Hall of Justice" in *Poems* (1807).

Apart from Wordsworth there are two poets working around the turn of the century whose success in finding a public may similarly have given Crabbe some encouragement to persist in his narrative experiments. The first is Southey, whose longer poems of the period were devoted to exotic or historical narrative of a grandiose kind, but whose shorter poems included a number of narratives with a more contemporary and realistic setting. The earliest of these were *Botany Bay Eclogues*, published in 1794, a group of four poems (two monologues, two dialogues) in which transported convicts relate their past histories. The poems in the sequel, *English Eclogues* (1799), are rather more varied in their subject matter, and the date of composition of most of them overlapped Wordsworth's putting together of the first volume of *Lyrical Ballads*. One of them seems, indeed, to be an almost plagiaristic reworking of Wordsworth's "Old Man Travelling"—a dialogue between a traveler and a woman journeying to Plymouth to see her sailor son who has been blinded in the war at sea. Southey gives more prominence to the narrative element, which Wordsworth kept in the background in his first version and subsequently suppressed. In the eclogue the woman's son went to sea because he was caught poaching and was offered a choice between prison and the ship; the traveler's consolatory comments are complacently sententious and patriotic. More sensational than most, but also more effective, is "The Grandmother's Tale," written in 1798, in which the grandmother tells to her two grandchildren the horrible story of "how the smuggler murdered / The woman down at Pill." Later, pursued by a guilty conscience, which ensured that his victim's cries were always in his ears and her figure always before his eyes,

> he confess'd it all, and gave himself
> To death; so terrible, he said, it was
> To have a guilty conscience. . . .

The motif here prefigures an aspect of the fate of Peter Grimes, though the resemblance is not perhaps close enough to suggest any direct relationship.

In the 1803 edition of *English Eclogues* Southey added two further poems. The first, written in 1800, "The Wedding," offered an unusually savage presentation of rural poverty and of the miseries that follow on marriage among the poor. The second, "The Alderman's Funeral," written in 1803, interestingly prefigures a short character sketch in letter 17 of *The Borough* in a way that does not preclude the possibility of a direct, though probably unconscious, influence. Southey's alderman, though rich, widely famed and respected, was

> one in whose heart
> Love had not place nor natural charity.

The moral issue involved is by no means new and only moderately subtle, but it has been framed and defined in terms of a character sketch whose particularity gives to it a satirical force unusual in Southey:

> This man of half a million
> Had all these public virtues which you praise:
> But the poor man rung never at his door,

> And the old beggar, at the public gate,
> Who all the summer long, stands hat in hand,
> He knew how vain it was to lift an eye
> To that hard face. Yet he was always found
> Among your ten and twenty pound subscribers,
> Your benefactors in the newspapers.
> His alms were money put to interest
> In the other world . . . donations to keep open
> A running charity account with heaven . . .
> Retaining fees against the Last Assizes. . . .

Despite the difference in tone, this certainly puts one in mind of Crabbe's character sketch of an unnamed governor of the hospital that opens as follows:

> Again attend!—and see a man whose cares
> Are nicely placed on either world's affairs,—
> Merchant and saint; 'tis doubtful if he knows
> To which account he most regard bestows;
> Of both he keeps his ledger:—there he reads
> Of gainful ventures and of goodly deeds;
> There all he gets or loses finds a place,
> A lucky bargain and a lack of grace.
>
> (*The Borough*, letter 17, 214–21)

Crabbe slides here almost mechanically into his customary balanced style, and it cannot really be claimed that the effect he achieves is markedly either neater or less verbose than Southey's.

The third poet whose verse-tales about humble rural people may have helped to pave the way for Crabbe was Robert Bloomfield, who had already introduced a couple of narrative fragments into his descriptive poem *The Farmer's Boy* (1800). In the same volume there was included a further poem in heroic couplets, "Good Tidings; or, News from the Farm," which was essentially a tribute to (and propaganda for) Dr. Jenner's discovery of vaccination, but which encompassed two rather more lengthy anecdotes that are much the best section of the poem, being vivid and affecting, while much of the remainder does not escape bathos. Both anecdotes deal with the effects of smallpox, the first being about a previously healthy child who had been blinded by the disease, while the second is about the death of Bloomfield's father. Bloomfield's second volume, *Rural Tales* (1802), contains some half-dozen ballads, mostly in quatrains, that show unmistakably the influence of Wordsworth, though they regularly slump into just those pitfalls (of false simplicity or sentimentality) that Wordsworth usually avoids. There are also, however, two longer tales in heroic couplets that can plausibly be seen as precursors of Crabbe. The first of these is "Walter and Jane; or, The Poor Blacksmith. A Country Tale." It recounts how Jane, a milkmaid, and Walter, a blacksmith, fall in love but find their courtship interrupted by the death of Jane's mistress, as a result of which Walter has to walk twelve miles each Sunday to see her at her new place of work. There is some use of dialogue, and at times Bloomfield even achieves something approaching Crabbe's pointedness, an effect verging on conciseness and epigram. But the pattern of the story is too neatly, and indeed tritely, resolved when the squire appears with a small legacy from Walter's dead uncle, together with a gift on his own account and the promise of a cottage to live in. The other tale, "The Miller's Maid," which is slightly longer, does exhibit a little more complication of narrative structure, but here again all ends happily with marriage and an atmosphere of cheerful benevolence all round. The fact is that Bloomfield lacks any complexity of moral or poetic vision, and lacks also any capacity for sustained realism. Only occasionally does he use the typical resources of the heroic couplet, such as balance, contrast, antithesis, and repetition. When he does, he comes rather nearer to Crabbe, as for instance in the following lines where the returned sailor-brother is speaking:

> Keen disappointment wounded me that morn:
> For, trav'lling near the spot where I was born,
> I at the well-known door where I was bred,
> Inquir'd who still was living, who was dead. . . .
>
> (147–50)

Bloomfield's next volume, *Wild Flowers: or, Pastoral and Local Poetry* (1806), is predominantly non-narrative, but it does contain one rather mawkishly sentimental ballad, "Abner and the Widow Jones," and one longish tale in heroic couplets, "The Broken Crutch." The plot construction of this is clumsy, naïve, and sentimental, while the conclusion is a positive wallowing in sloppy, virtuous good-fellowship. Here and there, nevertheless, Bloomfield has made some advance in dexterity in his use of the couplet for dialogue. Here is Peggy Meldrum's father speaking:

> From honest poverty our lineage sprung,
> Your mother was a servant quite as young;—
> You weep; perhaps *she* wept at leaving home;
> Courage, my girl, nor fear the days to come.
>
> (7–10)

And here is an extract from later in the poem:

> "News?" cried a stooping grandame of the vale,
> "Aye, rare news too; I'll tell you such a tale:
> But let me rest; this bank is dry and warm;
> Do you know Peggy Meldrum at the farm?
> Young Herbert's girl? He's clothed her all in white,
> You never saw so beautiful a sight!
> Ah! he's a fine young man and such a face!
> I knew his grandfather and all his race;
> He rode a tall white horse, and look'd so big,
> But how shall I describe his hat and wig?"
> "Plague take his wig," cried Gilbert, "and his hat,
> Where's Peggy Meldrum? can you tell me *that?*"

(193–204)

Occasional passages such as this do seem to suggest that Crabbe may have taken a hint or two as to the lines his own vastly more subtle and complex poetic development was to take.

There is no independent evidence as to whether Crabbe had read Bloomfield's poetry. As far as Wordsworth is concerned, Crabbe's son (as will be shown later) does seem to imply that his father was among the early readers of *Lyrical Ballads*, though neither Wordsworth nor Coleridge figure in the (evidently incomplete) list of books in the poet's library at Trowbridge. The evidence that Crabbe had read Southey's eclogues soon after their publication is rather stronger; at any rate the three volumes by Southey in the library at Trowbridge certainly included his *Metrical Tales*. In any case, whether or not Crabbe had read them, the poems discussed in this chapter exemplify a clear trend around the turn of the century towards the presentation in narrative verse of ordinary people and mundane events, and should therefore help to explain why there was a ready audience for his next volume, *Poems*, when it appeared in 1807.

4

The Tale in Embryo

Unfortunately, little information is available about the writing that Crabbe engaged in between 1785 and 1807, the bulk of which was destroyed in the periodical "grand incremations" so much enjoyed by his children. Crabbe's son does tell us that one of the casualties was a treatise in English on botany that was burnt because the vice-master of Trinity College, Cambridge objected to "the notion of degrading such a science by treating of it in a modern language." It is probable, however, that most of Crabbe's compositions during this period were in verse, since his son makes it clear that it was as an exception to his usual practice that

> During one or two of his winters in Suffolk, he gave most of his evening hours to the writing of *Novels*, and he brought not less than three such works to a conclusion. The first was entitled "The Widow Grey"; but I recollect nothing of it except that the principal character was a benevolent humourist, a Dr Allison. The next was called "Reginald Glanshaw, or the Man who commanded Success"; a portrait of an assuming, overbearing, ambitious mind, rendered interesting by some generous virtues, and gradually wearing down into idiotism. (*Life*, 159)

There is little in this description to suggest any direct relationship between the prose novels and Crabbe's later narrative verse, though it is perhaps of interest that as early as this Crabbe was already depicting the development of insanity in one of his characters. About the third novel Crabbe's son remembered even less:

> I forget the title of his third novel; but I clearly remember that it opened with a description of a wretched room, similar to some that are presented in his poetry, and that on my mother's telling him frankly that she thought the effect very inferior to that of the corresponding pieces in verse, he paused in his reading, and after some reflection, said, "Your remark is just." (*Life*, 159)

Probably the "corresponding pieces in verse" were descriptions rather than extended attempts at narrative. However two pieces of evidence show that before the turn of the century Crabbe had already started to write narratives pieces in verse. The first is the poet's own statement, in his preface to *Poems* (1807), that "The Hall of Justice" (he calls it "Aaron, or The Gipsy") had been written nine years earlier—i.e., in 1798. The second is the testimony of Crabbe's son that

> In the course of the year 1799, he [Crabbe] opened a communication with Mr Hatchard, the well-known bookseller, and was encouraged to prepare for publication a series of poems, sufficient to fill a volume—among others, one on the Scripture story of Naaman; another, strange contrast! entitled "Gipsy Will"; and a third founded on the legend of the Pedlar of Swaffham. (*Life*, 160)

Clearly two out of the three narrative poems mentioned can have borne little significant relationship to Crabbe's later development; the third, however, "Gipsy Will," does suggest an affinity with "The Hall of Justice" (particularly in the light of the poet's alternative title for the latter), and compels a conjecture that it may have been an early version of the published poem, in which Crabbe altered the name of the protagonist. Some uncertainty remains, nevertheless, since the conjecture is incompatible with the assertion of Crabbe's son that his father "finally rejected the tales I have named altogether" (*Life*, 160).

"The Hall of Justice" is in some ways the most fully developed narrative in *Poems* (1807); but, most exceptionally for Crabbe, it is written in octosyllabic quatrains, varied occasionally by the insertion of a six-line or eight-line stanza. In two parts, it takes the form of a dialogue, adjourned in the middle, between a female vagrant guilty of stealing food for her starving grandchild and a magistrate who adds significance to the title of the poem by being evidently more concerned for the spiritual welfare of the offender than for the administration of mere worldly justice. The greater part of the poem consists of the vagrant's story of her life. As an orphan she "wander'd with a vagrant Crew" and fell in love with Aaron the Gipsy Boy whose father was the "Party's Chief." But Aaron's father is himself attracted to the young vagrant, drives his son away from the group by deliberate brutal violence, and then rapes the girl and forces her to "wed" him. When Aaron returns he secretly murders his father in Blackburn Forest, "weds" the vagrant in his turn, and unlike the bride feels no guilt for his crimes. The ensuing crisis in the narrative is told with chilling economy:

I brought a lovely Daughter forth,
    His Father's Child, in Aaron's Bed;
He took her from me in his wrath,
    "Where is my Child?" —"Thy Child is dead."

(49–52)

Some time later Aaron dies in a fight, and she takes a third husband who forces her into prostitution. After this husband dies, she manages to subsist for a time by "fraudful Arts," and then, in prison, encounters her long-lost daughter whom Aaron had in reality given to

wander with a distant Clan,
The Miseries of the World to brave
And be the Slave of Vice and Man.

(94–96)

The daughter is transported for her crimes, leaving to her mother's care the illegitimate child for whom the vagrant has now committed the crime of stealing food.

In its subject matter, as well as in its language and metrical form, "The Hall of Justice" owes an obvious debt to that strain in the magazine poetry of the 1790s that contributed to the formation of some of Wordsworth's *Lyrical Ballads.* Crabbe's solitary published incursion into this genre is marked by an unusual starkness and sordidness of detail as well as by the power of its psychological depiction—a quality that enables him to avoid the temptation of sentimentality. In addition, Crabbe imprints his own Christian prepossessions upon the emergent moral pattern. The magistrate frowns and cuts short the vagrant's narrative at the end of part 1 when she impiously curses the gypsy chief who wronged her; at the end of part 2 he insists that God's pardon is available to the vagrant herself (given the necessary dread and repentance) as well as to the innocent child for whom she had sought it. Despite a certain artificiality about its pseudodramatic framework, the poem is an impressive one and seems to mark out a possible line of narrative development that Crabbe did not in fact take.

There is, however, one surviving poem, not published until 1960, which shows that Crabbe did not immediately abandon his attempts to work this vein. This is "Hester," a poem in stanza form (the stanzas being slightly irregular in length, but all basically derivative from the quatrain), 520 lines in length and extant in "fair draft" in an ms. notebook dated "Glemham, 1804." In it an elderly female vagrant tells her own life story as a warning against human failure to shut out with sufficient care the voice of temptation.

As the virtuous daughter of the gamekeeper on a large estate, she had been taken up as a personal maid by the countess at the castle, had learnt to tolerate the profligate manners of the servants' hall, and after the countess's death had become her son's mistress, universally recognized and deferred to. But after her lord's unexpected and sudden death, she was reduced to becoming a common prostitute, and her distress and suffering at this period of her life are described with considerable frankness. It may perhaps have been the fear that this part of the poem was too outspoken for the contemporary audience that led Crabbe to decide against publishing it in *Poems* (1807). It has, taken as a whole, a certain power, though its merits are not of a kind we associate particularly with Crabbe, and it shares with its prototypes among the magazine poems of the 1790s a tendency to stereotyping of both character and situation.

The only other anomalous narrative poem in the 1807 volume (and indeed in the whole of Crabbe's narrative development) is "Sir Eustace Grey," which like "The Hall of Justice" has a semidramatic framework. The scene is a madhouse, and the speakers are the Visitor, the Physician and the Patient. According to a note in FitzGerald's copy of the 1834 edition, it was "composed at Muston, in the winter of 1804–5 in a great snowstorm."[1] This poem, also, is in octosyllabics and consists of 53 eight-line stanzas. The greater part of it is given over to extended descriptions of the madman's hallucinations, while the narrative element is confined to a dozen stanzas early in the poem. Because of its subject matter, this rather strange poem (well received in its day) will be held over for discussion until a later chapter, which deals with Crabbe's various treatments of insanity.

It may well be that Crabbe had learnt something from his experiments in these various narrative genres, both in prose and in verse; but it seems clear in retrospect that they were "false starts." The true growth-point around this time was the composition of *The Parish Register*, started shortly after his decision in 1799 not to proceed with the volume of poems discussed with Hatchard, and "nearly completed . . . by the latter part of the year 1806" (*Life*, 174). Admittedly the new start is not immediately apparent at the beginning of this long poem, since it opens with an extended introduction (276 lines) devoted mainly to the contrast between the dwellings of the "industrious" peasantry and those of "the Poor when improvident and vicious"; this seems at first to presage another "verse-essay" similar to *The Village*, though rather more lively in the detail and vividness of its descriptions. Only when Crabbe abruptly turns to the first recorded birth of the year (the "Child of Shame" born to Lucy the Miller's daughter) do we discover that what he has in store for us is a series of thirty character sketches, anecdotes, or brief tales prompted by a country clergyman's browsing over a year's entries in the pages of his parish register, under the headings of "Baptisms," "Marriages," and "Burials." Returning with increased mastery to his favorite verse form of the heroic couplet, Crabbe is able to develop the embryonic narrative implicit in some of Pope's short character sketches (particularly those in *Epistles to Several Personages*), while at the same time carrying forward the possibilities hinted at in the more homespun narrative experiments of Wordsworth, Southey, and Bloomfield. Moreover, the "narrative voice" adopted is particularly well suited to enable Crabbe to utilize his own firsthand observations of characters and of rural life over twenty-odd years.

The thirty or so entries in the parish register can be categorized under three main headings. First, and most numerous, are the straight character sketches in which any narrative element plays only a small part; second, there are some embryonic anecdotes in which the interest begins to shift away from characterization and toward narrative as such; third, there is a small group of half-a-dozen short but fully developed tales, each quite capable of standing on its own as a story. Though rather arbitrary, this classification has a certain convenience; but it should be made clear that there is no evidence to suggest that any one group was written earlier than the others.

A few of the straight character sketches are extremely general and in regard to characterization offer little more detail than the sketch of, say, the "hoary swain" in *The Village*. Thus, in "Burials" (3.208) we learn little about "The Lady who yon Hall possess'd" beyond the fact that she was an absentee landowner who left all the administration of her estate to her steward. Instead, what is striking is Crabbe's vivid physical evocation of the forsaken and decaying hall—a passage clearly indebted to Pope's description of Cotta's house in "Epistle III (To Bathurst)"—and the savagely farcical indictment of the "mimic miseries" of the paid mourners at her funeral. In his brief character sketches in "Epistle I (To Cobham)" Pope structures his vignettes around the thesis that everyone has some "ruling passion" that determines his or her character and behavior throughout life.

> Time, that on all things lays his lenient hand,
> Yet tames not this; it sticks to our last sand.
>
> (224–25)

The lady of the hall's determined avoidance of any knowledge about her tenants' problems or about the "Sufferings of the Poor" is perhaps too negative a trait to be deemed a "Passion," but in its unidimensionality Crabbe's portrayal of her may be thought to have an analogue, and even a precedent, in

Pope's brilliant miniatures. The moral upshot of the entry is a grimly appropriate one, moreover; since she paid no heed to the sorrows of her village dependents, it is fitting that the tears shed at her funeral should be as "feigned" as those of the stone cherubs upon her tomb.

More typically, however, Crabbe presents the dominant trait in his characters not as a "given" but as a manifestation that is explicable if seen in its historical-biographical context. Thus in the entry concerning the "Rambler" Robin Dingley, one of the small number of developed and self-contained narratives, Dingley's compulsion to wander is known to be based on the real-life character of a certain Richard Wilkinson—"a parishioner of Muston who every now and then disappeared" for no evident reason, but later came home "to be again clothed and fed at the expense of the parish." What Crabbe has added is the incident that caused Robin's mental aberration. A "keen attorney" (very much a stock figure from eighteenth-century fiction in his self-interested promotion of litigation) persuaded Robin that he had an unshakable title to the fortune of the newly deceased "rich old Dingley"; when the claim failed, Robin had built so much on his expectations that "the failure touch'd his brain."

Again in the entry concerning Catharine Lloyd (one of the more detailed and fully elaborated character sketches) the genesis of her "ruling passion" is carefully filled in. The "Treasures" to which she has become so immutably attached had originally been left to her by her cousin (a "Captain . . . rich from India") and may be supposed to have had a sentimental value on that score; but over the years during which she displayed their "Splendour" to her circle of women friends the "Delight" she took in them had increased beyond all bounds. The "Treasures" themselves are described with the same vividness of detail Crabbe uses in evoking the physical appearance of Catharine herself (see p. 25 above), while the intensity of her attachment to them gains credibility from the superbly realized emotional emptiness of her spinster's life.

> Her neat small Room, adorn'd with Maiden-taste,
> A clipt French-Puppey first of Favourites grac'd.
> A Parrot next, but dead and stuff'd with Art;
> (For Poll, when living, lost the Lady's Heart,
> And then his Life; for he was heard to speak
> Such frightful Words as tinge'd his lady's Cheek;)
> Unhappy Bird! who had no power to prove,
> Save by such Speech, his Gratitude and Love.
> A grey old Cat his Whiskers lick'd beside;
> A type of Sadness in the House of Pride.

The polish'd Surface of an India-Chest,
A glassy Globe, in Frame of Ivory, prest;
Where swam two finny Creatures; one of Gold,
Of Silver one; both beauteous to behold:
All these were form'd the guiding Taste to suit:
The Beasts well-manner'd and the fishes mute:
A widow'd *Aunt* was there, compell'd by Need,
The Nymph to flatter and her Tribe to feed;
Who, veiling well her Scorn, endur'd the Clog,
Mute as the fish and fawning as the Dog.

(3.352–71)

Some constituents of this picture (the lapdog, the parrot, the dependent companion) had formed part of the fictional stereotype of the aging spinster from Richardson onward,[2] though Crabbe has added his own ironic twist in making the parrot a stuffed one. What is especially noticeable, however, is the skill with which carefully selected details have been knitted together to convey, in their atmosphere and interrelationships, a clear sense of the character of the room's owner. Crabbe relies a great deal on physical detail, but uses it above all, as there will be frequent occasion to note, for psychological purposes.

These details turn out to be highly relevant also to the moral dimension of the portrait. The culminating theme is Catharine's painful and ultimately unsuccessful attempt "in the sad Summer of her slow Decay" to wean her affection away from her possessions as death approaches, and to fix her heart upon otherworldly concerns. In presenting this, the closing section of the sketch achieves a genuine poignancy, partly because Crabbe gives full weight to the difficulty of the spiritual task set for her, partly because the beguiling attraction of the "Bawbles" that fill her "Trunks and Chests" has been given a powerful presence by the earlier detailing of them. Ironically, even the book that she knows she now ought to fix her attention on is "a rich-bound Book of Prayer," a gift from the Captain who had, perhaps, at one time been her lover. The profusion of detail in this sketch may seem to lend support to the charge of "excessive minuteness" that reviewers repeatedly leveled against *The Parish Register*, but closer attention shows the detail to be fully justified in terms of its relevance to the artistic purpose in hand.

Two of the most masterly of the character sketches proper are those of Andrew Collett and the Widow Goe near the beginning of part 3 ("Burials"). Both were based on real-life figures whom Crabbe's son has identified. Andrew Collett, "The blind, fat landlord of the Old Crown Inn," is, as Peter New has commented, "an early example of Crabbe's ability to

dramatise the zest of a character whose moral attitude he totally rejects."[3]
Here again is a character driven on by a single unvarying trait—one made
convincing in this case by the diversity of detail surrounding it. Crabbe
starts with the external and objective moral vision and embodies it in the
traditional antitheses and parallelisms of the heroic couplet form.

> Each night his string of vulgar Tales he told;
> When Ale was cheap and Bachelors were bold;
> His Heroes all were famous in their Days,
> Cheats were his boast and Drunkards had his praise;
>
> (3.81–84)

From this he moves on to using the verse medium to impersonate the voice
and tone of the innkeeper, sliding almost imperceptibly from direct to indirect speech and back again. At the same time he adroitly indicates his dis-
approbation through an ironical heightening of the occasional extravagant
word or phrase.

> He prais'd a Poacher, precious child of Fun!
> Who shot the Keeper with his own Spring-gun;
> Nor less the Smuggler who the Exciseman tied,
> And left him hanging at the Birch-wood side,
> There to expire; —but one who saw him hang,
> Cut the good Cord—a Traitor of the Gang.
>
> (3.93–98)

Here the application of the epithet "good" to "Cord" tells its own story
without any need for explicit comment by the poet, and so too, in the inap-
propriateness of their context, do the phrases "precious child of Fun" and
"Traitor of the Gang." As Crabbe pursues this technique further, the heroic
couplet itself becomes more flexible, colloquial, and relaxed:

> He told, when angry Wives, provok'd to rail,
> Or drive a third-day Drunkard from his Ale;
> What were his Triumphs and how great the Skill,
> That won the vex'd Virago to his Will;
> Who raving came;—then talk'd in milder strain, —
> Then wept,—then drank and pledg'd her Spouse again.
>
> (3.107–12)

Here the ordered freedom of the verse form both enacts the vulgar self-
satisfaction of the boastful toper and at the same time "places" it for the

reader, while the syntactic structure and the overrun between lines and couplets begin to develop a forward-moving narrative impetus that foreshadows the poet's subsequent ease in verse storytelling. There is perhaps a slight slackening of impact in the concluding paragraph, with its overdependence on a final line quoted intact from Young's *Night Thoughts* ("Beware, *Lorenzo*, the slow-sudden Death"); but taken as a whole the character sketch is both a remarkable achievement in itself and a pointer to later developments.

A similar mastery is displayed in the entry about the Widow Goe— another character portrayal whose unidimensionality is effectively concealed by the skilful marshalling of much significant detail. This builds up unerringly the picture of an "active" and "commanding" dame, busying herself incessantly with running the affairs of the parish and of her own family, and relishing thoroughly the power and consequence that that exercise of sway carries with it. The culminating triumph of the piece comes in Crabbe's rendering of her spoken reactions and of her persisting divided allegiances when she realizes that her end is near. These are epitomized for the reader in her superbly telling line : "A Lawyer haste, and in your way a Priest"; even now she is unable to give up "those Signs of Sway" that have become so important to her, so that she

> trembling, dropp'd upon her knees,
> Heav'n in her Eye and in her Hand her Keys:
>
> (3.183–84)

Ironically, the sketch ends with her sons' peremptory assumption, the minute she is dead, of the power she has kept from them:

> In haste her Sons drew near,
> And dropp'd, in haste, the tributary Tear,
> Then from th'adhering Clasp the Keys unbound,
> And Consolation for their Sorrows, found.
>
> (3.187–90)

As will appear later, this episode of the keys, so placed as to give symbolic significance to a naturalistic detail small in itself, foreshadows a narrative device that Crabbe was to use to even stronger effect in some of his subsequent tales.

The entry in "Burials" concerning Leah Cousins, the parish midwife, falls somewhere midway between character sketch and brief tale. Like a number of the later full-length tales, this is the story of a whole life; and its structure is that of a contrast in time between two states, an earlier and a later. The "Before" is represented by Leah at the height of her career "with Honours crown'd," a "Matron . . . whom every Village-Wife / View'd as the Help and Guardian of her Life." The "After" is her old age, when she has been displaced by the satirically named "Doctor Glibb," and the "Honours" as well as the "Profit" of her calling have dropped away. Significant in the narrative development is the amount of detail with which Crabbe here fills in the transition from the earlier stage to the later—detail that is presented in quasi-dramatic form by the quoted utterances of the two contending practitioners. In his handling of the conflict between the two, Crabbe exhibits a characteristically evenhanded balance. Dr. Glibb's success in the parish results largely from the way in which "Fame (now his Friend)" disseminates his unstinted self-praise; moreover, the element of hubris in this self-congratulation is given full weight. He scornfully characterizes his rival as "A whining Dame, who prays in Danger's view," and goes on with gross insensitivity to prate:

> And what is Nature! One who acts in aid
> Of Gossips half asleep, and half afraid:
> With such Allies I scorn my fame to blend,
> Skill is my Luck and Courage is my Friend:
> No Slave to Nature, 'tis my chief delight,
> To win my Way and act in her despite;—

(3. 685–90)

At the same time the uneasy suspicion remains that "Luck" (to which she herself pays tribute) has perhaps played an unduly large part in Leah's successful record of bringing to birth "healthy Boys and handsome Girls." Crabbe resolutely refuses to sentimentalize her in her decline, recording on the one hand that the contentious words she utters when fortified by "her well-spiced Ale and aiding Pipe" are "too strong and plain"; and on the other hand recording her increasing recourse to the "insidious Aid" of "th'inspiring Cup" as "her Powers decay'd" and she grew "poor and peevish." The anecdote of Leah Cousins thus displays in miniature a number of the characteristics that were later to give strength to many of Crabbe's full-length tales.

Mention should be made also of two expanded anecdotes that though impressively well shaped and rounded in their narrative form, yet remain a little external in their characterization, lacking as they do that degree of sympathetic insight which in the mature tales takes the reader inside the consciousness of the protagonists. The first of these, the story of Roger Cuff in part 3, is one of those that seem to owe a large debt to fictional models, both in its conception and in its mode of presentation. "Shipwreck'd in Youth," Roger had strongly resented the unkind treatment he received at the hands of his three "Landman" brothers. Forty years later, his brothers all dead, he decides to return home and share his wealth with his surviving relatives. However, he decides first (and here the contrivance of the novelist shows through) to test out the genuineness of their goodwill by appearing before them "in Tatters dress'd" and appealing to them as their pauper uncle. The response of each of the three nephews is splendidly impersonated by the verse, which represents in turn the sternness of George ("Let them who had thee Strong, / Help thee to drag thy weaken'd Frame along"); the insincerity of "pious James" ("thy Sorrows pierce my breast; / And had I Wealth, as have my Brethren twain . . ."); and the coldness of Peter ("The rates are high; we have a-many Poor). The hypocritical disclaimer of the "sprightly Niece" is even more acutely rendered:

> "Avaunt! begone!" (the courteous Maiden said,)
> "Thou vile Impostor! Uncle Roger's dead:
> I hate thee, beast; thy Look my spirit shocks;
> Oh! that I saw thee starving in the Stocks!"
>
> (3.775–79)

Roger turns finally to a more distant relative, surly John the woodman, who offers him work rather than charity and is rewarded by a carefree life, enlivened by indulgence in beef and brandy, beer and biscuits, and tobacco's "glorious fume." After John's death Roger resists the blandishments of the remaining relatives and

> dying, built a Refuge for the Poor;
> With this Restriction, That no *Cuff* should share
> One meal, or shelter for one Moment there.
>
> (3.798–800)

The tale is a lively one, and in its telling displays to the full Crabbe's already remarkable skill in accommodating stylized yet naturalistic dialogue within the confines of the heroic couplet. A doubt arises, however, as to the extent to which it displays Crabbe's accustomed moral weight and seriousness. The second line of the tale suggests that the poet intended to convey a reproof to Cuff for the stubbornness with which he nurses his familial resentment. However, the wrongs offered to him are more forcefully presented than any other aspect of the narrative, so that at the conclusion his resentment is not felt to be quite as unreasonable and unchristian as the intention seems to require.

The second tale, the tale of Sir Richard Monday in part 1, can justly be seen as constituting in its spare 79 lines the most flawless of all the entries in *The Parish Register*. Particularly striking is the way in which every detail in the tale has been chosen not merely to unfold the structure of the narrative but also to enforce its significance—a significance organized round a vision that sees the mean-minded and selfish spirit in which poor relief is administered as a moral outrage and one that has the inexorable consequence of perpetuating itself for generations to come. Thus, we can hardly fail to be impressed, in the opening account of the parish meeting, by the artistry that ensures that each item in the sequence at once forwards the movement of events and at the same time underlines with dispassionate, straight-faced irony the inhumanity of the solemnly prolonged debate with which the prudent "Village-sires" greet their "unwelcome guest."

> Some harden'd knaves, who rov'd the country round,
> Had left a Babe within the Parish-bound.—
> First, of the fact they question'd— "Was it true?"
> The Child was brought— "What then remained to do?"
> "Was't dead or living?" This was fairly prov'd,
> 'Twas pinch'd, it roar'd, and every doubt remov'd;
> Then by what name th'unwelcome guest to call,
> Was long a question, and it pos'd them all:
> For he who lent it to a Babe unknown,
> Censorious men might take it for his own;
> They look'd about, they gravely spoke to all,
> And not one *Richard* answer'd to the call;
> Next they enquir'd the day, when passing by,
> Th'*unlucky* peasant heard the stranger's cry;
> This known; how Food and Raiment they might give,
> Was next debated—for the rogue would live;
> At last with all their words and work content,
> Back to their homes, the prudent Vestry went,
> And *Richard Monday* to the Workhouse sent.
>
> (*The Parish Register*, 1.692–710)

We must pay tribute here to the resonances set up between the phrase "hardened knaves" (the vestry's term?) as applied to the vagrant parents who had abandoned their baby, and the vestry's own callousness in pinching the infant till it roared, in order to establish that the "rogue" insists on remaining alive; and also to the sophisticated effortlessness of the effect achieved by holding back the outcome of the naming process till the clinching final line, thus resolving two narrative uncertainties with a single clause.

In the couplet linking this opening "scene" with the summarizing section that succeeds it, the coalescence of hard-hearted insensitivity and grudgingly performed charitable duty is rendered with telling concentration:

> There was he pinch'd and pitied, thump'd and fed,
> And duly took his beatings and his bread.
>
> (711–12)

And in the extended summary itself, the sequence of workhouse indignities to which the boy is subjected is held together by a further duality that brings out, on the one hand, the depth of the covert resentment they provoke in him, and, on the other hand, their efficacy in schooling him in the ignoble qualities that will fit him to go far in later life. The items in this sequence are not, however, individual incidents but general categories of situation (errands, thefts, disputes, rebellions, detections), chosen to conjure up vivid though unspecific events all of which are highly pertinent to the tale's central moral concern. And in the bridging paragraph that carries us cursorily over Richard's life after he has run away, this theme, though restated in the most general terms conceivable, still carries conviction: what Richard learnt during his years in the workhouse—his single-minded devotion to self-interest and his skilled concealment of this drive from others—are indeed, we recognize, precisely the attributes needed for worldly success.

The closing section of the tale returns us, nevertheless, to specifics that balance those of the opening "scene":

> Long lost to us, at last our man we trace,
> Sir *Richard Monday* died at *Monday-place*;
> His lady's worth, his daughter's we peruse,
> And find his Grandsons all as rich as Jews;
> He gave reforming Charities a sum,
> And bought the blessings of the Blind and Dumb;
> Bequeath'd to Missions money from the Stocks,
> And Bibles issu'd from his private box;
> But to his native place severely just,
> He left a pittance bound in rigid trust;
> Two paltry pounds, on every quarter's-day,
> (At church produc'd) for forty loaves should pay;
> A stinted gift, that to the parish shows,
> He kept in mind their bounty and their blows!
>
> (753–66)

The poet's organization of detail again constitutes a telling demonstration of vital causal relationships in human affairs. Selfishly mean and stinted performance of duty leads inexorably (we have been shown) to tragic deformation of character in the unfortunate recipient. In the longer run it leads to petty retaliation of a sourly comic "biter bit" kind, and ultimately to the perpetuation of mean-mindedness all round. Surely this tale is a masterpiece in miniature, more than worthy to stand beside Pope's "Sir Balaam."

A further transitional stage between anecdote and full-fledged tale can be studied in three quite lengthy entries that are concerned, in their differing ways, with the seduction and betrayal of a village maiden. The most compact of these is the one in part 2 relating to Lucy Collins, who despite her betrothal to Stephen Hill ("A sturdy, sober, kind, unpolish'd Youth") finds herself irresistibly attracted to the pseudofashionable grandeur of Footman Daniel when he visits "his native Green." Lucy Collins herself, however, is a mere cipher in this entry, in which much of the space and most of the poetic energy is given over to the depiction of the "idle Coxcomb," Daniel, whose elegance is described in such a way as to make clear that his pretensions are both spurious and presumptuous. By contrast, Stephen's steady self-advancement is sketched in by a passage where a Pope-like verbal patterning is imposed, without sense of strain, upon more mundane subject matter:

> *Stephen*, meantime, to ease his amorous Cares,
> Fix'd his full mind upon his Farm's Affairs;
> Two Pigs, a Cow, and Wethers half a Score,
> Increas'd his Stock and still he look'd for more;
> He, for his Acres few, so duly paid,
> That yet more Acres to his lot were laid;
> Till our chaste Nymphs no longer felt disdain,
> And prudent Matrons prais'd the frugal Swain;
> Who thriving well, through many a fruitful Year,
> Now cloth'd himself anew, and acted Overseer.
>
> (2.341–50)

The economical narrative skill shown here is matched by the conciseness of the denouement in which the disgraced Lucy appeals to Stephen for charity and

> was chidden first, next pitied and then fed;
> Then sat at *Stephen*'s Board, then shared in *Stephen*'s bed:

And the formal symmetry of the final couplet brilliantly underscores the woman's incurable frivolity and moral insentience:

> All Hopes of Marriage lost in her Disgrace,
> He mourns a flame reviv'd, and she a love of Lace.
>
> (2.354–57)

The only faint reservation that seems to be in place is that Crabbe has been guilty of a certain sleight of hand in placing this episode in the part of the poem entitled "Marriages."

By contrast with this admirable tautness, the story of Phoebe Dawson and her fall (also in "Marriages") strikes us as somewhat too leisurely and expansive. Yet this entry was often singled out for special praise in contemporary reviews, was frequently quoted and reproduced as an example of Crabbe's poetry at its most affecting, and was read, as Crabbe tells us in his 1807 preface, with particular pleasure by Charles James Fox on his deathbed. The very fact of its contemporary popularity may give a clue as to what is wrong with it; its pathos contains a strain of vulgarizing oversimplification (uncommon in Crabbe) that must have made a strong appeal to Regency taste. The thrice-repeated refrain ("Ah! fly temptation, Youth, refrain! refrain!") is in itself an index of this. Even more noteworthy is Crabbe's failure to give much psychological reality to his portrayal of Phoebe (although according to Crabbe's son she was based on a real-life original) or to elaborate a convincing social setting for the account of her downfall. A "Rustic Beauty," Phoebe's earlier and uncorrupted state is described in terms of unqualified approval not only for her physical charms, but also for her "Air" and "Manners" and the "untutor'd elegance" of her dress. Yet her successful suitor (and seducer) appears to be distinguished only by his brash self-confidence, and no special reasons are made out as to why the Phoebe Dawson who has been described for us should have been "pleas'd by Manners most unlike her own" or why she should have taken her lover "for his sparkling Eyes / Expressions warm, and love-inspiring Lies." The youth himself is indeed portrayed somewhat perfunctorily; the first couplet in the following quotation seems particularly lacking in the closely reasoned inner logic that we normally find in Crabbe's couplets:

> Loud though in Love and confident though young;
> Fierce in his air and voluble of tongue;
> By trade a Tailor, though, in scorn of trade,
> He serv'd the Squire and brush'd the Coat he made;
> Yet now, would *Phoebe* her Consent afford,
> Her Slave alone, again he'd mount the Board;
> With her should years of growing Love be spent,
> And growing Wealth: —She sigh'd and look'd consent.
>
> (2.157–64)

There is more coherently and convincingly detailed narrative progression in the account of the evening walks that Phoebe takes with her lover:

> Now, through the lane, up hill, and cross the Green,
> (Seen by but few and blushing to be seen—
> Dejected, thoughtful, anxious, and afraid,)
> Led by the Lover, walk'd the silent Maid:
>
> (2.165–68)

It is as a result of her "Compassion" for "all his suffering, all his bosom's smart" that these walks are followed by her downfall.

In this tale the seduction is followed by marriage, even though a "Warrant" has been needed to bring "the Boy-Bridegroom" to the point of surrendering his liberty; and the opening paragraph consists of an unvarnished description of the wedding ceremony, complete with the shame, anger, and "savage gloom" of the reluctant youth (his "Brain confus'd with muddy Ale") and the self-conscious and hopeless attempt of the bride to conceal "by long rent cloak, hung loosely" her advanced state of pregnancy—a description that Jeffrey justly commended as "perfect in this style of drawing." The color of this garment, later referred to as a "red rent cloak" is a detail taken from the same poetic tradition as the "scarlet cloak" of Martha Ray in Wordsworth's poem "The Thorn."

Crabbe, however, unlike Wordsworth, is clearly committed to making the most of his narrative pattern; and there is a considerable amount of artifice, even if not exactly of artistry, in his sequencing of events. He starts with the wedding itself, then moves back two summers to a picture of Phoebe Dawson at the height of her youthful beauty, and then on again to a contrasting portrait of her deplorable condition a year or more after the marriage. Now, burdened with an infant in her arms and the consciousness of another "nearer Cause" for anxiety because she is again pregnant, she is nevertheless obliged to fetch water from the pool in her broken pitcher—a task that has now become for her exacting and physically laborious. When she puts a foot disastrously wrong in "the clinging clay," the mishap causes her "Cup of Sorrow" to brim over. Of particular interest is the use Crabbe makes of this hysteria; she reaches home, places her infant on the floor, and gives way to a fit of uncontrolled sobbing, so that, as New puts it, the trivial incident that has triggered her outburst "stands as a kind of symbol of her anxious, clogged life."[4] This passage, in fact, carries a little further the unforced use of a naturally occurring symbol, which we noted in the reference to Widow Goe's keys.

In this tale, however, the contrastive pattern as a whole is too deliberately contrived for the pathos to take a full hold on our imaginative sympathies. In the key couplet that describes Phoebe in her "first state":

> Two summers since, I saw at Lammas Fair,
> The sweetest flower that ever blossomed there;
>
> (2.131–32)

there is a conscious "prettiness" and striving for effect that is not characteristic of Crabbe at his best, however much it may have appealed to his contemporary audience.

By contrast, there is no empty rhetoric in *The Parish Register*'s third story of seduction, that of Lucy the Miller's daughter. Even in the moralizing that prefaces the tale, reproof, regret, compassion, and didactic intent are blended together with an admirably balanced control of tone :

> With evil omen, we that Year begin;
> A Child of Shame,—stern Justice adds, of Sin,
> Is first recorded;—I would hide the deed,
> But vain the wish; I sigh and I proceed:
> And could I well th'instructive truth convey
> 'Twould warn the Giddy and awake the Gay.
>
> (1.277–82)

The claim made for Lucy herself is a modest and temperate one:

> Of all the nymphs[5] who gave our village grace,
> The Miller's daughter had the fairest face:
>
> (1.283–84)

The miller, with his pride in his wealth, is sharply characterized; and Lucy shows herself keenly aware of her father's coldheartedness and proud possessiveness in regard to herself:

> To me a Master's stern regard is shown,
> I'm like his steed, priz'd highly as his own;
> Stroak'd but corrected, threaten'd when supplied,
> His slave and boast, his victim and his pride.
>
> (1.317–20)

It is indeed the miller's barroom boasting about his daughter and her expected compliance with his wishes that first sets off the "youthful Sailor" on his mercenary pursuit of such a desirable "prize":

My ebbing purse, no more the Foe shall fill,
But Love's kind act and *Lucy* at the Mill.

(1. 295–96)

Notably adroit and resourceful, in this tale, is Crabbe's use within the couplet form of slightly stylized dialogue that is suited both to the speaker and to the situation and that carries forward the narrative with a swift economy. This quality is particularly apparent when the sailor responds thus to Lucy's warning about her father:

Cheer up, my Lass! I'll to thy Father go,
The *Miller* cannot be the Sailor's foe;
Both live by Heaven's free gale that plays aloud
In the stretch'd canvass and the piping shroud;
The rush of winds, the flapping sails above,
And rattling planks within, are sounds *we* love;
Calms are our dread; when Tempests plough the Deep,
We take a Reef, and to the rocking, sleep.

(1.321–28)

This speech starts out as one addressed to Lucy, but it concludes as the young man's bluffly overconfident approach to her father, and as such it is contemptuously rejected in tones that Crabbe catches to perfection:

"Ha!" quoth the *Miller*, mov'd at speech so rash,
"Art thou like me? Then where thy Notes and Cash?
Away to *Wapping*, and a Wife command,
With all thy wealth, a Guinea, in thine hand;
There with thy messmates quaff the muddy cheer,
And leave my *Lucy* for thy Betters here."

(1. 329–34)

As a consequence of this rebuff it is not love, nor even cupidity, that leads the sailor to seduce the unfortunate Lucy, but desire for revenge.

Crabbe vividly evokes the "stolen moments of disturb'd delight" that persuade Lucy to give her suitor "not her Hand—but ALL she could"; and her subsequent feelings when she finds she is with child are tactfully but effectively conveyed, as are the means by which the news reaches the mill. At this point her father's reaction is wholly in character:

"Go! to thy curse and mine," the father said,
"Strife and confusion stalk around thy bed;

Want and a wailing Brat thy Portion be,
Plague to thy fondness, as thy fault to me."

                                                            (1.361–64)

The dual significance of "fondness" (as meaning on the one hand "tenderness," on the other hand "foolishness") is incorporated into the texture of
the miller's speech here with that appositeness which is so characteristic of
Crabbe's choice of words. There follows a moving but wholly unsentimen-
talized passage describing the unhappy condition of Lucy, who is consigned
by her father to the poverty of the higgler's cottage, awaiting news of
her lover who is now at sea, bearing her child in the seclusion of disgrace, and registering his birth similarly. Into this portrayal, which is
neither overstated nor understated, the news of William's death comes
with a flat finality:

No Sailor came; the months in terror fled!
Then news arriv'd; He fought, and he was DEAD!

                                                            (1.383–84)

After this we are given a brief but vivid cameo of her lonely life at the
cottage, whence she has to walk to the mill for her "weekly pittance" and
witness there the "mean seraglio" that her father now keeps and "whose
mirth insults her." The tale concludes with a passage all the more telling for
its restraint, in which we see the poor girl fearing that her reason may break
down under the strains she is enduring. The tale as a whole is realized with
a remarkable concreteness, given its comparative brevity, and also with an
acuteness of moral insight that shows Crabbe to be already fully mature as
an artist. It is surely the finest treatment of this frequent turn-of-the-century theme to be found anywhere. In addition, it interestingly anticipates in
its structure those later tales, in the 1812 and 1819 volumes, in which the
action is generated by the interplay of a small group of characters.

    In concentrating on the qualities to be observed in individual entries,
we have inevitably left out of account the degree of skill with which Crabbe
weaves them together to form a unified sequence. The overall structure is
in fact often a fairly loose one. Thus one entry may contrast with the next,
as when the baptism of Lucy's bastard is followed by that of the boy born in
wedlock to Robert and Susan, for whom :

Love all made up of torture and delight
Was but mere madness in this couple's sight.

                                                            (1.409–10)

Or there may be a parallelism between two successive entries, as with the "Relation of the Accomplishments of Phoebe Dawson" and the anecdote of the unnamed "well-dress'd pair" that follows it; though the social sphere of the two couples is widely different, in each case the bridegroom has been drawn reluctantly into a marriage that bodes ill for the future. Only in part 3, "Burials," does the poet come near to integrating his material within a genuine thematic unity. Here his starting point is the rarity, in his own observation, of the "perfect resignations" that the good Christian ought to be able to achieve on his "dying-bed." Apart from three divagations from this central theme (in the persons of Robin Dingley, Leah Cousins, and Roger Cuff) the generalization is then enforced by a series of well-varied illustrations culminating in the final extended sequence prompted by the death of the sexton, old Dibble. Dibble, though in his eightieth year, took satisfaction in having outlived five rectors and had cherished the hope of outliving yet another; and this leads very naturally into an eloquent closing passage that begins:

> Yes! he is gone and WE are going all;
> Like flowers we wither and like Leaves we fall:
>
> (3.957–58)

Nevertheless, it is true that in general the reader's attention does tend to focus on the individual character sketch, anecdote, or short tale as though it were a discrete item rather than part of an extended argument; and there is a certain degree of unevenness in these items, the outstanding high spots being the sections inspired by Lucy the Miller's daughter, Sir Richard Monday, the unnamed blacksmith, Andrew Collett, the Widow Goe, Catharine Lloyd, Leah Cousins, and old Dibble. All the same, as we read our way through this superb long poem (undoubtedly among the most successful long poems of the period) there does accumulate a rich sense of the varied life of a rural parish, encompassing both different social levels, different occupations, and different ages and stages, and establishing a compassionate yet discerning social and moral vision well matched with the sincere, reasonable, well-judging Christian priest who acts as narrator. In this way the vividly particularized character sketches and neatly turned narratives add a unique further dimension to what is recognizably an extension into another period of the Augustan poetic tradition.

5

Further Narrative Development in *The Borough*

Crabbe's next volume was *The Borough*, published in 1810, a lengthy poem of nearly eight thousand lines, cast in the form of twenty-four letters from "an imaginary personage . . . a residing burgess in a large sea-port" to "the inhabitant of a village in the centre of the kingdom." In many respects the borough described asks to be identified with that of Aldeburgh, although it is only intermittently that the reader experiences any very strong sense of place. The town seems to have been expanded considerably in size in order to accommodate Crabbe's descriptive interests; consequently, some of its features (the street plan, the number of inns and clubs, the range of religious sects) are more suggestive of the larger neighboring towns of Woodbridge or Beccles.

In the first line of the poem Crabbe issues to his "imaginary personage" the injunction, "Describe the Borough"; but it soon becomes clear that he has not conceived the term "describe" in any narrow sense. In the preface, indeed, he writes, "What I thought I could best describe, that I attempted:—the sea, and the country in the immediate vicinity; the dwellings, and the inhabitants; some incidents and characters"; and the relative formlessness of the poem seems to have followed from this broad definition of "description." Lilian Haddakin has justly characterized the result as "a medley of descriptions, portraits, reflections, anecdotes and tales—more of a medley than the letter-headings suggest, since many letters are miscellaneous in content."[1]

Canon Ainger in his volume on Crabbe in the Men of Letters series seems to have associated the amorphousness of *The Borough* with the fact that it was "'in the making' during at least eight years." This, however, seems rather to overstate the length of the poem's gestation. There can be no real doubt that the poem was completed in October 1809. In regard to the starting-date, however, the probabilities are that in 1804 (three years before the publication of *The Parish Register*) Crabbe set to work upon a long poem that was ultimately to be published as *The Borough*, but that as he worked he incorporated into it, where he conveniently could, passages that he already had by him and that had not been written with this specific poem in mind. Of these passages the most important were those relating to the "Hospital Directors" in letter 17 and to Sir Denys Brand in letter 18.[2]

No manuscripts have survived of *The Borough* (any more than of *The Parish Register* or of *Tales* [1812]), so that we can do no more than speculate about the order of composition of the various letters, which must have been composed over a period of at least five years. Sigworth evidently believed it possible to infer a sequence from an examination of the development of narrative technique within the poem, for he wrote that in *The Borough*

> we can trace very clearly the course of Crabbe's development as a narrator, particularly if we assume that the poem was written more or less in the order in which Crabbe finally arranged it. If we accept the growing in narrative as a development in technique, we are safe in making the assumption of order, for in the course of the poem we can watch the art of story-telling absorb more and more of the poet's concern.[3]

However, what little we know about the poem's composition surely suggests that Sigworth's assumption here must be an extremely hazardous one. And, indeed, if we examine the material dispassionately we shall find that our impression that "in the course of the poem we can watch the art of story-telling absorb more and more of the poet's concern" is based almost entirely upon seven letters near the end of the poem, namely letters 14, 15, and 16 and letters 19, 20, 21, and 22. These differ from all the other letters in proclaiming themselves to be the history of a single individual, either one of the "Inhabitants of the Alms-House" or one of "The Poor of the Borough"; and they unquestionably mark a development in which narrative technique is carried some way beyond anything in *The Parish Register*. We seem fairly safe, therefore, in assigning to them a date of composition later than the conclusion of that poem—later, in fact, than "the latter part of the year 1806."

These apart, the overwhelming majority of the letters take the pattern of a fairly lengthy section of description or of generalized discursive argument, followed by either a character sketch or an anecdote that illustrates what has gone before. These often make interesting and agreeable reading, and can at times be highly entertaining. In letter 10 ("Clubs and Social Meetings"), for instance, one cannot fail to admire the skill with which Crabbe has rendered the tipsy maundering of the "Midnight Conversation" at the Smokers' Club, or to enjoy his skill in capturing the acrimonious quarrelsomeness that develops over the whist table. Nevertheless, with the possible exception of the portrayal of the vicar in letter 3, it cannot justly be maintained that the character sketches or brief narratives in these seventeen letters show any demonstrable advance in either characterization or storytelling technique beyond the level achieved in *The Parish Register*. It is thus only in the histories of the "Inhabitants of the Alms-House" and of "The Poor of the Borough" that we can see Crabbe making a significant (and seemingly rather sudden) breakthrough to new levels as a storyteller in verse; and it is therefore to these seven letters that the bulk of the present chapter will be devoted.

Letters 14, 15, and 16 (subtitled "Inhabitants of the Alms-House") are given over to the histories of Blaney, Clelia, and Benbow. Each was admitted to the almshouse as the choice of Sir Denys Brand, the self-important and plaudit-seeking chairman of the trustees. Crabbe says they have been selected for detailed representation so that the reader may "still more . . . understand / The moral feelings" of this ill-judging public benefactor. But this seems to be little more than a pretext. Crabbe, we feel, has departed at this point from his general plan for *The Borough*, because his imagination has been seized by the possibilities inherent in an extended narrative. One of the more influential models working in his mind has clearly been the eighteenth-century Progress, though it is not really possible to point to a specific exemplar. He was undoubtedly acquainted with some of the "progress pieces" in verse from the earlier decades of the eighteenth century, such as George Granville's "Cleora" (1712), Swift's "Phillis, or The Progress of Love" (1719), Pope's "Sir Balaam" (1735), or Soame Jenyns's "Modern Fine Gentleman" (1746) and "Modern Fine Lady" (1750). But any relationship here is by no means obvious, and in any case this was a subgenre that virtually died out after midcentury. New has urged an influence from the "preceptive tale" as found in the periodical essays of Johnson and Hawkesworth; but here again the resemblances are not very convincing. More relevant are the points of contact with Hogarth's great series of Progresses, a matter that will be taken up more fully in chapter 9. What can be said here is that not only are these tales single-person histories, but they also record in each case a "degress," a downward movement in the protagonist's social or moral condition or both, and this decline is attributed, either explicitly or implicitly, to some identifiable vice, weakness, or error.

Clelia (in letter 15) was based, according to Crabbe's son, upon a real-life provincial flirt "known to Mr Crabbe in early life"; but what is striking is the amount of elaboration and development that has gone into Crabbe's poetic treatment of his raw material. Crabbe's son reports (in an ms. note on the same page) that "The incidents are imaginary." It is, however, the detailed instances and circumstances marking the steady decline of Clelia's fortunes that make up the real substance of the tale. One (fairly small) element that has contributed to this elaboration can be pinpointed with confidence. One of the two quotations prefaced to this letter is from Richardson's *Clarissa*; and this hint makes it clear that, in his portrayal of Clelia when young, Crabbe has had in mind to depict his own provincial Sally Martin. Richardson's Sally Martin was seduced by Lovelace, whom she had hoped to "catch" as a husband; the relevant letter from Lovelace to Belmont contains significant parallels ("she holds ready a net under her apron, he another under his coat; each intending to throw it over the other's neck") with the maneuvering that goes on when Clelia (unsuccessfully) engages in a similar "strife of hearts" with "the Lovelace of his day."

In general, Crabbe's narrative convicts Clelia of folly and error rather than of innate viciousness, though these faults do lead her into vicious conduct that she deludedly expects to serve her own self-interest. Self-delusion is indeed a trait in her at all stages of her career. The "spirit quick and gay" that enables her to maintain a certain resilience amidst her declining fortunes is essentially a manifestation of her refusal to face the truth—a refusal announced at the outset in her determination "In time's despite, to stay at twenty-five."

Crabbe's opening fifty-four-line characterization of her as a young woman is so skilful in its marrying of neatness, objectivity, and subtlety that it needs to be read as a whole and cannot fairly be excerpted from. It is followed by an effective, though fairly unspecific, account of her disastrously unsuccessful attempt to entrap Henry (the "Lovelace" in question) into marriage. Ten years later we glimpse her as the mistress of an attorney who had at one time sought to marry her; she fatuously keeps up her spirits by fond talk about her "higher friendships," which are now no more. Another ten years pass and we see her a few rungs further down the social ladder— now the mistress of the landlord of the *Griffin*, where she is ready enough "Gaily to dress and in the bar preside," but proves ineffectual in the more mundane duties required of the landlady of an inn. (She and her protector try to drown their differences in strong drink, and he dies insolvent.) After yet another ten years we see her going rapidly downhill as her powers decline: keeping house for widowers among whom she still hopes, fruitlessly, to catch a husband; writing a novel; and unsuccessfully keeping a toy shop.

At this point compassion enters into Crabbe's depiction of her plight:

> Now friendless, sick and old, and wanting bread,
> The first-born tears of fallen pride were shed—
> True, bitter tears; and yet that wounded pride,
> Among the poor, for poor distinctions sigh'd.
>
> (174–77)

Crabbe's unfailing concern for "th'instructive truth" compels him to record dispassionately her persistence, even at this lowest ebb in her fortunes, in reprehensible triviality and self-delusion—her attempts to give "flirtish form" to the "piteous patchwork" of her only dress, her "strange delight" in joining "the menials crowding to the wall" to watch the dancing in which she had once participated, the "degraded vanity" with which she boasts (no longer quite accurately) of her former triumphs. Nor does she show any signs of repentance or even of moral regret; after being admitted to the almshouse by Sir Denys, she becomes the crony of the unspeakable Blaney. Together,

> Hour after hour they sit, and nothing hide
> Of vices past; their follies are their pride;
>
> (210–11)

Although there is no psychological development in Crabbe's portrayal of Clelia, there is psychological continuity, and this continuity both supports and enhances the variety of particularized detail that the poet excels in supplying.

The story of Blaney in letter 14 is also a "degress," but this time with certain variations. Blaney starts at a higher point in the social scale than Clelia, and consequently has farther to fall. The opening phase is indeed a conventional one:

> Blaney, a wealthy Heir at twenty-one,
> At twenty-five was ruin'd and undone:
> These Years with grievous Crimes we need not load,
> He found his Ruin in the common Road;
>
> (13–16)

A second chance comes his way; he is lucky enough to ensnare "a kind wealthy Widow," and this time his wife's dowry lasts them "ten long Winters" before it is used up. Even then his luck does not desert him, and a kind relation finds a "place" for him in a colony overseas; from the rather more limited opportunities for debauchery now offered he and his lady are eventually delivered by his remarkable good luck in inheriting a huge fortune from a previously unknown relative.

The psychological development that Crabbe has worked into this "progress" belongs essentially to these earlier stages in Blaney's history. We are told at the outset that there is in Blaney's makeup "much innate vileness," though the vicious practices that swallowed up his first fortunes had been of a commonplace, undistinguished kind. As Crabbe puts it, he

> Gamed without Skill, without Enquiry bought,
> Lent without Love, and borrow'd without Thought.
>
> (17–18)

In his second round of debauchery, paid for out of the dower of his "kind wealthy Widow," he aspires to "loftier flights of Vice," but these are represented as the slightly ridiculous exploits of a self-regarding young rake, taking such forms as the hiring of "singing Harlots of enormous price" and the intimate friendship of *"Hounslow Dick*, who drove the Western Stage." It is only when he is busy spending his third fortune that his vicious propensities come into full play, for now his jaded appetite requires that his "vicious Pleasure" must be "season'd and refin'd" by the consciousness of ruining and destroying an innocent victim. In this portrayal of progressive moral degradation Crabbe shows acuteness of insight. Less fully convincing is his accompanying description of how Blaney stilled an uneasy conscience by reading "Tales of *Voltaire*, and Essays gay and slight." Indeed, the references to the harmful influence of "the cooler reasoners" such as Blount, Mandeville, Chubb, and Hume (it is admitted that Blaney didn't read them himself but accepted their "faith" at second hand) seem to have been dragged in a little arbitrarily as an outlet for the poet's animus against these writers. Crabbe's denunciatory power comes into its own again, however, in the final stage of Blaney's "degress" after he has given away his last guinea in a devil-may-care gesture and is reduced to the miserable straits of "A Man of Pleasure when he's poor and old":

> Lo! now the Hero shuffling through the Town,
> To hunt a Dinner and to beg a Crown;
> To tell an idle Tale, that Boys may smile;
> To bear a Strumpet's Billet-doux a mile;
> To cull a Wanton for a Youth of Wealth,
> (With reverend view to both his Taste and Health);
> To be an useful, needy thing between
> Fear and Desire—the Pander and the Screen;
>
> (142–49)

Since Blaney clearly belongs to an earlier world of eighteenth-century debauchery that Crabbe cannot have known at first hand, the particularization that clothes this penultimate phase of his career is more convincing
than one might expect. Admittedly it does not approach the unquestion-
able authenticity of Clelia's depiction. On the other hand, since Crabbe
has evidently moved well beyond poor "Major Dade of Dennington," the
"half-pay major in a garrison town on the east coast" whom Crabbe's son
nominates as the real-life original for this portrait ("though the extreme
degradation is exaggerated"), one feels that he has made exceptionally well-
judged use of what he could glean from the more disreputable of eighteenth-century novels and (perhaps) from oral tradition. The markedly
unsympathetic moral judgment is, at any rate, more than justified by the
case presented. Even Sir Denys Brand, in pleading for Blaney's admission
to the almshouse, concedes that "The Fellow's quite a Brute— / A very
Beast." Crabbe's own concluding description of him as "an old licentious
Boy" has a mildness explicable only if we see it as deliberately bringing to
the fore Blaney's constitutional incapacity for taking in, in moral terms, any
of the lessons of experience. In the almshouse the temperance and solitary
life enjoined upon him makes him miserable; he is shunned by all the inmates except Clelia, and yet even now he "will nothing learn" and "Not
one right Maxim has he made his own."

In his history of Blaney, Crabbe evaded the constrictions of the
"progress" form by expanding the earlier prosperous phases that precede
the obligatory downward movement of the protagonist. In the story of
Benbow, letter 16, the diversification is differently achieved, by adding three
other separate but related character sketches. Benbow's own "progress" is
told in extremely foreshortened form. Having inherited from his father "a
worthy Name and Business," he sold the "fair Possessions," and spent all
the proceeds in drinking, thereby acquiring the "glowing Face" that Crabbe
compares with Bardolph's "fiery Front." There is some shrewd description
of the empty self-inflation supplied by "the Midnight bowl," which "when
the *Gas* from the *Balloon* is gone" leaves the toper "grov'ling on the Ground";
but the bulk of the letter is occupied by Benbow's retrospective eulogies of
three of his former boon companions. The first and longest of these concerns "the good *Squire Asgill,*" and this gives opportunity for a vividly pic-
tured reconstruction of an "Old England," loose-living, easygoing, licentious, which has now vanished under the new regime introduced by the late
squire's son. Secondly, Benbow celebrates, with wholly inappropriate encomia, Captain Dowling, a toper who was ready to drink with anyone like "a
Man" at all times of day, despite his gravel, gout and short breathing, and
who died unrepentant at the age of fifty-five, having just called for his glass

to be filled, very much in the spirit of Pope's Helluo.[4] The third of Benbow's exemplars is Dolly Murrey, a compulsive cardplayer, who, satisfied by a sweepingly successful game at "gay *Quadrille,*" died at the card table "as one taught and practis'd how to die."

These three sketches (and particularly that of the old Squire Asgill) are supreme examples of what Peter New called, in relation to Andrew Collett, "Crabbe's ability to dramatize the zest of a character whose moral attitude he totally rejects." It is surprising therefore that the same critic should so misinterpret the poet's tone here as to write of "the barely criticised zest" of Benbow, and even go so far as to claim that "our sympathies are drawn powerfully towards Benbow's and the elder Asgill's values, for they seem to be the values of life as against death."[5] Crabbe himself evidently found Benbow an even more repugnant character than either Blaney or Clelia, as can be seen from his comment in the 1810 preface:

> Benbow may be thought too low and despicable to be admitted here; but he is a Borough-character, and however disgusting in some respects a picture may be, it will please some, and be tolerated by many, if it can boast that one merit of being a faithful likeness.

The poetic texture itself repeatedly underscores an irony that tells all the time against taking Benbow's encomia at face value. For it is Benbow whose voice we hear enthusing about these three worthless specimens, and in doing so he is being encouraged by the poet to damn himself out of his own mouth—and his drinking-companions with him.

> Topers once fam'd, his Friends in earlier days,
> Well he describes, and thinks Description Praise;
> Each hero's Worth with much delight he paints,
> Martyrs they were, and he would make them Saints.
>
> (57–60)

Appropriately enough, the letter ends with the following triplet:

> The Bell then call'd these antient Men to pray,
> "Again," said *Benbow,* "tolls it every Day?
> Where is the life I led?" —He sigh'd and walk'd his way.
>
> (230–32)

This conclusion to his "degress," bereft of liquor, of cards and of congenial cronies, is clearly presented by Crabbe as his just desert.

Though they vary between themselves in their treatment of the "progress" form, each of the three letters dealing with "Inhabitants of the Alms-House" remains in some sense a "history"—a narrative whose structure is formed by successive stages in the unfolding of a human life story. Crabbe had still, in the four letters headed "The Poor of the Borough," to take the further step of weaving together the elements in his narrative so that they constitute an interlinked "plot." He moves a little closer to this with letter 20, "Ellen Orford," where certain of the incidents are more organically interrelated, though the total effect is still that of a "history" rather than of a unified "tale." In this letter, which is discussed more fully in chapter 12, those elements that remain obstinately disparate are held together by a unity of feeling that contrasts the reality of ordinary human suffering with the highly colored agonies and distresses portrayed in novels. Ellen Orford's sorrows are ones "Too often seen, but seldom in a book."

Had it been more successful, letter 21, "Abel Keene," might have been seen as coming even closer to being a fully organized "tale," partly because the narrative starts when Abel is already "growing old," so that the timescale of his "degress" (from respectable right-thinking schoolteacher to despairing pauperized suicide) is necessarily much foreshortened. Abel's troubles start when he is taken on as a clerk (at a much improved salary) by a "kind Merchant." He finds that the young clerks and the merchant's son, who are his new workmates, lightheartedly combine together, in their skepticism and atheism, to undermine the Christian beliefs that have hitherto kept him moral. Hesitantly at first, but then with increasing abandon, he enters on the path of vice. The narrative is at its weakest in its failure to explain why, when the merchant dies suddenly, his son should dismiss and abandon Abel, so that after a prolonged spell on "Town-relief" he becomes a moody, solitary wanderer and is eventually found hanging, long dead, in a pedlar's shed. He has left behind him a paper with the infelicitous title "My Groanings and my Crimes" in which he blames for his misfortunes firstly the "Deluders," who took away his "simple Faith," and secondly a famous Calvinist preacher to whom he had turned in his distress of mind but who bade him do nothing but wait for a "Call," which in the event never came. Unfortunately, throughout this letter Crabbe's talent is working at unusually low pressure, and much of the poem is marred by a banality of expression foreshadowed in the unfortunate opening couplet:

> A quiet simple Man was *Abel Keene,*
> He meant no harm, nor did he often *mean*;
>
>   (1–2)

Clearly the verbal infelicities are symptoms of a failure of imaginative power, and this we can perhaps associate with an uncharacteristic narrowing of sympathy observable in Crabbe at times when his professional prejudices (against deists or against Calvinists, for instance) are strongly aroused.

It is with letter 19, "The Parish-Clerk" that Crabbe comes into his own as creator of a fully fledged "tale in verse"—a cohesive narrative sequence in which incident and character are woven together in such a way as to build up to a climax, followed by a dénouement, and winding down to a resolution. Though the tale itself has a certain slightness that keeps it from being one of his most powerful achievements, Crabbe shows himself here fully in command of his material and its form. The only feature that might arouse a trace of uneasiness is the use of the mock-heroic mode for the introduction of his protagonist ("hight Jachin"), followed by the overt dismissal of "the playful Muse" when the story proper commences, on the grounds that "There is no jesting with Distress and Crime." But even here Crabbe vindicates his procedure by using it to dramatize the self-regarding "Spirit's Pride" with which Jachin casts himself as a mighty opponent to Satan's omnipresent wiles. Jachin's "book-taught" self-importance, his disposition to see himself as a "Man of Letters," a cut above the unlearned members of the congregation, had perhaps for contemporary readers a socially typical appositeness that it is not easy for us to appreciate today. Originally one of the minor orders of the church, the office of parish clerk still had clinging to it at the end of the eighteenth century a certain tradition of clerical learning, even though it was normally filled by a layman with no formal education. In the opening mock-heroic section of the tale, Jachin's self-righteous complacence is conveyed to us through his own words as he boasts of his careful avoidance of the snares that "the sly Seducer" sets out in the form of inns, feasts, banquets, plays (which his vicar, like Crabbe in real life, is not averse to attending) and, most dangerous of all, "the Damsels pacing down the Street." His excessive zeal for the moral welfare of others excites the resentment of some parishioners who feel that he is overstepping his allotted role, and they make two unsuccessful attempts to tempt him away from the path of virtue. However, Crabbe is well aware that the temptations we are conscious of are frequently not the ones we most need to be on our guard against.

> Alas! how often erring Mortals keep
> The strongest Watch against the Foes who sleep;
> While the more wakeful, bold and artful Foe
> Is suffer'd guardless and unmark'd to go.
>
> (142–45)

Jachin's true Achilles' heel is his poverty, and now that he has dismissed the "playful muse," the poet gives circumstantial reality to the temptation this presents to a man who

> wanted not the sense
> That lowly rates the Praise without the Pence
>
> (124–25)

and who felt in any case that the "common Herd," having noted the worn condition of "his Doublet and his Shoes," did not accord him the reverence and respect they gave to less deserving but more wealthy parishioners. The parish-clerk's fall from grace follows period that is a particularly lean one for his finances:

> The year was bad, the Christening-fees were small,
> The Weddings few, the Parties Paupers all:
>
> (136–37)

There follows a graphic evocation of the physical setting within which the temptation takes root—the monthly Communion service during which the vicar reads and the clerk takes the collection, holding the collection box over the high partition that separates the pews and shields him from the view of the congregation. No less effectively and truthfully realized are the trains of thought that lead Jachin to think first about the seeming justice of appropriating for himself a portion of the "Off'rings'" intended for "the Poor" and then about the practicability of doing so without being detected. In these private musings Jachin is of course perverting reason for his own venal ends, looking in fact for "Reasons on his Passion's side"; and it is worth noting that although Crabbe is unquestionably a firm believer in "right Reason" as the basis on which behavior, values, and religious faith should be built, he is at the same time exceptionally alert to the human tendency to misuse reason. The reader needs therefore to be on guard to catch the ambivalences that surface from time to time in his use of the words "reasons" (particularly in the plural), "reasoning," and "reasoners." Jachin's case is, of course, an example of what we would nowadays call rationalization. He reassures his conscience by saying:

> But I'll be kind—the Sick I'll visit twice,
> When now but once, and freely give Advice.
>
> (184–85)

This kind of shift is ludicrous whether or not one recognizes the allusion to the similar good resolution uttered by Pope's Sir Balaam when he similarly yielded to temptation.[6]

Once Jachin, in a vividly rendered scene, has taken the plunge into sacrilegious pilfering, custom and practice harden his conscience so that he can eat and drink the sacramental bread and wine after completing his offense without feeling "th'electric Shock" that accompanied his first such fall. Suspicion, discovery, and retribution are shown to follow their inevitable course; and it is perhaps a superadded blow to the "book-taught" Jachin's pride that the instrument of detection should be

> A stern stout Churl, an angry Overseer,
> A Tyrant fond of Power, loud, lewd and most severe.
>
> (230–31)

This man's lewd (i.e., unlearned) energy and ingenuity have come into play partly because the circumstances have called into question his own honesty in the procedures involved in distributing the Communion offerings among the poor of the parish. Even the angry overseer, however, is content to leave retribution to the work of Jachin's own conscience once he has been removed from office, and there is a shrewd fittingness in the incongruous thought that comes into the clerk's mind when his misdeeds are first exposed: "I owe to *Satan* this Disgrace and Shame." Later, as he languishes away, he recognizes more rationally and justly the full extent of his own responsibility for what has happened.

> They saw him then so ghastly and so thin,
> That they exclaim'd, "Is this the work of Sin?"
> "Yes," in his better moments, he replied,
> "Of sinful Avarice and the Spirit's Pride;—
> While yet untempted, I was safe and well;
> Temptation came; I reason'd and I fell;
> To be Man's Guide and Glory I design'd,
> A rare Example for our sinful kind;
> But now my Weakness and my Fault I see.
> And am a Warning—Man, be warn'd by me!"
>
> (287–96)

This declension from the original vanity of hoping to be an example to the actual fate of being a warning is not, perhaps, an uncommon eighteenth-century theme—it certainly brings with it an echo of Richardson's *Clarissa*[7]— but as presented here it brings out to the full a tragic poignancy that lifts the tale above the level of a mere didactic exemplum. The preceding paragraph, too, has intensified our empathy with the disgraced parish clerk by evoking the setting in which he was destined to see hourly "how much more fatal Justice is than Law":

> In each lone place, dejected and dismay'd,
> Shrinking from view, his wasting Form he laid;
> Or to the restless Sea and roaring Wind,
> Gave the strong yearnings of a ruin'd Mind:
> On the broad Beach, the silent Summer-day,
> Stretch'd on some Wreck, he wore his Life away;
> Or where the River mingles with the Sea,
> Or on the Mud-bank by the Elder-tree,
> Or by the bounding Marsh-dyke, there was he;
> And when unable to forsake the Town,
> In the blind Courts he sate desponding down—
> Always alone . . .

These lines are an impressive early example of Crabbe's ability to use landscape or a feeling of place to define and underscore a state of mind.

The nature of the step forward in narrative development from "The Inhabitants of the Alms-House" to "The Poor of the Borough" deserves a little further discussion. We may start from E. M. Forster's offer, in *Aspects of the Novel*, to define the term "plot":

> We have defined a story as a narrative of events arranged in their time-sequence. A plot is also a narrative of events, the emphasis falling on causality. "The king dies and then the queen died,'" is a story. "The king died, and then the queen died of grief," is a plot. The time-sequence is preserved, but the sense of causality overshadows it.

Forster's "story" is clearly equivalent to what I have called a "history" ("chronicle" would be another alternative word). More recently Seymour Chatman has raised a doubt as to whether there can be such a thing as "mere sequence, a depiction of events that simply succeed one another but in no sense owe their existence to each other." Our minds, he suggests, "inveterately seek structure," and will seek to supply it if it appears to be absent. On the other hand, it may be questioned whether the presence of either explicit or implicit causation within a narrative sequence is in itself enough to constitute what we ordinarily call a "plot." Some further "point" or thematic concentration seems to be needed—as is perhaps recognized in Edwin Muir's classic definition in *The Structure of the Novel*:

> The term plot . . . designates for everyone . . . the chain of events in a story
> and the principle which knits it together.

But it will be better to return from such abstractions to specific examples.[8]

"Clelia," as we have said, belongs to a transitional stage in the development of Crabbe's narrative art—the point at which the influence of the Progress-form has produced something analogous to what Pat Rogers has called "a sharply cut-off narrative sequence of step-by-step external scenes" whose aims are "instructive and illustrative rather than explanatory and exploratory." Certainly the plot element here is still only rudimentary: the ten-year stages chart a steady decline in Clelia's status and worldly fortune, but there is no close linking of episodes within them, and Clelia, though older and poorer, remains at the end just as incurably vain, trivial, and self-deluding as at the beginning. The steps that mark the downward movement of her fortunes are so loosely bound together, and the causal relationships are so lightly touched in, that the emphasis falls more on the pathos of her continuing self-delusion than on her responsibility for her own fate. Thus in its total effect the letter seems to be concerned with events not so much for their intrinsic narrative interest as for their illustrative power as manifestations of the dominant traits in Clelia's personality—a combination of false moral values with feckless ineffectuality.

By contrast, "The Parish-Clerk" has a much more closely woven plot, the most salient parts of which trace in circumstantial detail the mechanics of Jachin's thefts from the church offering intended for the poor and his subsequent exposure and humiliation. Yet in any attentive reading of the poem this structure of outward events is necessarily subordinate to a more inwardly conceived narrative structure—one that is concerned above all with the moral and psychological dimensions of the temptation to which Jachin yields and of his devastation when his crime has been detected. There can be little doubt that in the selection, ordering, and presentation of his narrative Crabbe has been guided throughout by the intention to demonstrate a divinely ordained causality at work in human affairs, even though in the workings out his view of causality is neither as crude nor as lacking in compassion as some popular stereotypes of Crabbe might suggest. Crabbe places the node or hinge-point of his tale at the point in the narrative when Jachin is rehearsing to himself the self-justifying "Reasons" to whose tempting voice, after much inner debate, he finally succumbs, and the whole point of the fable depends on our accepting that this hinge-point is a genuinely open one—that Jachin had at the moment of his decision a free moral choice. Here is the "principle," in Muir's sense, that is at the heart of this plot—and it is one that reappears in varying guise in many other tales in Crabbe's oeuvre.

"The Parish-Clerk," then, can fairly be seen as a "progress" in which the chain of events has been knitted together, with the artifice characteristic of the novelist, into a "tale in verse" with a plot. "Peter Grimes," letter 22, by far the most powerful of the tales in *The Borough*, is rather different in that while there is indeed a taut interrelatedness between the events, so that incidents are seen to lead on, one to the next, with an almost tragic inevitability, there is no sense in which it can properly be called a progress. The poet's inspiration has patently been guided by Shakespearean influences, as is made plain by the choice of epigraphs from *Richard II* and *Macbeth*. Peter New's allusion[10] to "the motionless phase of what the general *Preface* calls his [i.e., Grimes's] 'progress'" is in fact misleading, since Crabbe is here using the word in a much more restricted context; his full sentence reads:

> The character of Grimes, his obduracy and apparent want of feeling, his gloomy kind of misanthropy, the progress of his madness, and the horrors of his imagination, I must leave to the judgment and observation of my readers.

For the poet the problem essentially was that of making convincing the operation of something akin to remorse in a mind so unfeeling as to appear incapable of it. Crabbe seems to have been fully aware of the difficulty of what he was attempting, for in the passage just quoted he continues:

> The mind here exhibited is one untouched by pity, unstung by remorse, and uncorrected by shame: yet is this hardihood of temper and spirit broken by want, disease, solitude, and disappointment; and he becomes the victim of a distempered and horror-stricken fancy . . . . The ruffian of Mr Scott [in *Marmion*] has a mind of this nature: he has no shame or remorse: but the corrosion of hopeless want, the wasting of unabating disease, and the gloom of unvaried solitude, will have their effect on every nature; and the harder that nature is, and the longer time required to work upon it, so much the more strong and indelible is the impression. This is all the reason I am able to give why a man of feeling so dull should yet become insane, and why the visions of his distempered brain should be of so horrible a nature.

In this prose comment Crabbe may give the impression of attributing rather too much to external, and even accidental, circumstances, whereas the tale itself enacts a process in which the "want, disease, solitude, and disappointment" follow on from and are the inescapable corollary of Grimes's own actions and temperament. The poem works on a level where any initial didactic intent has been transmuted into an almost Shakespearean moral horror at what a human mind can be capable of, but the essential driving force of its poetic vision is an intense and unflinching closeness to reality, both sociological and psychological.

The sociological authenticity appears first and foremost in the description of the parish-apprenticeship system, the "Slave-shop" to which Grimes is able to apply no less than three times to procure the "feeling Creature subject to his Power" that his sadistic impulses demand. Crabbe does not mince his words here:

> Peter had heard there were in London then—
> Still have they being?—workhouse-clearing men,
> Who, undisturb'd by feelings just or kind,
> Would parish-boys to needy tradesmen bind:
> They in their want a trifling sum would take,
> And toiling slaves of piteous orphans make.
>
> (59–64)

A similar steadfast percipience of social observation is manifested in the indifference to Peter's treatment of his boys shown by the majority of the townsfolk; in the callousness of the few who "on hearing Cries / Said calmly, '*Grimes* is at his Exercise'"; in the muted tone of the inquiries into the deaths of the first two boys; in the sentimentalizing intensification of concern on the part of the seamen's wives when they suspect that Peter's third boy is "Of gentle Blood, some noble Sinner's Son"; in the townsfolk's self-righteous hostility to Peter after the death of his third apprentice; and in their inhumane reactions (some curious, some censorious) to Peter's madness once his odd behavior has been noticed by "summer visitors" watching through their glasses.

But it is the psychological authenticity that is at the heart of the poem, and it is here that Crabbe has added to the bare outline of his raw material so much that is peculiarly his own. This raw material was twofold. The 1834 footnote by Crabbe's son reads:

> The original of Peter Grimes was an old fisherman of Aldborough while Mr Crabbe was practising there as surgeon. He had a succession of apprentices from London, and a certain sum from each. As the boys all disappeared under circumstances of strong suspicion, the man was warned by some of the principal inhabitants, that if another followed in like manner he should certainly be charged with murder.

To this Crabbe's son later added in a manuscript note on the same page: "Tom Brown. The death of the apprentices was most suspicious. The Terrors imaginary, I believe." In addition it must be remembered that throughout the eighteenth century cases of apprentice-cide (as *The Anti-Jacobin Review* dubbed them) were by no means uncommon; and they sometimes attracted a good deal of attention and were turned into ballads or broadsides. Thus, according to A. L. Lloyd, the short ballad "The Cruel Ship's Captain" was a pared-down version of a longer broadside ballad in the form of a wordy gallows confession based upon a case in which a whaler skipper was charged in King's Lynn with the murder of an apprentice. By far the most famous of such cases, however, was that of John Bennett, a fisherman living at Hammersmith, who was indicted for the murder of his apprentice, George Main, a boy about eleven years old, "on the High-Seas, near Sheerness in England by beating him with a stick called a Tiller on the Head, Back, Shoulder and Arms and thereby giving him several Mortal Wounds."[11] There are too many parallel details in the stories of Bennett and Grimes to leave room for doubt that Crabbe must have heard of Bennett's case and, whether consciously or not, made use of it. Thus G. Sugg, Bennett's colleague and employee, gave evidence of continual whipping, bullying, and maltreatment of the boy and said that he had had "but one shirt to his back" in the three months he was with his master. Moreover, according to Sugg, Bennett "said that [the boy] fell from the Mast-head and kill'd himself, but that was impossible, for the Mast is so low, that a man may stand upon his Boat's head and reach the top of it." (It will be recalled that Grimes's second apprentice was said by him to have fallen "From the Boat's Mast and perish'd in her Well," and that the jury were doubtful whether this story could be true.) Finally, it was stated that Bennett had returned to Hammersmith with the corpse of the boy *and* with a load of fish that he got another fisherman to tranship and take to Billingsgate for sale—a detail closely paralleled in the fate of Grimes's third apprentice. It seems, then, that the details of the poem have been fused from two separate real-life instances. At the same time, the comment by Crabbe's son, "The Terrors imaginary, I believe," reminds us that it is precisely the poet's evocation of Grimes's state of mind as his guilt-induced delusions take hold over him that makes the tale so hauntingly powerful.

Crabbe's choice of the surname "Grimes" for his own protagonist (so much more fitting for his purpose than Bennett or Brown) may have been suggested by the young man Grimes in Chapter 7 of Godwin's *Caleb Williams*, a novel that we know the poet to have possessed in his library at Trowbridge. Godwin's Grimes was "in an inconceivable degree boorish and uncouth," with a complexion scarcely human, and features "coarse and strangely discordant and disjointed from each other." At the same time he was a total stranger to tenderness and had "an incapacity to conceive those finer feelings that make so large a part of the history of persons who are cast in a gentler mould." In any case, we have to accept as a "given" in Crabbe's young Peter Grimes an inborn self-centered, antisocial disposition to evil. His obdurate rebelliousness against all social claims upon him is evidently neither inherited nor the result of early ill-treatment. Indeed, it is "the good Old Man" his father whom Peter not only reviles but also first rebels against "to prove his freedom," even to the extent of felling him with a "sacrilegious Blow.'" In a shrewd foreshadowing of feelings that assert themselves more strongly later in the tale, his father's death leads Peter to an outburst of maudlin grief, but the strength and significance of this apparent remorse is discounted for us by his intoxication at the time. Released from parental restraint, Peter now thinks it hard that he should be "debarr'd / From constant Pleasure" by the need to "acquire the Money he would spend" and embarks upon a career of pilfering and depredation that leads him increasingly to look on "all Men as his Foes." But this kind of success in flouting the conventions of property cannot satisfy him, and it is his cruel soul's wish for "one to trouble and control" (to torment, in fact, out of sheer sadism) that leads him to acquire his first apprentice. The relationship that ensues is described in a passage that shows how flexibly Crabbe is now able to adapt the heroic couplet to purposes very different from those hitherto associated with it:

> Pinn'd, beaten, cold, pinch'd, threaten'd, and abus'd,—
> His Efforts punish'd and his Food refus'd,—
> Awake tormented,—soon arous'd from sleep,—
> Struck if he wept, and yet compell'd to weep,
> The trembling Boy dropt down and strove to pray,
> Receiv'd a Blow, and trembling turn'd away,
> Or sobb'd and hid his piteous face. . . .
>
> (79–85)

After the relentless battering sequence of the first line, it is the well-tried poetic resources of parallelism and antithesis that are deployed in series to enforce the grimly compassionate realism with which the boy's wretched and hopeless situation is portrayed.

The first boy's death passes with relatively little question or comment. When a second boy dies, there is a full-scale inquiry that "sturdy Peter" outfaces brazenly; and this time an unemphatic rider added by the jury who dismiss him strikes home in a way that subtly demonstrates that there is a side to him that will in the end prove susceptible to shame, if not to remorse.

"Keep fast your Hatchway, when you've Boys who climb."
This hit the conscience, and he colour'd more
Than for the closest questions put before.

(115–18)

The third boy, "of manners soft and mild," lasts a surprisingly long time, partly because the sympathetic seamen's wives surreptitiously give him "Fire, Food and Comfort" and partly because Peter, made more cautious by the last inquiry, now exercises "self Pity" in dealing "his vile Blows." The crisis, when it comes, is rendered with a chill economy. Having caught more fish than he can sell in the Borough, Peter sets sail with them for "London-mart":

the Boy was ill,
But ever humbled to his Master's will;
And on the River, where they smoothly sail'd,
He strove with terror and awhile prevail'd;
But new to Danger on the angry Sea
He clung affrighted to his Master's knee:
The Boat grew leaky and the Wind was strong,
Rough was the Passage and the Time was long;
His Liquor fail'd, and *Peter*'s wrath arose . . . :
No more is known—the rest we must suppose,
Or learn of *Peter*,—"*Peter*," says he, "spied
The Stripling's danger and for Harbour tried;
Meantime the fish and then th'Apprentice died."

(140–52)

The bathetic parallelism in the last line (a device borrowed directly from Pope)[12] here underscores with devastating irony the distorted value scale that animates Grimes's actions.

This time the Mayor's verdict is that Peter shall never again be allowed to take a boy apprentice; but the permitted alternative, that of hiring a freeman, is not in sober fact open to him either, since he has made himself so hated that no one will work for him. Consequently he is condemned to be "employ'd alone / At bootless labour" by which he cannot adequately support himself—the precondition of the "hopeless want" mentioned in the Preface, which in its turn leads eventually to "the wasting of unabating disease." In the poem, however, the stress falls more strongly upon "the gloom of unvaried solitude" that afflicts Peter now that he is "by himself compell'd to live each day"; and the well-known passages describing the bleak river landscape are both vividly evocative in their own right and unerringly matched to the progressive development of Peter's "gloomy kind of misanthropy."

Initially what we see are the views forced upon Peter by his circumstances, compelled as he is

> To wait for certain hours the Tide's delay,
> At the same times the same dull views to see,
> The bounding Marsh-bank and the blighted Tree;
> The Water only, when the Tides were high,
> When low, the Mud half-cover'd and half-dry;
> The Sun-burnt Tar that blisters on the Planks,
> And Bank-side Stakes in their uneven ranks;
> Heaps of Entangled Weeds that slowly float,
> As the Tide rolls by the impeded Boat.
>
>   (172–80)

Later, as his misanthropy deepens, we find Peter choosing "from Man to hide" and actually nursing "the Feelings these dull Scenes produce." At each stage there is a masterly precision and accuracy about the way in which the landscape of the River Alde is evoked, along with its accompanying marine life and bird sounds. These passages provide powerful ammunition for F. R. Leavis's assertion that "in the use of description, of nature and the environment generally for emotional purposes he [Crabbe] surpasses any Romantic."[13]

There is a well-judged art, too, in the successive stages by which the progress of Grimes's madness is revealed to us. Our first view of him petrified by some horrifying apparition is an external one:

> At certain stages he would view the Stream,
> As if he stood bewilder'd in a Dream,
> Or that some Power had chain'd him for a time,
> To feel a Curse or meditate on Crime.
>
>   (243–46)

Later, fear of mankind leads him to run away from his boat:

>   new terror fill'd his restless Mind:
> Furious he grew, and up the Country ran,
> And there they seiz'd him—a distemper'd man:—
> Him we receiv'd, and to a parish-bed,
> Follow'd and curs'd, the groaning Man was led.
>
>   (250–54)

Now we hear in fragmented form his own account of his experiences, but told in such a way that, even though he is near to death, we cannot be sure that we are being told the true story or the whole story:

He knew not us, or with accustom'd art
He hid the knowledge, yet exposed his Heart;
'Twas part Confession and the rest Defence,
A madman's Tale, with gleams of waking Sense.

(286–89)

As we piece the tale together, it seems that, under pressure of prolonged solitude and adversity, belated feelings of guilt and terror have conjured up before him, at three places in the river, a vision of two of his victims, but that this manifestation has become fused in his mind with his dead father's admonition to his undutiful son, so that it is the "Father-foe" ("the hard Old Man" as he most inappropriately terms him) whom he deludedly blames for all his sufferings. Listening to his deathbed recital of the "Horrors" that have afflicted him, our feelings go along with those of the "gentle Females" who perceive "Compassion on their Anger steal," even though we are aware of an admixture of brazen insensibility and self-exculpation in Grimes along with the more fragmented intuitions of "tortur'd guilt." "Peter Grimes" has its patches of weak writing, lines where the verbal expression is more clumsy than the evident underlying intention, but the intensity of the poet's vision is powerful enough to carry us over these. There will be more subtle, complex, and masterly tales to come in the poet's two succeeding volumes, but we can surely agree that in "Peter Grimes" the "tale in verse" has reached its full maturity as an art form.

If we attempt an overview of these seven single-character "Letter-tales" that were so crucial for Crabbe's development into a major poet, we see that the two subgroups prompt rather different reflections. There can be little doubt about the predominantly Augustan provenance and ethos of the three Letters concerned with "The Inhabitants of the Alms-House." Drawing much of their inspiration from the Progress form, they depict, in Blaney, Clelia, and Benbow, three characters whose social standing would have qualified them for portrayal in a verse-progress in the high Augustan era. The norms against which they are judged (with some compassion as regards Clelia, more harshly in the case of the other two) are the characteristically Augustan values of good sense, reasoned Christian belief and conduct, and good breeding. The extension beyond Augustanism here is essentially in the highly particularized detail and penetrating psychological insight with which their shortcomings are recorded.

The four letters under the heading of "The Poor of the Borough" are more varied among themselves and more difficult to characterize. The "low" nature of Crabbe's choice of subject matter necessarily carries him well outside the bounds prescribed by old-style Augustan theory and custom, and the feelings and spiritual experience of his humble protagonists are treated with a seriousness of concern that seems to fuse Crabbe's pastoral preoccupations as a country clergyman with an influence from the kind of pre-Romantic and early Romantic poems that were surfacing around the turn of the century. The poet's values, while more broadly based socially, are still largely Augustan in their essential ethos, and there is little suggestion of any generalized social protest on behalf of the underprivileged. Nevertheless, both the themes and their treatment, together with the highly particularized mode of characterization, leave with us a strong impression that these four tales could only have been written by a poet who had exposed himself, sensitively though not uncritically, to the new currents of feeling that were stirring in England and its literature from the 1790s onwards. What does seem to be in evidence, moreover, is a growing fascination with the possibilities of narrative as a means of embodying and representing these newly evolving values—and this is a radical innovation that carries the poet to the utmost fringe of Augustanism, and arguably beyond it.

6

The Goal Achieved:
Tales (1812)

Crabbe's next volume, *Tales*, was published in September 1812 and consists of twenty-one separate and unrelated tales, ranging in length between 298 lines ("The Wager," tale 18) and 727 lines ("The Patron," tale 5). Unfortunately, no manuscript material has survived for these tales, nor is there any information about the date or order of their composition. Judging from the technical mastery of all of the tales, it seems unlikely, however, that they can predate the final group of tales ("The Poor of the Borough") in *The Borough*.

The twenty-one tales are strikingly varied in subject matter, setting, theme and artistic purpose. It is true that, with a few exceptions, the characters dealt with belong to the middle rank of society—tradesmen, shopkeepers, merchants, farmers, clergyman's families; and it is undoubtedly the case that in each tale there is some focus of moral concern. This is often such as to distil from the sequence of events an explicit moral lesson, though there are also some tales in which Crabbe, without any diluting of his own Christian stance, seems rather to be preoccupied with defining the subtlety and complexity of the moral issues involved. Within this general framework, nevertheless, the overwhelming impression left behind by the collection is one of remarkable diversity; indeed, one feels that Crabbe is fully justified in making a virtue in his preface of the "greater variety of incident" made possible by a collection of separate tales, as opposed to the unified longer poem that the *Edinburgh Review* had recommended to him.

In the same sentence in his preface Crabbe seems to imply that his arrangement of the separate tales is designed to bring out the contrasts among them, so that "in these narratives we pass from gay to grave, from lively to severe, not only without impropriety, but with manifest advantage." It is difficult, however, to detect any special significance in Crabbe's chosen order for his tales, so it seems best to start instead with the tales that follow on most directly from the achievement of *The Borough*. Thus each of the four final tales in *The Borough* charts the life history of one individual; among the few 1812 tales that fall into a similar pattern, one of the more interesting is tale 19, "The Convert." This we know to have been suggested by the *Memoirs* of the bookseller, James Lackington, though the relationship seems to be a fairly distant one. Crabbe owes something to the general outline and spirit of Lackington's volume, but has borrowed only a few of the details.[1]

Crabbe's John Dighton grows up "an active boy" in a market town, obliged by his illegitimate birth to make his own way in the world. He soon proves himself "a ready knave" well able to find various odd and incongruous tasks or errands to fill his purse, and when in funds he is unrestrainedly ready to lead a thoroughly dissolute life. His conversion is accomplished by a "Teacher" who comes to pray with him when he is terrified of dying from a fever. So "mighty" is the "change" that his resolve to reform long outlasts his recovery from his illness. It is crucial to the intention of the tale that the poet here makes clear what it is that is lacking in Dighton's conversion—a lack that is wholly unrecognized by his Methodist mentors, to whom it never occurs that "one so passive, humble, meek" can still have need for "a creed and principles" as a basis for his religious life. Crabbe's extended explicit statement has key significance for an understanding of the poet's own beliefs, since the distinction between the faith that relies solely on feelings and the faith that is fortified also by reason is central to his whole outlook:

> The Faith that Reason finds, confirms, avows,
> The hopes, the views, the comforts she allows, —
> These were not his, who by his feelings found,
> And by them only, that his faith was sound;
> Feelings of terror these, for evil past,
> Feelings of hope to be receiv'd at last;
> Now weak, now lively, changing with the day,
> These were his feelings, and he felt his way.
>   Sprung from such sources, will this faith remain
> While these supporters can their strength retain:
> As heaviest weights the deepest rivers pass,
> While icy chains fast bind the solid mass;
> So, born of feelings, faith remains secure,
> Long as their firmness and their strength endure:
> But when the waters in their channel glide,
> A bridge must bear us o'er the threat'ning tide;
> Such bridge is Reason, and there Faith relies,
> Whether the varying spirits fall or rise.

(85–102)

The weak point in this passage is surely the opening couplet of the second paragraph. What the argument requires here is an assertion that this kind of faith (based only on feelings) will last as long as (and only as long as) its supporting feelings retain their strength; but the movement of the verse allows the syntactic inversion ("will this faith remain") to offer only a faltering attempt at this. Moreover, it may be felt that the simile of the fast-frozen river, if scrutinized closely, lacks some of the compelling internal consistency that characterizes Crabbe's imagery at its best. One wonders how far the poet has thought through the implications of an opposition between the bridge, a man-made artifact liable to prove impermanent, and the immutability of the river's tide, a force of nature . The passage as a whole, however, does establish the contrast between a feeling faith and a reasoning faith with a power that will help to make convincing Dighton's subsequent backsliding.

The humble convert still, Dighton is placed by his friends in a stationer's shop, where he sells pious pamphlets. He earns enough to take a wife, who is duly found for him from within the sect. But his zeal slackens as he grows more prosperous, and he extends the scope of his trade to include books of all kinds, whether religious or not. Crabbe ironically records his self-justification as the traditional commercial one:

> He had no office but to sell and buy;
> Like other traders, profit was his care;
> Of what they print the authors must beware;
> He held his Patrons and his Teachers dear,
> But with his trade—they must not interfere.
>
> (142–44)

As a next step he starts to sample the bolder and more freethinking titles among the books he is now selling, and he resembles Lackington in that he has begun to observe in his mentors defects of character ("craft, conceit, and spleen") that undermine his deference to them. Consequently when a deputation from the sect calls in order to reprove him, John vigorously rebuts their interference while at the same time accusing them of the faults (in particular "the frail and carnal appetite" manifested in a fondness for "ducks and peas") that he has noted in them. Freed now from any lingering restraints or scruples, Dighton finds that "Best of his books he loved the liberal kind." He disregards his wife's misgivings, and when she dies marries again, this time outside the sect.

Though his continuing increase in wealth and "consequence" buoys him up for a time, at the age of sixty-five Dighton begins to question once again the principles on which his life has been conducted, and to feel saddened and hurt by the strictures of the brethren who stand outside the shop (as they had done in real life outside Lackington's) to make their severe comments on his retreat from "the chosen track." His directionless disillusionment is compassionately rendered in the seesawing rhythms of his final monologue, when he knows that he has only another year or two to live:

> "No more!" he said, "but why should I complain?
> A life of doubt must be a life of pain:
> Could I be sure—but why should I despair?
> I'm sure my conduct has been just and fair;
> In youth indeed I had a wicked will,
> But I repented, and have sorrow still:
> I had my comforts, and a growing trade
> Gave greater pleasure than a fortune made;
> And as I more possess'd and reason'd more,
> I lost those comforts I enjoy'd before,
> When reverend guides I saw my table round,
> And in my guardian guests my safety found:
> Now sick and sad, no appetite, no ease,
> Nor pleasure have I, nor a wish to please:
> Nor views, nor hopes, nor plans, nor taste have I,
> Yet sick of life, have no desire to die.
>
> (430–45)

Since this tale is above all else an affirmation of the importance of basing one's religious faith on reason, it is somewhat striking that even in this context Crabbe's latent uneasy ambivalence towards the word "reason" should lead him to use it as a verb (line 438) in a sense that brings out the human tendency to misuse rationality for unworthy purposes. However, in his closing paragraph Crabbe unequivocally reasserts his dominant theme by restating a regret that at the crucial time Dighton did not find a friend to show him "the grounds of hope and fear" in reason and virtue, in which case his faith would have rested upon "the solid rock" and not "upon the sand / Where long it stood not, and where none can stand."

Peter New has described this tale as "in a conventional 'progress' form," but surely it should more properly be seen as essentially "spiritual biography." Its affinities are above all with those numerous biographies and autobiographies (mainly of Quakers during the early half of the century, and of Methodists in the later half) that led on the one hand to a democratization of the art of biography during the eighteenth century, and on the other hand to an increasing preoccupation in this newly developing art form with the "life within."[2]

Another tale with certain features in common with "The Convert" is tale 14, "The Struggles of Conscience." Here again is a spiritual biography, the novelty being that in this case conscience is personified as an inner presence with whom the protagonist, Fulham, is almost incessantly at war. Fulham was nephew to a toyman whose fanciful whims led him to sample a variety of sects, fixing finally on an obscure and unprosperous one, "precious and elect," small enough to meet "all in an attic room." Having followed his uncle's various conversions in a dutiful but skeptical spirit, Fulham had his conscience awakened for the first time by "a warm preacher" who "found a way t'impart / Awakening feelings to his torpid heart." Once he inherits his uncle's business, Fulham's desire for increased profits leads him into a protracted conflict with conscience—at first over trifles, where compromise can usually be attained, later over more serious issues. (There is some intriguing detail here about the various kinds of sharp practice on the part of shopkeepers, which Fulham either witnesses or engages in.) The final breach with his conscience, however, comes as a result of Fulham marrying for her money a wealthy maid "not quite an idiot" but "pretty, trifling, childish, weak." Unexpectedly he finds it impossible to control his newlywed wife; and to the accompaniment of conscience's steadily increasing alarm, he starts to think up ways of getting rid of her. At this point Crabbe seems to be thinking of Steele's Ephraim Weed, a tobacco merchant who had married for money three times and who in his letter to the *Spectator* wrote of his third wife, who had given him "a great deal of plague and vexation by her extravagances."

> I knew it would be to no manner of purpose to go about to curb the fancies and inclinations of women that fly out the more for being restrained; but what I could I did. I watched her narrowly, and by good luck found her in the embraces (for which I had two witnesses with me) of a wealthy spark of the court-end of the town; of which I recovered £15,000 which made me amends for what she had idly squandered. . . .[3]

Fulham's objective is not to obtain damages from the guilty party who cuckolds him, but merely to be able to divorce his wife without having to return the dowry she had brought him; to this end he "seem'd to leave her free" while remaining in reality "as watchful as a lynx." Unfortunately for his plans, the wife, though "without virtue," had "no wish to stray"; and he has to resort finally to provoking her into adultery as an act of revenge against his own petty tyrannizing over her:

> "Revenge," said he, "will prompt that daring mind;
> Refus'd supplies, insulted and distress'd,

Enrag'd with me, and near a favourite guest
Then will her vengeance prompt the daring deed,
And I shall watch, detect her and be freed,"

(401–5)

The infamous plan succeeds; but this time Fulham has gone too far to be able to square his "troubled Conscience," whatever expedients he may try. The final section of the tale recounts the various twists and turns by which the man tries to no avail either to forget or to appease the "watchful foe" within; and we are left with a powerful sense of a ruined life in which the sinning mortal has no hope of escape from pangs of conscience that have now become unbearable.

These two tales are each histories of a single life, and as such probably owed something (as did the final tales in *The Borough*) to the vogue that had developed in the course of the eighteenth century for prose biographies of people of no great social standing. Augustanism had always found peculiarly apt to its purposes the use of contrast, not merely as a local rhetorical device but also as a strategy for organizing larger structural patterns. The development of biography, with its built-in tendency to focus on change in the individual human being throughout a lifetime, led naturally to a penchant for narrative organized by means of contrast in time—contrast between an earlier and a later state. Contrast in time is indeed Crabbe's favorite structure for the verse-tale, as will be seen repeatedly both in this and in later chapters.

Among the biographies widely read was *Plutarch's Lives*, in the translations both of Dryden (1683–86) and of John and William Langhorne (1770). As D. A. Stauffer has shown, Plutarch's striking invention of parallel lives in pairs had been either explicitly or implicitly taken up in a number of eighteenth-century imitations. It seems possible therefore that this model lies behind the three tales in Crabbe's 1812 volume that follow a pattern of synchronous contrast between pairs of individual characters. Plutarch's practice, it is true, had been to recount the two lives separately and then to follow them up with a lengthy "Comparison," drawing out points of resemblance and difference. Crabbe's technique is to intermingle the two narratives and to allow the contrasts to develop in the process of the telling. (A similar contrastive pattern, used for didactic purposes, can be noted in some fiction of the period, notably that of Maria Edgeworth, though one thinks also of Jane Austen's *Sense and Sensibility*, published in 1811 but written a good deal earlier.) In the earlier part of "The Brothers" (tale 20), a series of swift cameos builds up the characters of the pair: George is a bluff, openhearted sailor, careless of money and solicitous for his brother's welfare; he rents for him a house where in return he himself spends his shore leave. Isaac is a physically weak but crafty and unscrupulous landsman, well-skilled in flattery and subservience. This eventually earns him a humble port-place, and he is ready to exercise the same guile upon his unsuspecting brother. In this phase of the narrative each character can fairly be seen as little more than a stereotype, leavened by an occasional touch of individuality. After George has spent some years at war and has bestowed two windfalls of prize-money upon his brother's family, he returns, a cripple with only one leg, intending to "lie at anchor" at his brother's house, innocently confident that he will receive a hero's and a benefactor's welcome. From this point on, the mode of presentation changes; it becomes a sequence of more extended scenes, realized with convincing detail and often with an adroit use of dialogue. There is charted for us the painful course of George's disillusionment, as he comes to understand that Isaac and his wife are treating him at first with indifference ("the mask of kindness now but seldom worn"), then with increasing callousness, and finally even with cruelty. Soon their young son is the only member of the family who values his uncle or wants to hear his sea yarns; then even he is forbidden access to George, who becomes consigned to solitary exile in the garret. Aware that his uncle is grievously ill, the boy persists nevertheless in clandestine visits to him. The action moves to a climax when Isaac follows the boy to the garret door and from outside it violently upbraids George for encouraging disobedience in his nephew—only to find when he eventually pushes the door open that his brother is already dead.

The enhanced vividness of these later episodes goes hand in hand with an added complexity in Crabbe's characterization of Isaac. It has been revealed that even while his harsh treatment of his brother was at its most extreme he has at times experienced "qualms of discontent" when contrasting the present with the past, and that his attribution of blame to his wife is not wholly unjustified, even though the main cause for his disregard of his better impulses is his own "av'rice, peevishness, or pride." The access of acute remorse that overcomes him when he realizes the outcome of his own actions has thus been prepared for; and we can see too that a practiced artistry is at work in the way Isaac's son's references to his late uncle heap coals of fire upon his father's head:

> An ague seiz'd him, he grew pale, and shook, —
> "So," said his son, "would my poor uncle look."
> "And so, my child, shall I like him expire:"
> "No! you have physic and a cheerful fire."
>
> (366–69)

Nor does the poet soften in any way the agony that Isaac is now condemned to feel; although indulgence in remorse and sorrow brings him some comfort, repentance cannot in the end palliate or diminish the gravity of his fault, and the tale concludes:

> Dark are the evil days, and void of peace the best.
> And thus he lives, if living be to sigh,
> And from all comforts of the world to fly,
> Without a hope in life—without a wish to die.

(408–11)

These final paragraphs of the tale bring home to the reader once again the remarkable power and penetration that Crabbe is always able to draw upon when he is rendering a sense of guilt in one of his characters.

The other two tales that rely on concurrent contrast instead of contrast in time are less serious in tone and amount really to contrastive anecdotes rather than contrasted lives. Thus tale 18, "The Wager" tells of two partners, Counter and Clubb, who, though "as men in trade alike," choose their wives according to markedly different criteria. Counter, who is vain and "must ever of [his] house be head," brings home

> a young complying Maid;
> A tender creature, full of fears as charms,
> A beauteous nursling from its mother's arms;

(63–65)

while Clubb, more realistic, looks for an equal, not a slave, and has no difficulty in finding a mate to suit his requirements. The wager, entered into after a convivial evening among neighbors at which the wine has flowed freely, is designed to show, by means of an excursion to Newmarket, which of the partners can demonstrate that he wears the trousers in his own household. Of course it succeeds in its object, showing clearly that, contrary to Counter's expectations, "'Tis easiest dealing with the firmest mind." The tale itself, though something of a lightweight among its companions in this volume, is wittily engaging, uses a good deal of neatly managed colloquial dialogue, and is notable for the acuity of its psychological insight, both in its portrayal of the relationships between the two married couples and of the relationships between Counter and Clubb themselves. (Clubb perceives that Counter's compulsion to chaff his partner about the extent to which he wields authority in his home "plainly proves him not at perfect ease"—as indeed turns out to be the case.) In "The Wager" Crabbe has taken up again, in slightly different and expanded form, a pattern of anecdote first attempted with Dawkins and Ditchem in part 1 of *The Parish Register*, but the comparison shows at once how much Crabbe has advanced in the intervening five years in sophistication, in lightness of touch, and in mastery of his medium.

The other tale with a pattern of synchronous contrast is tale 1, "The Dumb Orators; or, The Benefits of Society," and this also is an expanded anecdote designed to illustrate the theme, explicitly stated in the opening ten lines, that man's courage ebbs and flows according to whether he is surrounded by enemies or friends. Justice Bolt, who is unduly fond of holding forth on all manner of topics in an overbearing way, visits a midland city and goes along to a debating club, which turns out to be a nest of Socinians, Deists, Reformers, and Radicals. Here he finds himself compelled to listen to Hammond ("a sharp, shrewd, sallow man") abusing church, government, law, and lawyers, and extolling French liberty (this stage of the tale is evidently dated early in the 1790s). Though Bolt lets his disapproval appear by emitting a groan, he does not dare to speak out, a failure of courage that leads him later, on his home territory, to moderate the fierceness of his harangues—for a time at any rate. Some years later Hammond appears at Justice Bolt's dining club; he has come to the town to read one of his "Historic lectures where he lov'd to mix / His free plain hints on modern politics." Justice Bolt recognizes him as the cause of his former discomfiture and takes the appropriate revenge. Surrounded by a formidable array of clergy (and pluralists) Hammond can manage no more in reply than a halting mumble about "the Rights of Man" before he flees in confusion. What is most striking about this highly entertaining piece is the balance Crabbe accomplishes, a mature balance of attitude reflected in the formal structure of the tale as well as in the measured antitheses of the versification. The footnote by Crabbe's son states that "The original of Justice Bolt was Dr Franks of Alderton on the Norfolk coast—a truly worthy man, but rather a pompous magistrate," while an ms. note in FitzGerald's copy changes "Norfolk" to "Suffolk" and adds the phrase "and a most implacable Tory." Crabbe was no Tory himself, but there are signs in the tale that his own sympathies lie with Bolt's opinions rather than with those of Hammond. Nevertheless, his handling of the radical Hammond is marked by a scrupulous fairness, and Bolt is portrayed with an astute irony that does not fail to bring out his love of applause, his wish to domineer, his tedious overindulgence in the sound of his own voice, his cowardice at the crucial moment, and his subsequent self-righteous self-deception about his own motives. The extended mock-epic simile in which the enraged Justice

Bolt, safe on his own home ground, is compared to a turkey merits quotation for the aptness of the associations invoked:

> As a male turkey straggling on the green,
> When by fierce harriers, terriers, mongrels seen,
> He feels the insult of the noisy train,
> And skulks aside though mov'd by much disdain;
> But when that turkey at his own barn-door,
> Sees one poor straying puppy and no more;
> (A foolish puppy who had left the pack,
> Thoughtless what foe was threat'ning at his back,)
> He moves about as ship prepar'd to sail,
> He hoists his proud rotundity of tail,
> The half-seal'd eyes and changeful neck he shows,
> Where, in its quick'ning colours, vengeance glows;
> From red to blue the pendant wattles turn,
> Blue mix'd with red as matches when they burn;
> And thus th'intruding snarler to oppose,
> Urg'd by enkindling wrath, he gobbling goes.
>
> So look'd our Hero in his wrath, his cheeks
> Flush'd with fresh fires and glow'd in tingling streaks;
>
> (368–85)

By such means the poet controls the flow of the reader's sympathy, so that it shall be detached and impartial, owing its allegiance to a Christian good sense, a tolerant "right reason" against whose yardstick both Hammond and Bolt show themselves deficient.

In these tales Crabbe is clearly moving away from the narrative that is concerned with a single life history towards a tale that takes as its center the interaction between two or more characters; and the predominance of such tales is one of the features distinguishing *Tales* (1812) from the tales in *The Borough*. A preoccupation with individuality, and in particular a concern to recognize the uniqueness of the individual human being, has been commonly regarded as a characteristic feature of Romanticism, and Crabbe's change of direction at this point might be seen as a reassertion of those Augustan values that placed the major emphasis on human life in its social aspects. It must be remembered, however, that for Pope and his contemporaries interest in the "social" was focused above all on the behavior of their protagonists in their public roles. This emphasis does continue to appear in a few of Crabbe's 1812 tales. Thus tale 5, "The Patron," is directed mainly against Lord Frederick's callous indifference to the fate of the young would-be poet whom he has irresponsibly encouraged in his role as patron; in tale 15, "The Squire and the Priest," it is the archetypal role of the two contestants that gives a serious sociopolitical content to their disagreement. In tale 9, "Arabella," it is clear that the heroine's marital choices gain an added significance because in the public view she is seen as a representative of the enlightened bluestockings of the period. But for the most part Crabbe's interest in the "social" is located (in a way that points forward interestingly to Jane Austen) in the domain of the family and the responsible exercise of the domestic virtues. Belonging very much to its period, and undoubtedly helping to endear him to the new middle-class reading public, this interpretation of man's social role is another of those subtle modifications of Augustan values that make Crabbe's mature poetry so unmistakably sui generis.

An impressive success in this vein is tale 8, "The Mother." The central character is a vain, self-centered, wealthy beauty, irretrievably spoilt in childhood by her doting parents and now, as widow, finding contentment in the companionship of her equally beautiful older daughter:

> They were companions meet, with equal mind,
> Bless'd with one love, and to one point inclin'd;
> Beauty to keep, adorn, increase, and guard,
> Was their sole care, and had its full reward:
>
> (79–82)

The main events of the tale, however, concern her younger daughter, "a child / With a plain face, strong sense, and temper mild," whom the mother has contemptuously allowed to take herself off to live with her "pious aunt." Lucy is presented with an almost Wordsworthian note of lyricism:

> A Village-maid, unvex'd by want of love,
> Could not with more delight than *Lucy* move;
> The village-lark, high mounted in the spring,
> Could not with purer joy than *Lucy* sing. . . .
>
> (88–91)

> There was such goodness, such pure nature seen
> In *Lucy*'s looks, a manner so serene;
> Such harmony in motion, speech, and air,
> That without fairness, she was more than fair. . . .
>
> (98–101)

She is wooed by, and grows to love, a youthful rector, a younger brother of good family whose only spiritual weakness is a certain pride in his lineage. Persuaded thereto by the aunt's discreet representations, the mother scornfully agrees to the match, on the condition that Lucy wait until her sister's expected "high marriage" has taken place. But quite unexpectedly "The Beauty died, ere she could yield her hand," and the mother now withdraws her consent to Lucy's marriage to the rector, ordering that as an heiress she has a duty to make an advantageous marriage with a suitor of noble blood. Despite Lucy's insistent appeals, the reasoned arguments of her aunt, and the urgings of the young rector himself, the mother remains adamant:

> she never chang'd her mind;
> But coldly answer'd in her wonted way,
> That she "would rule and *Lucy* must obey."
>
> (216–18)

Lucy remains steadfast in her opposition to her mother's plans, but she is denied any communication with her lover, and the rude discouragement and even insult he has received at the mother's hands strike home to the weak spot in the rector's armor, so that he sacrifices "his passion to his pride" and marries another woman.

> Some spirit *Lucy* gain'd; a steadfast soul,
> Defying all persuasion, all controul;
> In vain reproach, derision, threats were tried;
> The constant mind all outward force defied,
> By vengeance vainly urg'd, in vain assail'd by pride. . . .
>
> (255–59)

Her soul is reconciled to her fate in true Christian spirit; but her body pines away. Peter New finds the ensuing description of Lucy's death "runs dangerously close to a convention of third-rate sentimental novels"; but this judgment seems to underestimate the power of Crabbe's religious faith to imbue with conviction his portrayal of serene Christian resignation at the approach of death. It is, after all, the mother who "once with a frown" cries, "And do you mean / To die of love—the folly of fifteen?" The poet's view of the case stresses rather the girl's calm and pious acceptance of the inevitability of her "withdrawal" from a world in which there are no longer any hopeful prospects to detain her. Moreover, Lucy's vivid deathbed visions of her Savior, though recounted in some detail, are explicitly presented as aberrations, the product of her bodily fever. In her final hours they are dispelled.

Then grew the soul serene, and all its power,
Again restor'd, illum'd the dying hours;
But Reason dwelt where Fancy stray'd before,
And the mind wander'd from its views no more. . . .

(335–38)

Though the account of Lucy's life and death is not Crabbe in his most characteristic vein, it is decidedly powerful in its own way.

Yet the tale, we must remind ourselves, is entitled "The Mother," and the mother's character is indeed its central subject. The story of Lucy has the function of hammering home her mother's appallingly hard and callous egotism, and it is framed by two shorter sections that present this egotism directly in its earlier phase and also in its final state. They are so consummately done as to transform our response to the tale as a whole. After an opening description of her childhood upbringing, Crabbe moves on to an account of her twelve years of marriage to

a man so mild,
So humbly temper'd, so intent to please,
It quite distress'd her to remain at ease,
Without a cause to sigh, without pretence to teaze. . . .

(33–36)

The account of their marital discord has an unerring verve and brilliance that demands extended quotation:

She tried his patience in a thousand modes,
And tir'd it not upon the roughest roads.
Pleasure she sought, and, disappointed, sigh'd
For joys, she said, "to her alone denied;"
And she was "sure her Parents, if alive,
Would many comforts for their Child contrive:"
The gentle Husband bade her name him one;
"No—that," she answer'd, "should for her be done;
How could she say what pleasures were around?
But she was certain many might be found:"
Would she some Sea-port, *Weymouth, Scarborough,* grace?"
He knew she hated ev'ry watering-place:
"The Town?" —"What! now 'twas empty, joyless, dull?"
"In winter?" —"No! she lik'd it worse when full."
She talk'd of building —"Would she plan a room?"
"No! she could live, as he desir'd, in gloom:"
"Call then our friends and neighbours;"—"He might call,

And they might come and fill his ugly hall;
A noisy vulgar set, he knew she scorn'd them all:"
"Then might their two dear girls the time employ,
And their improvement yield a solid joy;"
Solid indeed! and heavy!—oh! the bliss
Of teaching letters to a lisping Miss!"
"My dear, my gentle Dorothea, say,
Can I oblige you?" —"You may go away."

Twelve years this patient soul sustain'd
This wasp's attacks, and then her praise obtain'd,
Grav'd on a marble tomb, where he at peace remain'd.

(37–64)

The starting point for this superb tour de force must surely have been Pope's thumbnail sketch of Papillia in epistle 2 of *Epistles to Several Persons:*

Papillia, wedded to her doating spark,
Sighs for the shades—"How charming is a Park!"
A Park is purchas'd, but the Fair he sees
All bath'd in tears—"Oh odious, odious Trees!"

(37–40)

Yet, as we can see, Crabbe has elaborated his treatment of conjugal perversity far beyond his neatly laconic source, weaving into his verse texture a subtle counterpointing of the two contrasted voices, such that the wife's voice comes to us distanced and muted by an oblique form of reported speech that only by courtesy takes quotation marks around it. This device ensures that when we finally hear her voice directly in the biting "You may go away," the effect is all the more devastating. The appropriateness of the phrase "this wasp's attack" has been acted out for us in the dialogue, and there is consequently a supreme irony in the fact that when her husband does at last obtain her praise it is "Grav'd on a marble tomb."

In the final "scene" of the tale we see Dorothea, quite unrepentant and even unmoved, it would seem, by the death of her two daughters, standing in front of her own portrait, comparing it with the reflection of her living form in a tall mirror, and exacting from her dutiful dependents an agreement with her own assertion that the portrait lacks the "living grace" of its original. In its context, this concluding "scene" acquires a symbolic significance, summing up for us, in a vividly realized cameo, the narrative drift of the tale as a whole. Completely unaltered by all that has happened, impervious to experience, the mother is a living embodiment of Pope's principle

of the inextinguishable "ruling passion," so that for all its narrative sophistication the tale is seen to have as its central conception a view of character
that is more simplistic than that which we associate with most of Crabbe's
work of this period. Yet though the elements within it are decidedly disparate, Crabbe's art has succeeded in integrating them and unifying them to a
quite remarkable extent.

Another tale centered on intrafamilial relationships is tale 17, "Resentment." This is one of the tales that open by expounding a moral generalization, in this case the statement that there exist two types of women, one
comparable to wax and the other to "smelted iron." The former, time and
again, will forgive those who deceive them, while the latter, once injured,
bear a lasting resentment and will "never melt again." Once made, the
generalization is left hanging in the air, a reference point to which the poet
will revert later in the tale, while the narrative busies itself with the fortunes
of "a serious merchant," Paul, who left his native town when his children
died and has recommenced his trade in a busy port. His wife too dies not
long afterward; and "civil, sober and discreet" he pays judicious court to a
well-off spinster who is pathologically suspicious of the motives of any ar-
dent-sounding lover. The exchanges between them are neatly hit off; Paul's
approach, astute almost to the point of deviousness, is a cool business-like
one that avoids any overt flattery while at the same time indicating matter-
of-factly his shrewdly appraising valuation of both "her person and her
prudence." Well pleased by a mode of proposal that "romantic maidens
would have scorn'd," she accepts him, and her jointure is fixed without
debate. As an ironic contrast to her suspicious attitude towards all her former
suitors, she now places a complete reliance on him:

> In his engagements she had no concern;
> He taught her not, nor had she wish to learn:
> On him in all occasions she relied,
> His word her surety, and his worth her pride.
>
> (118–21)

Some time later, when she is preparing for a "bounteous feast" to celebrate
the launching of a ship, her husband calls her into his study to sign a docu-
ment ("a trifling business") in the presence of a black-garbed lawyer who
gabbles off the explanation in legal jargon. So complete is her trust in Paul
that she signs without even listening. In fact, however, the merchant, under
his assumed veneer of prosperity, has long been in financial difficulties, stav-
ing off disaster first with the aid of his former marriage, now with the aid of
the present one.

The "evil day" comes, nevertheless; and with her husband bankrupt she finds that what she has done is to sign away her jointure.

> His guilt, her folly—these at once impress'd
> Their lasting feelings on her guileless breast.

> (166–77)

It is at this point that she reveals herself to be a member of the "smelted iron" division of the female sex. Her resentment toward him is extreme, and despite his appeals she resolves "from his meanness" to part and to live in solitary poverty in a humble cottage.[4] Her bitterness finds expression in a lengthy monologue in which she bemoans her "hard fate" yet proclaims such hardship

> easier to sustain
> Than to abide with guilt and fraud again;
> A grave impostor!

Lilian Haddakin, in discussing Crabbe's "varying modes of treating the passage of time" very aptly writes of this tale as follows:

> His favourite method, well exemplified in "Resentment," consists of a "timeless" or static exposition, followed by a series of significant "scenes" linked by compressed and laconic narrative, the story proper ending in a "scene."[5]

The linking narrative that immediately follows carries us rapidly over a number of years. Befriended (unasked) by a rich uncle, she learns from him the satisfaction afforded by a combination of frugality and charitable works, inherits his wealth on his death (carefully secured to her by law as "her own peculiar right"), and returns to her former residence. There she lives as a widow and follows the same chosen mode of life, actively seeking out "the objects of her alms" and personally administering relief to their needs. Her assistant in the exercise of this "free bounty" is now "the gentle Susan," an archetypal example of the "waxen " division of females, one who is repeatedly deceived and unfailingly forgives her deceiver. The final "scene," which occupies nearly a third of the tale, is acted out in a superbly realized series of conversational exchanges between these two women. Years have now passed, and the mistress observes with curiosity an "aged pauper" who makes shift to live by selling grit that he obtains from a mason's yard that is visible from her window. When she asks her maid, "Who is he, Susan? who the poor old man?," the "conscious damsel's" confused silence immediately reveals to her that, although she has not recognized him, this is her husband. He, we learn, has returned to the town after repeated failures in various "small employments" elsewhere and has been restrained by "some remains of spirit, temper, pride" from applying to his wife for charity, which he knows would be denied him.

Once she knows his identity, the "bounteous lady" does indeed show her resentment to be implacable, and the stage is set for the tale's denouement.

> A dreadful winter came, each day severe,
> Misty when mild, and icy-cold when clear;
> And still the humble dealer took his load,
> Returning slow, and shivering on the road:
> The Lady, still relentless, saw him come,
> And said, —"I wonder, has the Wretch a home?"
> "A hut! a hovel!" —"Then his fate appears
> To suit his crime;" —"Yes, Lady, not his years;
> No! nor his sufferings—nor that form decay'd"
> "Well! let the Parish give its Paupers aid:
> You must the vileness of his acts allow;"
> "And you, dear Lady, that he feels it now:"
>
> (351–62)

The exchange, a fine example of Crabbe's ability to combine the cut-and-thrust of naturalistic dialogue with the rhetorical constraints of the heroic couplet, continues over days, with the mistress's mind able to dwell only on the vileness of the victim's past behavior to herself, while the maid can speak and think only of his present miseries. The steady accentuation of these miseries is vividly detailed by the compassionate Susan, and eventually her mistress so far relents as to send her maid to him with food, wine, and a chilly lecture that Susan privately determines to hold back for a later occasion. But when the servant returns, it is to report to her mistress (who sits "self approving" with "a pious book" in her hand) that the husband is dead—not, it seems, of actual starvation, but from exhaustion and exposure. The mistress, sensitive now to the consequences of her inexorable resentment, supposes her servant to be reproaching her: "Blame me not, child; I tremble at the news." But it is herself and not her mistress whom Susan is blaming, and a further turn is given to the screw by the self-accusatory speech that closes the tale:

> "Tis my own heart," said Susan, "I accuse:
> To have this money in my purse—to know

> What grief was his, and what to grief we owe;
> To see him often, always to conceive
> How he must pine and languish, groan and grieve;
> And every day in ease and peace to dine,
> And rest in comfort!—what a heart is mine!"—

(483–90)

"Resentment" is unequivocally a moral tale in verse, but it embraces complexities of characterization, motivation, and moral discrimination that must immeasurably enlarge our conception of what that term can mean.

Tale 9, "Arabella" is more open-ended in its central moral discrimination (so much so that the poet felt it necessary to append a lengthy footnote to preclude any possible misunderstanding of his position). It seems clear that its primary concern is to convey an ironically tolerant psychological insight rather than to spell out any didactic lesson. Crabbe opens directly with a lively characterization of Arabella herself—the only daughter of the vicar of "a fair town," beautiful, accomplished, and virtuous beyond reproach. Her accomplishments (she has studied Latin literature and English philosophers, as well as the "moral muse" of history) recall those of the Bas Bleu ladies whose fame was at its prime in the 1770s, and Crabbe does indeed mention that Arabella's conversational powers were equal to those of Mrs. More and Mrs. Montague; however, the central issue of the tale (what should be the moral judgment of a prospective bride upon the previous sexual transgressions of her future husband?) remained a live one throughout the latter decades of the eighteenth century and even into the nineteenth. There follows a comically precise specification of the "store of virtues" Arabella requires in any future husband, and so exacting are her demands that it is hardly surprising that the first three contestants fail to match up to them. Evidently her familiarity with "Berkeley, Bacon, Hobbes and Locke" has had no harmful effect on the religious principles of "this reasoning maid," for she rejects "with high disdain" the suit of the deist, Mr. Campbell, who incautiously acknowledges to her the freethinking that underlies his hypocritical compliance with religious observances. Vicar Holmes ("the good old Vicar") does not fare any more successfully, however; and only a slightly more extended consideration is given to Captain Bligh:

> On Captain Bligh her mind in balance hung—
> Tho' valiant, modest; and reserv'd, tho' young:
> Against these merits must defects be set—
> Tho' poor, imprudent; and tho' proud, in debt:

In vain the Captain close attention paid;
She found him wanting, whom she fairly weigh'd.

(110–15)

As an instance of the relaxed skill with which Crabbe now matches his versification to its context, we may note how admirably the movement of the first four lines enacts the judicial balancing and weighing, and is in sharp contrast to the brisk decisiveness of the succeeding couplet. Like so much of Crabbe's workmanship the effect is unobtrusive but wholly effective in its economic forwarding of the narrative.

Seemingly "the man indeed," her next suitor, Edmund Huntly, enjoys the triumph of becoming her accepted lover; but, apparently as a trial of his affection (in order that he may prove himself more attentive to her desires than to his own), Arabella keeps postponing the date set for their marriage. From Huntly's standpoint she defers too long:

> "Let *June* arrive." —Alas! when *April* came
> It brought a stranger, and the stranger, shame;
> Nor could the lover from his house persuade
> A stubborn lass whom he had mournful made;
> Angry and weak, by thoughtless vengeance mov'd,
> She told her story to the Fair belov'd;
> In strongest terms th'unwelcome truth was shown,
> To blight his prospects, careless of her own.

The gentle irony by which the "lass's" justified complaints are counterpointed against the lover's adjectival deprecations reminds us again of the alertness that Crabbe's verbal detail must exact if it is to be properly appreciated.

Once she has learnt of his lapse from chastity, Arabella has "too firm a heart" to yield to the entreaties of either her suitor or his mother. Indeed, the terms in which his mother applies to "the reason of the nymph"—

> It well becomes thee, Lady, to appear,
> But not to be, in very truth, severe;

(157–58)

—are too patently those of prudential worldly consideration for them to be approved by the "Reason" that is the guiding spirit of the poet himself. On the other hand, Arabella's rejection of these appeals is not to be attributed solely to Reason either, since "the lofty lass" reveals in the course of her indignant answer that personal pride is one of the motivating forces underlying her obduracy. As she puts it:

> Say that the crime is common—shall I take
> A common man my wedded lord to make?
> See! a weak woman by his arts betray'd,
> An infant born his father to upbraid;
> Shall I forgive his vileness, take his name,
> Sanction his error, and partake his shame?
> No! this assent would kindred frailty prove,
> A love for him would be a vicious love:
> Can a chaste maiden secret counsel hold
> With one whose crime by every mouth is told?
> Forbid it spirit, prudence, virtuous pride. . . .
>
> (165–75)

The complacent self-regard that underlies this speech is rendered with a consummate skill and insight that at the same time makes clear the speaker's complete lack of self-knowledge. One feels that Crabbe was overmodest in supposing that there was a necessity to justify himself in a concluding footnote that explains that "motives may in a great measure be concealed from the mind of the agent: and we often take credit to our virtue for actions that sprang originally from our tempers, inclinations, or our indifference." In response Huntly transfers his affections to "one more mild," while Arabella's "remorseless" reflection of him is vigorously praised and defended by her elderly "virgin friend." What we are now shown is:

> the gradual change in human hearts
> That time, in commerce with the world, imparts;
> That on the roughest temper throws disguise,
> And steals from Virtue her asperities.
>
> (212–15)

The transition from Arabella's triumphs to her later phase of existence is effected by a lengthy paragraph of generalization and brief illustrative anecdote that seems more than usually close to Pope in its atmosphere, flavor, and even diction. Then we learn that twelve years later ("Twelve brilliant years . . . / Yet each with less of glory than the last") Arabella has accepted the attentions of Beswell, whose status as a merchant represents in itself a decline from her former pretensions. The course this courtship follows is in ironic contrast to the earlier courtship by Huntly, and this contrast is enforced by some neat parallelisms in both structure and language. Very different this time, for instance, is the lady's attitude towards the date proposed for the marriage:

> Now was the Lover urgent, and the kind
> And yielding Lady to his suit inclin'd;
> "A little time, my friend, is just, is right;
> We must be decent in our neighbour's sight;"
> Still she allow'd him of his hopes to speak,
> And in compassion took off week by week;
> Till few remain'd, when, wearied with delay,
> She kindly meant to take off day by day.
>
> (250–57)

At this point Arabella's spinster friend comes with ill-concealed triumph to bear the information that Beswell is secretly keeping a colored mistress who has borne him "a spurious race" of "brown ugly bastards." Taken aback at first (her "look / Was like a school-boy's puzzled by his book") Arabella declines to probe further into her friend's story, despite the latter's offer to substantiate her charge. With an evenhanded self-delusion as to her motives, she proclaims that if he is innocent, to marry him will be a just reward for virtue, and that if he is guilty, to marry him will be the best way of reclaiming him. We cannot but remember her pronouncement in the case of Huntly twelve years earlier:

> "The way from Vice the erring mind to win
> Is with presuming sinners to begin,
> And show, by scorning them, a just contempt for Sin."
>
> (177–79)

This time her verdict is different indeed:

> She spoke; nor more her holy work delay'd,
>   'Twas time to lend an erring mortal aid;
>   "The noblest way," she judg'd, "a mortal soul to win,
>   Was with an act of kindness to begin,
>   To make the sinner sure, and then t'attack the sin."
>
> (333–37)

The paired triplets point the contrast between "the false sublime" idealism of the youthful "lofty lass" and the self-deceiving realism of the mature spinster grasping at what may be the last opportunity of marriage. The device enables the author to round off with panache one of the most subtle and penetrating of his tales.

In "Procrastination" we engage with another of the most masterly of Crabbe's narrative performances. The theme is announced at once, both

in the title and in the opening twelve lines of moral generalization. In no
spirit of cynicism but rather with a resigned Christian acceptance, the ex-
piry of love is presented as the universal human lot; but Rupert and Dinah
belong among the most luckless of the lovers who have in varied ways to
experience this fate. They are to be

> the prey
> Of long-protracted hope and dull delay;
> 'Mid plans of bliss, the heavy hours pass on,
> Till love is wither'd, and till joy is gone.
>
> (9–12)

Aside from Rupert's lack of prospects the main external obstacle is the
wealthy widowed aunt on whom Dinah ("the prudent Dinah") is dependent and who selfishly presses on them a continued postponement of their
marriage.

> The Dame was sick, and when the Youth applied
> For her consent, she groan'd, and cough'd, and cried;
> Talk'd of departing, and again her breath
> Drew hard, and cough'd, and talk'd again of death.
>
> (34–37)

When Rupert has an opportunity to seek his fortune abroad, the aunt, intent on her own purposes, urges acceptance:

> "You now are young, and for this brief delay,
> And *Dinah's* care, what I bequeath will pay;
> All will be yours; nay, love, suppress that sigh,
> The kind must suffer, and the best must die:"
> Then came the cough, and strong the signs it gave
> Of holding long contention with the grave.
>
> (56–61)

The plight of the lovers is underscored with characteristic neatness by the
shrewd irony implicit in the ambiguity of this last couplet.

With Rupert overseas, a telling series of vignettes shows Dinah becoming progressively more enamored of her future possessions, and steadily
more neglectful and more prosaic in her correspondence with her lover.
There follows a passage that brilliantly exemplifies Crabbe's ability to develop in his verse a forward movement and impetus that overrides the constraints of the heroic couplet—a quality that he may have learnt from

Dryden, whose *Fables Ancient and Modern* (translations from Chaucer and the Latin poets) are notably flexible and onward-surging in their narrative movement:

> Seldom she wrote, and then the Widow's cough,
> And constant call, excus'd her breaking off;
> Who, now oppress'd, no longer took the air,
> But sate and doz'd upon an easy chair.
> The cautious Doctor saw the case was clear,
> But judg'd it best to have companions near;
> They came, they reason'd, they prescrib'd,—at last
> Like honest men, they said their hopes were past;
> Then came a Priest—'tis comfort to reflect,
> When all is over, there was no neglect;
> And all was over—by her Husband's bones,
> The Widow rests beneath the sculptur'd stones
> That yet record their fondness and their fame,
> While all they left the Virgin's care became;
> Stocks, bonds, and buildings; it disturb'd her rest
> To think what load of troubles she possess'd:
> Yet, if a trouble, she resolv'd to take
> Th'important duty, for the donor's sake;
> She too was heiress to the Widow's taste,
> Her love of hoarding, and her dread of waste.
>
> (106–25)

The insistent onward movement here is achieved partly by an occasional syntactic overrunning of the couplet ("Who now oppress'd . . ."; "That yet record . . ."), but even more by the marked rhythmical and rhetorical variety that Crabbe insinuates into the framework of his verse form.

After Dinah has duly inherited from her aunt not only her wealth but also her "love of hoarding" and her "love of splendour," the tale moves to a vividly realized episode in which Rupert, broken down by his travels and appearing now as "a huge tall sailor" with "tawny cheek" and "pitted face," confronts her in the splendor of her sitting room only to have all his hopes shattered by the devious insincerity of her evasive replies. We see him after this a recipient of parish alms in "thickset coat of badge-man's blue," while Dinah, in her costly attire, "walks the street with stately air." The chance encounter between them that concludes the tale makes its point on two levels, first as a rounding-off of the external chain of events, second as a symbolic revelation (almost equivalent to one of James Joyce's "epiphanies") of the moral distance that now separates the two of them.

Behold them now! see there a Tradesman stands,
And humbly hearkens to some fresh commands;
He moves to speak—she interrupts him—"Stay!"
Her air expresses,—"Hark! to what I say":
Ten paces off, poor *Rupert* on a seat
Has taken refuge from the noon-day heat,
His eyes on her intent, as if to find
What were the movements of that subtle mind:
How still!—how earnest is he!—it appears
His thoughts are wand'ring through his earlier years;
Through years of fruitless labour, to the day
When all his earthly prospects died away;
"Had I," he thinks, "been wealthier of the two,
Would she have found me so unkind, untrue?
Or knows not man when poor, what man when rich will do?
Yes, yes! I feel that I had faithful prov'd,
And should have sooth'd and rais'd her, blest and lov'd."

Dinah moves—she had observ'd before,
The pensive *Rupert* at an humble door:
Some thought of pity rais'd by his distress,
Some feeling touch of ancient tenderness;
Religion, duty urg'd the Maid to speak
In terms of kindness to a man so weak:
But pride forbad, and to return would prove
She felt the shame of his neglected love;
Nor wrapp'd in silence could she pass, afraid
Each eye should see her, and each heart upbraid;
One way remain'd—the way the Levite took,
Who without mercy could on misery look
(A way perceiv'd by Craft, approv'd by Pride,)
She cross'd and pass'd him on the other side.

(319–49)

Crabbe has created here a culminating episode that encapsulates, with an admirable unforced concreteness and concision, the whole drift of his narrative—the divergence that events have imposed on the two characters, the sad hopelessness of Rupert's ill and poverty-stricken condition, the moral deterioration that has wrapped itself around the wealthy and self-important Dinah.

We cannot fail to notice that in this tale the motivations encompassed are remarkably complex and indeed multidimensional. The opening homily (and the title) lead us to expect that it will be delay itself that works the mischief, and to some extent this expectation is fulfilled. Nevertheless, in the course of the actual narrative the emphasis falls not so much on the "heavy hours" of "long-protracted hope" as on the growing strength of the competing impulses within Dinah that in the end strangle her love—the "avarice" she learns from her aunt and the satisfaction she comes to feel in showing off her elegant and costly treasures. And as far as Rupert's feelings for her are concerned, these seem to have been undiminished either by his long wait or by his disappointments overseas; it is only after Dinah has repulsed him with her pious cant about her commitment to "other spousal" (as bride of Christ, evidently) that his love dies in "Indignation." In the closing scene the count against Dinah once more seems to have shifted slightly. Rupert's bitterness relates not only to her breaking of the vows that bound them, but also to the sense that her repudiation of his claim upon her in his present state of poverty and distress represents a failure in the Christian duty of compassion—a judgment endorsed by the narration when it equates Dinah's action with that of the Levite in the parable. What we find ourselves required to take into account in this tale taken as a whole is the extent to which human behavior is the outcome of overlapping multiple causes and motivations—is, indeed, in Freudian terminology "overdetermined." This more fully developed awareness of the intricacy of human motivation in "Procrastination" seems (as in many other tales in the 1812 volume) to be associated with a broadening of the poet's intention, away from the explicitly didactic and toward a more relaxed interest in defining the subtlety and complexity of human behavior.

The last of the 1812 tales to be discussed here is tale 6, "The Frank Courtship," a supreme example of the complex yet closely unified structure that the poet is capable of achieving within the individual tale. The events themselves are straightforward enough, since, as Jeffrey pointed out in his appreciative review of the 1812 volume, "The Frank Courtship" contains "even less than Crabbe's usual moderate allowance of incident." A well-to-do merchant belonging to an austere dissenting sect allows his only daughter, Sybil, to be brought up at a distance from her family by a widowed aunt, whose way of life has become more frivolous and worldly. The girl acquires tastes and views that at first are concealed from her father, but that come out into the open when he plans to marry her to an eligible but sober-minded young dissenter. Shocked by the independence of her outlook, he tries to threaten or cajole her into submission, but she remains stubbornly determined to exercise her own judgment in regard to the suitor, whom she has not yet seen. When finally an interview is arranged between the two young people, each approaches it with misgiving and suspicion, and they spend their time shrewdly pointing out each other's faults and weaknesses. Nevertheless, the tale ends with the certainty that the marriage will after all take place in a spirit of mutual compromise.

But this bald summary gives no indication of the rich pattern of vividly observed detail that makes up the real interest of Crabbe's ironic social comedy. The complexity of this pattern is, as so often in Crabbe, a matter of holding a just balance between conflicting attitudes and values, each of which has something to be said for it. The conflict is even observable in Sybil herself, for she is a character "in the round," recognizably her father's daughter as well as the protégée of her more worldly aunt. The way her delightful vivacity verges at times on impudence is admirably rendered in her pert exchanges with her parents and with her suitor Josiah, yet at the same time we are convinced of the "secret bias to the right" that gives her qualms of conscience over her deception of her father. But this is only one instance of the more general juxtaposition of Puritan and worldly values that is so arranged as to throw into relief the faults and limitations of each side. Thus any anxieties her father Jonas might feel that his daughter may learn from his sister "the manners of the world" are suppressed with the reflection that the aunt is "rich and frugal" and that ultimately some financial gain may be expected from the arrangement. Yet when the nineteen-year-old Sybil returns home spoiled (in the parent's eyes) by her protracted absence, what disturbs her father is only in part the fact (unpalatable, certainly) that her spirits are too high, her manners too free, and her dress too gay; above all, what outrages him is the realization that her "ductile spirit" has been "defiled"—that, as far as he is concerned, she is no longer biddable. Again in the "courtship" encounter we are compelled to recognize the element of justice in Josiah's denunciation of Sybil's vanity, as well as in her attack upon his "formal ways." It is in keeping with the spirit of the poem that their interview should end as a drawn battle.

This main theme is supported by several lesser but related themes. A balance has also to be struck, for instance, between Sybil's insistence upon being loved—

> "I must be lov'd," said *Sybil*, "I must see
> The man in terrors who aspires to me."

> (294–95)

—and her mother's recommendation (based upon sad experience) of a sober, prudent union based upon "esteem" and aiming only at domestic peace. Related to this is the way in which, as she grows to maturity in her aunt's home, the pleasures of whist and visits that so pleased Sybil as a girl have now begun to pall, so that her romantic fancy (nurtured upon "amusing books") now prefers "the nut-tree shade," "the pensive gloom," and the "evening bird." Ironically enough, the tears on parting that the aunt attributes to love of herself are due in reality to the disturbance of mind caused by her father's letter; it has excited in her "various, soft, contending passions." The descriptions of the Kindreds' household (both its physical aspect and its domestic habits) are closely relevant to the tale's artistic purpose. They define for us the complacent conviction of their own worth that lies behind the austere manners of the "saints"; and they point, by way of the treasured and ingeniously concealed portrait of the Protector Cromwell ("Forc'd, though it griev'd his soul, to rule alone") to the connection between this attitude of self-satisfied righteousness and the father's overbearing domestic tyranny—the same tyranny that later shows itself comically baffled by Sybil's unlooked-for defiance. The insight thus established into the motive force behind Puritan austerity lends deeper point to Sybil's perception, later on, that in Josiah's plain and formal attire there is

> something of the pride
> That indicates the wealth it seems to hide.
>
> (349–50)

Like the novels of Jane Austen in this respect, "The Frank Courtship" is a tale that benefits from reading again and again; and only with such re-reading do we come to appreciate at all fully the way in which the local wit and point continually reach out both backwards and forwards, with a sort of ironic counterpointing, to every corner of the poem.

The extended encounter between Sybil and Josiah is, of course, the set piece by whose success the tale must stand or fall, and it should by now go almost without saying that this conversation, crucial in its import, is worked into the strict yet flexible verse pattern with a superb naturalness and wit. As a local demonstration of Crabbe's mastery of his medium in this tale it is more appropriate, however, to quote the closing dialogue between the "wrathful father" (who knows that Josiah is captivated by Sybil but mistakenly believes that Sybil intends to reject him) and the "smiling maid" (who has privately decided that her suitor has acquitted himself more promisingly than she expected):

> *"Sybil,"* said he, "I long, and yet I dread,
> To know thy conduct—hath *Josiah* fled,
> And, griev'd and fretted by thy scornful air,
> For his lost peace, betaken him to prayer?

Couldst thou his pure and modest mind distress,
By vile remarks upon his speech, address,
Attire and voice?" —"All this I must confess." —
"Unhappy Child! what labour will it cost
To win him back!" — "I do not think him lost." —
"Courts he then, (trifler!) insult and disdain?" —
"No: but from these he courts me to refrain." —
"Then hear me, *Sybil*—should *Josiah* leave
Thy Father's house?" — "My Father's Child would grieve;"
"That is of grace, and if he come again
To speak of love?"— "I might from grief refrain."
"Then wilt thou, Daughter, our design embrace?" —
"Can I resist it, if it be of grace?" —
"Dear Child! in three plain words thy mind express —
Wilt thou have this good Youth?" — "Dear Father! Yes."

(478–95)

In the sophisticated art of this exchange the demure teasing of the girl is as brilliantly rendered as the comic incomprehension of her father. Particularly neat and appropriate in its context is the wording of Sybil's reference to grace in the last line but two. It may, indeed, include an allusion to the retort attributed to Wilberforce's mother when she carried off her son from the Methodistical aunt to whom he had been entrusted after his father's death: "You should not fear. If it be a work of grace, you know it cannot fail."[7] Once again, this tale is not one that offers the reader any simple or clear-cut moral lesson; but it does, on balance, leave us with the expectation that Sybil and Josiah will have a better chance than their parents of attaining in their marriage

that peace some favour'd mortals find,
In equal views and harmony of mind. . . .

(25–26)

Despite their diversity, the tales in this volume have certain common features that should be summarized here, since they mark off *Tales* (1812) both from Crabbe's earlier narrative experiments and from his subsequent more meandering and less highly concentrated tales. Concentration, tautness of structure, and economy of narrative line are indeed of the essence of these tales. The incident is realistic in tone and presentation, and there is in general an absence of violent action or improbable coincidence; the characterization is marked by psychological insight deployed in a more extended and individualized mode of portrayal than Crabbe had hitherto attempted except on rare occasions. At the same time, these highly individualized characters are quite deliberately representative on two levels. In the first place, they are socially typical; Arabella's accomplishments are those of the typical bluestocking of the period, while Jonas Kindred combines in his own person the characteristics most commonly found (or thought to be found) in members of his own social class and religious sect. Secondly, they typify what Crabbe clearly saw as permanent traits in human nature, so that the moral issues and conflicts they embody have a significance that extends far beyond their own particular time and place. In this respect (as examples of the "just representation of general nature") they remind us of the continuing Augustan affiliations of Crabbe's poetic art—affiliations that are in evidence also in the way each tale reveals itself as having a focus of strong moral concern. The values underlying this concern are also in the main Augustan, with a leaning towards moderation, good sense, modest expectations, and rational Christian endeavor, though there are two aspects indicative of an alert and sensitive response to those changes in intellectual and emotional climate characteristic of the turn of the century. The first of these is an undogmatic tendency to avoid formulating a clear-cut didactic lesson and to concentrate instead on the complexity of the moral questions involved. The second is a preoccupation with the domestic virtues and with issues arising from relationships within the family circle.

Apart from those few that are single-character narratives, the tales typically take as their subject matter the interaction of two or three leading characters, in the course of which some conflict of values gives rise to behavioral clashes and conflicts. These conflicts make up the substance of what can properly be called a "plot"—a sequence of causally related events that lead up to a climax and move subsequently either to a resolution of the conflict or to a condition of stalemate. Most typically the tale starts with an expository passage, which may take the form either of a character sketch or of an outline of the situation that is the announced theme of the tale; and this leads into a "scene" that the reader is enabled to visualize concretely and in some detail, often with the aid of some naturalistic but slightly stylized dialogue. Normally, development over time plays a significant part in the structure of these tales; and although the timescale is occasionally quite brief, more often it extends over a considerable number of years. This means that there will be, later in the tale, at least one further detailed "scene" and possibly several; and it is characteristic of the structure of these tales that the subsequent scenes are selected in such a way that they can be placed in a significant relationship with the first "scene," often providing either a parallel to it or a contrast. The significance, in any case, is sure to be formulated in the context of the moral issue or theme that forms the tale's overriding preoccupation. Inevitably, since the tales are of modest length, the high-lighted "scenes" are linked by highly compressed narrative that spans the years by means of a series of condensed and laconic cameos—a technique in which Crabbe's talent for concise expression shows to full advantage. The "scene" that brings the tale to a close may be one that resolves the conflict at the heart of the plot (as in "Resentment") or it may be an ap-pendage subsequent to the plot's resolution in which an intrinsically minor incident is made to symbolize retrospectively the main drift of the narrative (as in "The Mother" or "Procrastination").

One question that still remains is the frequently posed one, "Why in verse?" Much has no doubt to be attributed to Crabbe's habitual attach-ment to the medium of the heroic couplet over some four decades—an attachment that made the use of it almost second nature to him; he cer-tainly found it a more unforced mode of expression than prose, in which he always seemed stiff and ill at ease. In addition it must be said, however, that his particular method of using the heroic couplet, exploiting to the full its potentialities for pointed antithesis and parallelism, lends itself with great appropriateness to the kind of narrative structure he developed in *Tales* (1812). Consequently, the local neatnesses of phrasing and wit exhibit a peculiarly fitting congruity with the kind of alertness exacted from the reader in appreciating the relationships between the different "scenes" in the narra-tive structure. In this sense the small-scale verbal felicities present themselves essentially as local manifestations of Crabbe's art as teller of verse-tales. And in this art *Tales* (1812) shows the poet at the height of his powers—able to achieve a level that in his subsequent work he would equal at times but would never surpass.

7

The Downward Slope: *Tales of the Hall* and *Posthumous Tales*

Crabbe's next volume, *Tales of the Hall,* was not published until July 1819, and it is distinguished from its predecessor by the presence of a frame narrative that loosely links together eighteen separate tales plus four shorter anecdotes in a sequence of twenty-two books. As Jeffrey put it in his notice of the volume in the *Edinburgh Review:*

> Two brothers, both past middle age, meet together for the first time since their infancy, in the Hall of their native parish, which the elder and richer had purchased as a place of retirement for his declining age; and there tell each other their own history, and then that of their guests, neighbours and acquaintances.[1]

According to Crabbe's son these tales occupied the poet during the years 1817 and 1818, but the poet told John Murray in November 1818 that he had been working on the collection for four years, and surviving manuscripts show that at least half the tales existed in draft form by the end of 1816. It is probable, however, that the frame material relating to the brothers took its present shape at quite a late stage.[2] Despite its prolonged gestation, it has to be said that the structure of the resulting mélange, though acceptable, is not particularly successful; the reader has to take his satisfactions from some of the parts rather than from any unity of intention aimed at in the volume as a whole.

Three of the tales, all ones related only loosely to the frame narrative, are very much of a piece with the tales of the 1812 collection, though only the first two to be mentioned are among those known to have been in existence before the end of 1816. Book 9, "The Preceptor Husband," is fully up to the standard of the best of *Tales* (1812), and is in much the same vein; it displays the same firmly held moral standpoint, the same compassionate yet quietly amused portrayal of human weakness, and the same neatness and economy of narrative skill. Possibly suggested by a brief anecdote in Hannah More's *Coelebs in Search of a Wife*,[3] it recalls the marital misfortune of Finch who, having from boyhood always loved his studies and always declared that his wife must share his taste for learning, allows himself to be drawn in by Augusta Dallas, who is beautiful, apparently unmercenary, and shrewd enough to indicate modestly that she has a love for learning, even though "doomed so long to frivolous employ." Disregarding his mother's skepticism, Finch marries the girl only to discover, once the honeymoon is over, how mistaken he has been. His disillusionment is recorded in three brilliantly realized episodes. In the first, he offers to read Hume to his wife but is deterred by her unwitting revelation of the extent of her historical ignorance and miscomprehension; in the second, he attempts on their walks to teach her botany by reference to the plants and flowers they encounter; and in the third he asks her to expound her favorite reading (it turns out to be *Wanderings of the Heart, The Confessions of a Nun,* and other sensational fiction). In this tale the versification has become slightly more relaxed than in most of the 1812 volume and the diction slightly less stiff, while the couplets, though largely end-stopped, are organized into an admirable fluidity of forward movement. Moreover, the conversations between Finch and Augusta have great naturalness; Crabbe catches exactly the brainless vapidity of her replies as she rattles on, all the time giving herself away without in the least realizing it. In addition, Crabbe does not shrink from displaying the misjudgments into which Finch's learned enthusiasm betrays him; on their botanical walks he is led to indulge in a proliferation of complicated technical terms that would have bemused even an apt pupil.

Though it is not strictly a "tale," book 14, "The Natural Death of Love" also has close affinities in length, style, tone, moral attitude, and psychological acumen with the 1812 volume. It offers an extended dialogue between Henry and Emma some twelve months after their marriage, and though the narrative element is very slight, the ending does offer a certain dramatic resolution to the dilemma that their mutual recriminations have unfolded. Both agree to follow Henry's recommendation that, instead of sighing regretfully for the illusory bliss that was provided by "pleasant fallacies" about each other, they should now set to work to make the most of the real, though more humble, good qualities that both are blessed with.

The earliest surviving ms. version of book 17, "The Widow," belongs to sometime in 1817; but whatever its date of composition, this is certainly

one of the most successful of the tales in the 1812 style. The moral concern
here is with the degree of "rule" and control that it is proper for a husband
to exercise over his wife. Harriet's first husband, a wealthy merchant, is an
"easy man" who lets her have her own way over every fancy or whim that
comes into her head. Consequently, she is continually demanding some
new extravagance, though it comes to be not so much the "comforts" themselves that give her pleasure as the satisfaction she gains from prevailing
over husband's opposition. The husband himself, finding their wealth un-
equal to sustain her reckless expenditure, sinks into a state of ill health (which
gains him no sympathy at all from his wife), and finally dies leaving their
affairs in confusion. At this point, Harriet's inability to take sensible deci-
sions on her own account is concisely delineated in a passage of dialogue
that has the hallmark of Crabbe at his best:

> "My helpless babes," she said, "will nothing know,"
> Yet not a single lesson would bestow;
> Her debts would overwhelm her, that was sure,
> But one privation she would not endure;
> "We shall want bread! the thing is past a doubt."
> "Then part with Cousins!"— "Can I do without?"
> "Dismiss your servants!"— "Spare me them, I pray!"
> "At least your carriage!"— "What will people say?"
> "That useless boat, that folly on the lake!"
> "O! but what cry and scandal will it make?"
>
> (187–96)

Luckily for her, one of her late husband's clerks sees some hope of re-
trieving her affairs by judicious management, makes her a business-like
proposal of marriage, and then coolly and tactfully persuades her into ef-
fecting all the economies that she had previously thought impossible. To
her surprise she finds that whereas

> When every deed by her desire was done
> She had no day of comfort—no, not one;
>
> (275–76)

now, under the kind, polite, and well-judged guidance of her second husband, her heart has "comfort" and her temper "rest." It is, however, only in
material terms that Crabbe presents this marriage as an ideal arrangement;
the former clerk feels no affection for his wife and lives essentially with an
eye to his own advantage, looking forward to the time when he will be left a

widower and will be able to build himself an estate in the country, starting a new life with a younger wife. As it turns out, however, he is the one to be carried off by illness, and Harriet becomes a widow for the second time.

Her third husband (married after precisely that twelve-month interval that the proprieties decree) is the spendthrift tenant of her lakeside folly, and he exacts from her the same blind obedience that she had earlier demanded from her first husband. His tyranny is exercised in the cause of "pleasure," in pursuit of which he insists on traveling ceaselessly, even after she has become exhausted by the search and longs only for rest. She now foresees the same doom that her first husband had feared: "Debts, threats, and duns, bills, bailiffs, writs and jails" (512). Fortunately, however, the spend-thrift husband dies before they are completely ruined, and Harriet gathers up the fragments of her fortune and retires to a cottage (though still evidently ready to take on a fourth husband if one should offer). The only weakness in this neatly turned tale is that the moral conclusion Crabbe arrives at—namely the need for a "middle way" somewhere in between "rule" and blind submission—does not seem to arise with sufficient inevitability from the case as presented.

In most of the volume, however, the main impression left is that of a greater prolixity and leisureliness, a relative absence of tautness, compression, and economy. Not only are the tales inclined to run to a considerably greater length, they also seem to be more loosely structured, and their placing within the frame narrative often leads to a discursive and repetitive rehearsing beforehand, by the ostensible teller, of the point and significance that the tale itself is going to unfold. The change is apparent locally also in a more relaxed and meandering verse texture. The following extract from book 1 (it is taken admittedly from the frame narrative) is by no means untypical:

> Through ways more rough had fortune RICHARD led,
> The world he traversed was the book he read;
> Hence clashing notions and opinions strange
> Lodged in his mind; all liable to change.
>
> By nature generous, open, daring, free,
> The vice he hated was hypocrisy;
> Religious notions, in her latter years,
> His mother gave, admonish'd by her fears;
> To these he added, as he chanced to read
> A pious work or learn a Christian creed:
> He heard the preacher by the highway side,
> The church's teacher and the meeting's guide;

And mixing all their matters in his brain,
Distill'd a something he could ill explain;
But still it served him for his daily use,
And kept his lively passions from abuse;
For he believed and held in reverence high,
The truth so dear to man — "Not all shall die."

(216–33)

On the credit side this achieves an easy flow and also gives the effect of using a natural, everyday vocabulary. As one reads it one has, however, little conscious awareness of its being in heroic couplets. Antithesis is largely eschewed, and though there is some use of parallelism, this has little rhetorical force. The general impression is of verse that is equable and agreeable, but rather lacking in energy and tension. One cannot but be put in mind of the comment that the Old Bachelor in book 10 makes sardonically on his own conversational powers as he grows older—namely, that he has begun "to prose."

Nevertheless, this new style is perfectly capable of rising to the occasion if need be, particularly in descriptive passages. The following is taken from book 11, "The Maid's Story":

There was a day, ere yet the autumn closed,
When, ere her wintry wars, the earth reposed;
When from the yellow weed, the feathery crown,
Light as the curling smoke, fell slowly down;
When the wing'd insect settled in our sight,
And waited wind to recommence her flight;
When the wide river was a silver sheet,
And on the ocean slept th'unanchored fleet;
When from our garden, as we look'd above,
There was no cloud, and nothing seem'd to move.

(790–99)

This seems, if anything, to have gained from a relaxation of Crabbe's earlier compulsion to dwell rather too fully on "minute particulars"; we have instead an unerring mingling of generality and particularization, directed and controlled by a specific poetic purpose. Each item is beautifully selected to define with the utmost precision the atmosphere of this perfect day of an Indian summer. The general terms are used because they give just as much as the poet needs and no more; "wing'd insect" may be one of the images whose constant repetition in eighteenth-century nature poetry had "wearied and disgusted" Aikin,[4] but here it is wholly appropriate, because its undefined generality leaves the mind free to concentrate on the utter stillness conveyed by the rest of the couplet. There is precise observation in Crabbe's presentation of the insect's "settling" and "waiting," and this is the aspect of reality that he has needed to bring to the forefront of our consciousness. Similarly we feel no doubt that Crabbe, the botanist, could have named the yellow weed if he had chosen to do so; what is germane to his purpose, however, is the extreme gentleness with which its "feathery crown . . . fell slowly down," and greater particularity would only have distracted from the vividness of evocation actually achieved in the lines as they stand. (It should be added that, characteristically, this description is not an end in itself; in its context it is instrumental to the presentation of Priscilla's "ecstasies" as she proclaims her conviction of the future life—"a world beside." And these "ecstasies" too are placed with balanced detachment by her friend Martha, the narrator of the tale; they lead in their high flight and uncontrolled fancy to an undervaluing of actual earthly possibilities—"the real bliss"—in a way that Crabbe finds morally objectionable.)

In general, however, we do find an increased diffuseness and looseness of structure in the individual tales of the 1819 volume, setting limits of a new kind to Crabbe's narrative achievement. A fairly characteristic example is book 10, "The Old Bachelor," which runs to 768 lines in length and falls naturally into four distinct episodes. The bachelor's rambling account of his experiences has its effective passages. Thus, in the first episode, the brief period of blissful expectation of marriage to his first love and the years of bleak misery that follow the girl's sudden death are evoked with remarkable poignancy. Again, the second episode concludes with a brilliantly counterpointed dialogue between mother and son that enacts with undiminished skill their conflicting attitudes towards the way he has been unexpectedly jilted by the grave lady whom his mother has inveigled him into taking to wife "as a friend." Effective too are the closing paragraphs that realistically, but without self-pity, depict the tedious and motiveless cheerlessness of an old bachelor's existence. In the third episode, however, the denouement is unconvincingly handled when a middle-aged man's attachment to a "thin, tall, upright, serious, slender maid" founders on his chance discovery of the cosmetic secrets that underlie her swimming eyes and rosy cheeks. The fourth episode seems at times uncomfortably close to Crabbe's own disquieting experience during his frustrated epistolary courtship, in 1814, of the unidentified young woman Miss Charlotte W.[5] On the whole, the separate parts do not work together to make a whole; yet, despite this, the tale succeeds in maintaining its interest throughout its full length, and it even has a certain cumulative effect that forbids us to write it off as a complete failure.

The parallel tale of "The Maid's Story" in book 11 is even more rambling and discursive; and although it has occasional passages that are well done (notably the "tale within a tale" of Martha's spinster companion Priscilla and her unexpected reunion with her former suitor) the absence of any compelling narrative line makes its 1096 lines seem inordinately long in the reading. (Singularly ineffective is the attempt to provide a unifying thread through the reappearance at intervals of Frederick, who unsuccessfully woos Martha, first as a "youth from college," next as an evangelistic dissenting preacher, later as a soldier, and finally as an unsuccessful actor.)

Both these tales are told in the first person, and it is noticeable that in *Tales of the Hall* Crabbe experiments quite extensively with first-person narrative, a mode that hitherto he had used only once, in the tale of Ellen Orford in *The Borough*. Thus not only are the earlier experiences of the two brothers recounted in the first person, but so are the entire stories in three of the main tales (in books 10 and 11, as already mentioned, and in book 19, "The Cathedral Walk") and part of book 12, "Sir Owen Dale," and book 16, "Lady Barbara." In all these cases it is the main protagonist who narrates the events, but in another tale, that of "Ruth" in book 5, it is an intimately concerned spectator (the protagonist's mother) whose narrative viewpoint is adopted. In all these instances the abandonment of Crabbe's customary mode of omniscient third-person narration leads to a more strongly focused engagement with subjective inner experience as opposed to external events.

This is no doubt the point at which to mention Crabbe's marked preoccupation in this volume with problems of love and marriage—a preoccupation first noticed by Jeffrey, who observed:

> It is rather remarkable that Mr Crabbe seems to become more amatory as he grows older; the interest of almost all the stories in this collection turning on the tender passion, and many of them on its most romantic varieties.[6]

This preoccupation leads the poet to a greater reliance than hitherto upon situations and incidents that seem to derive, secondhand, from his fictional reading rather than from firsthand experience; and in consequence there is some dilution, overall, in the atmosphere of verisimilitude that has been a hallmark of his narrative up to this point. Thus it is chance coincidence that accounts for the recurring appearance on the scene of Frederick in "The Maid's Story," and this fact contributes a good deal to the unconvincingness of these episodes. A tale in which coincidence forms the nub of the plot is book 19, "William Bailey." Here the opening portrayal of the courtship of Fanny by William is convincing enough, if somewhat overleisurely; and the reader can relish too, as an example of Crabbe's best style, the young woman's awed reactions to the baronial hall where her spinster aunt is an esteemed upper servant. Nor is there any lack of vigor in the spirited exchange between Fanny's father and the lord whose son has disappeared with Fanny after a seduction that is tactfully left to be inferred without actually being described. Thoroughly unsettled by Fanny's desertion and fall, William uses a small legacy from his sister to wander aimlessly around the country, diverting himself as best he may in observation of the varied company he meets on the road. Though the circumstance is discreetly clothed in the telling of it, rather too heavy a burden is placed on the reader's credulity by the coincidence that has William meet his Fanny again as a comfortably-off widow who efficiently runs a respectable hostelry. The happy ending seems to have been wished upon us rather than to have arisen out of the inner nature of the situation.

Elsewhere Crabbe allows himself to rely too much upon extreme or unmotivated action, so that the tone of his narrative slides dangerously near to the melodramatic. An instance of this is book 21, "Smugglers and Poachers," the subject of which was, according to his son, suggested to Crabbe by the reformer Sir Samuel Romilly a few weeks before his death, presumably as an occasion for protest against the severity of the Game Laws. However, it may be doubted whether the tale as written is quite what Romilly had in mind, since Crabbe says nothing of the desperate want that at this period drove so many of the rural poor to illicit poaching in order to supplement their families' bread; instead, he sees the poachers as a "lawless clan" motivated mainly by an appetite for adventure and danger. Two brothers, Robert and James, very different in temperament, become respectively a smuggler and poacher, and a gamekeeper; yet each falls in love with the same admirable and upright young woman, Rachel:

> That child of gracious nature, ever neat
> And never fine; a flowret simply sweet.
> Seeming at least unconscious she was fair;
> Meek in her spirit, timid in her air. . . .

(97–100)

Rachel comes to love Robert, though anxious about his surreptitious nocturnal activities, of which smuggling seems to her much less blameworthy than poaching. Nevertheless, it is as a poacher, involved in a bloody affray with the forces of order, that Robert is captured, and certain to be condemned to death unless his brother intercedes on his behalf. James's price for this intervention is a promise by Rachel to marry him instead of his brother, and the girl undertakes a prison interview with her lover in order to ascertain which desperate choice he would wish her to take. Robert is weak enough to opt for life even on these terms, and Rachel, accepting his decision, marries James, though as it turns out a daring jailbreak frees Robert, along with the other members of his gang, before the trial can take place. In reality the escape has been covertly permitted by the authorities as part of a plan to capture even more of the gang. One wild and windy night the poachers make a last attempt to pursue their vocation, and, betrayed by an informer, they meet the gamekeepers in a bloody battle in which one on each side is killed. Disturbed by her fears, Rachel follows her husband to the scene of the encounter, where she finds the two brothers lying on their deathbed, each killed at the other's hand.

FitzGerald seems to have thought, perhaps mistakenly, that in suggesting the subject Romilly also outlined the plot of this tale, for he wrote in the margin of his copy of the 1834 edition:

> This Tale, like "Lady Barbara," seems an instance of a Poet's disadvantage in writing to order or "My Particular Desire." One must let the Poet go his own way, and choose any subject: the very best, suggested by others, may not take hold of his Imagination so strongly as some much less striking one which has of itself taken root in his mind. In both these cases the simple outline of the story is better than its laborious filling-up.[7]

"Lady Barbara" will be discussed in chapter 8. In the case of "Smugglers and Poachers" FitzGerald's comment does not seem to be really justified, for the tale has been vividly imagined and is a telling and effective example of its own genre. That so melodramatic a narrative should seem not particularly out of place in the volume as a whole is nevertheless an implicit commentary on the direction Crabbe's work had been taking since the 1812 volume.

It would be wrong, however, to give the impression that Crabbe's adoption of a more relaxed and expansive style never produces a wholly successful tale. A convincing proof to the contrary is supplied by book 13, "Delay has Danger," at the opening of which the Elder Brother (the narrator in this instance) announces that the theme to be exemplified will be

> "When hope can sleep, there's Danger in Delay . . .
> And—hear me, Richard—man has reptile-pride
> That often rises when his fears subside . . .
>
> There is a wandering, wavering train of thought
> That something seeks where nothing should be sought,

And will a self-delighted spirit move
To dare the danger of pernicious love."

The situation now unfolded is that young Henry has gained the promise of
Cecilia's hand after some conventionally expected demurrals on her part,
countered by the appropriate degree of persistence on his. His worldly-
minded father has no objection to the match but insists that his son should
first pay a visit to their patron, from whom some benefit has come and from
whom more may still be expected. Reluctantly, Henry sets off to spend
some weeks at his lordship's mansion. There he meets, seemingly by chance,
the shy Fanny, "a mild and blue-eyed lass" who is an orphan living with her
uncle and aunt, the steward and his wife. Repeated meetings lead to a self-
deluded sentimental "friendship"—a "virtuous friendship," as he describes
it to himself. Crabbe's more leisurely and extended narrative pace pays off
here, because his detailed rendering of their repeated chance encounters in
the mansion and in the grounds helps to make convincing the gradual development of their relationship, almost unnoticed at first and apparently
innocent enough, but with an increasing undertone of intimacy that Henry
tries to disregard or deny to himself. Eventually he recognizes the danger,
but still lingers, mainly out of vanity and the conviction that his meetings
with the girl are unobserved, but partly also through resentful pique at the
warning letter of remonstrance he has received from Cecilia.

Then one morning the odiously self-important steward descends upon
the young couple as they are walking in the park. Ably seconded by his
wife, he virtually shanghais Henry into a marriage with Fanny, refusing to
let him get a word in edgewise, by the assumption that he has always intended to marry the girl anyway and by a subtle mixture of implicit threat
and appeal to the promised approval of his lordship as the ultimate sanction. This protracted conversation-piece marvelously enacts the couple's
complicity, and at the same time brings out with telling effect their vulgar
servility. A brief sample from the aunt must suffice to illustrate this:

> 'Nay, be not so surprised,
> In all the matter we were well advised;
> We saw my Lord, and Lady Jane was there,
> And said to Johnson, "Johnson, take a chair:"
> True, we are servants in a certain way,
> But in the higher places so are they;
> We are obey'd in ours, and they in theirs obey
> So Johnson bow'd, for that was right and fit,
> And had no scruple with the Earl to sit —'

(591–604)

Though he sees no alternative but lamely to submit, Henry realizes what a dupe he has been, and an impressive and much-quoted passage of description underlines his feelings when he wakes next morning, linking them with the cheerlessness of a late autumn landscape (lines 701–24). Five years later Henry finds himself, though materially prosperous, "the most repining of repenting men," burdened with a "fond teasing anxious wife" who is stupid, spiritless, and doleful. The brief closing "scene" is one of those that Crabbe uses to recapitulate symbolically the drift of his tale; an unexpected chance meeting brings Henry face to face with Cecilia, and he is so overcome with embarrassment and "the self-contempt that no self-love can cure" that he betrays himself as hopelessly and idiotically tongue-tied.

It seems likely that the character and situation of Henry was suggested in part by that of Vivian in chapters 4 to 7 of Maria Edgeworth's 1812 novel *Vivian*, though the resemblance is not so much in the details of events as in the makeup of the protagonists, and in the general feeling that is concerned in each case with the human weakness of "infirmity of purpose." Although engaged to Miss Sidney, Vivian allows himself, while separated from her, to be led into a platonic friendship with Mrs. Wharton and is too weak to detach himself from it. Even when he does decide to extricate himself, he is piqued by his mother's rebuke into continuing; he knows the inferiority of Mrs. Wharton but is vain of her attention and flattered by his power over her. He believes that Wharton is ignorant of the relationship, only to learn later that it is Wharton who has laid a plot to ensnare him and sue him for damages. Of Vivian, Richard Edgeworth wrote in his preface to the novel:

> Vivian expresses one of the most common defects of mankind—To be *infirm of purpose*, is to be at the mercy of the artful, or at the disposal of accident. Look around, and count the numbers, who have, within your own knowledge, failed from want of firmness! (P. 11)

Crabbe's tale on the same theme, though it lacks the tautness of his very finest tales, is nevertheless convincingly realized; and it does bring out with considerable poignancy the agony of guilt that can afflict a weak man when he realizes his own irrevocable folly and the price that will inexorably be exacted for it.

A brief reference to *Posthumous Tales* is all that is necessary, since the bulk of this volume offers only melancholy if unsurprising evidence of the decline of Crabbe's powers during the final thirteen years of his long life. Tales 6 to 22, inclusive, form a sequence, "The Farewell and Return," which Crabbe planned and first drafted in 1822, worked on over a period of years, and seems in 1831 to have thought "fully prepared for the press." However, his son found in fact (as the published version confirms) that the ms. was still in need of considerable revision. The general intention of the sequence—to present a series of narratives based on the contrasts in condition and character of former friends and acquaintances revealed to a man who returns to his native town after an absence of twenty years—seems one that might have offered interesting possibilities to Crabbe, who had over a long period occupied in relation to Aldeburgh this role of a "former native now returned" and might be expected to have a rich store of relevant experience and insight to draw on. In the event, however, these tales are thin and monotonous in their verse structure, generally lacking in vitality, and incompletely realized in both characterization and narrative shape. Of greater interest are the five tales that do not belong to the "Farewell and Return" sequence, though two at least of these, "Rachel" (tale 4) and "Villars" (tale 5), are "leftovers" from the earlier period when Crabbe was working on *Tales of the Hall.* Much the best tale in the volume is "Silford Hall," whose date of composition is uncertain; it will be discussed in chapter 8. Meantime we may conclude this chapter with some comments on tale 2, "The Family of Love," which belongs to 1826–27 and is probably the poet's last tale.

New dismisses "The Family of Love" as "an extremely long and shapeless tale, of no intrinsic interest";[8] Chamberlain, though finding it too long, considers that "otherwise, it betrays no falling away of powers whatsoever."[9] The truth lies somewhere between these two extremes. It is indeed a very long tale (1071 lines), and although it never actually loses the reader's interest, its leisurely expansiveness does mean that the subsidiary points are spelt out with a degree of explicitness that often blunts their force. In a large industrial town an elderly stranger takes up his residence. Evidently comfortably off, sociable in disposition, and apparently a seafaring man, he comes to be called (unprotestingly) "Captain" Elliott. He shows a particular interest in one family, the Dysons, and we learn at some length about the characters and idiosyncrasies of the two brothers,—James (a merchant) and David (a doctor)—and their two sisters, one widowed, and the other a spinster (though not without her elderly admirer). The four keep to themselves the differences that sometimes cause ill-feeling between them and publicly call themselves "a Family of Love"—a phrase that Crabbe seems to have taken from Miss Charlotte Grandison's boast to Mr. Reeves (in Richardson's *Sir Charles Grandison*)[10] that Sir Charles Grandison and his two sisters are "a family of love." (It may also have been recalled to his mind by Elizabeth Hamilton's use of the term[11] in *The Cottagers of Glenburnie,* a novel published in 1808; we know Crabbe to have possessed a copy.) However, when Captain Elliott discloses that he knows their uncle, John Dyson, then tells them the full story of his friend's adventures at sea and in foreign countries, and explains that he has been commissioned to find out about the now-wealthy John's relatives and report on them, paying particular attention to the question of whether they "live in love"—then in the next day or two the facade of unity and goodwill is dissolved by the prospect of legacies. Each of the four seeks a private interview with the captain, in order to expatiate upon the primacy of his or her own financial need, and to purvey tattle that reflects discreditably upon the others. Meantime Captain Elliott has come across an unacknowledged junior member of the family, an orphan nephew who is made use of as an ill-paid general factotum at James's factory and who asks the captain to make it possible for him to escape his unhappy lot by going to sea. At a formal gathering the captain now reveals that he is in reality John Dyson in person, announces his intention of providing honorably for "the Orphan boy," and assures the other members of the family that they will in due course be remembered in his will according to their merits. He also recommends that in the meantime they should all live in a sincere, open, forgiving relationship with one another.

As this summary will have made plain, the tale is essentially a long-winded and more benevolent reworking of the laconic, indeed almost elliptical, "entry" about Roger Cuff in part 3 of *The Parish Register* (see pp. 56–58 above). The rough and caustic wit of the earlier version has been replaced by an amiably Christian benignity of tone; but the more extended narrative pace has brought an implausibility to the failure of the family to recognize the impersonation practiced by their uncle—an artistic risk that did not arise in Cuff's brief encounters with his relatives. In general this tale— expansive, warmhearted, and a little too bland—serves as a fitting exemplar of the distance that Crabbe traveled, in his later work, from the crisp economy and incisiveness that were present in the developmental stage of his narrative art and that reached their apogee in the *Tales* of 1812.

Part II

8

Crabbe's Verse-Tales
and Romanticism

In 1798, when Crabbe was in his forty-fourth year, Wordsworth and Coleridge published the first volume of *Lyrical Ballads*. The impact of this epoch-making event was slow to make itself apparent, though Crabbe's son seems to imply that the poet was among the early readers of the volume:

> He was for several years, like many other readers, a cool admirer of the earlier and shorter poems of what is called the Lake School; but, even when he smiled at the exceeding simplicity of the language, evidently found something in it peculiarly attractive; for there were few modern works which he opened so frequently—and he soon felt and acknowledged, with the public, that, in that simplicity was veiled genius of the greatest magnitude.[1]

Since in the early 1800s Southey was often regarded as the leader of the group of poets who later became known as the Lake School, it is perhaps uncertain whether Crabbe's son had in mind Wordsworth and Coleridge when he penned this phrase.[2] There may indeed be some significance in the fact that the catalog (admittedly incomplete) of Crabbe's library at Trowbridge does not record the possession of any volumes by either Wordsworth or Coleridge, whereas it does record three volumes of Southey. Nevertheless, the account of Crabbe's son finds further confirmation in the following extract from a letter from Crabbe to Sir Walter Scott dated 5 March 1813, in which the poet writes of *The Rejected Addresses:*

> where you & I & Mr Southey & I know not who shine in the eye of the Public & Wordsworth whom I read & laughed at till I caught a touch of his disease & now really like many of the simplicities. . . .[3]

It is true that the same letter, in the course of eulogistic comments on "The Rime of the Ancient Mariner," betrays ignorance of the authorship of this poem and even speculates that it may be by "a Friend Mr Lambe [*sic*]"; but even so, the evidence suggests that in addition to his enthusiasm for the songs of Burns and the narrative poems of Scott, Crabbe did develop, during the fifteen years after the first publication of *Lyrical Ballads*, a considerable acquaintance with the poems of Wordsworth, Coleridge, and Southey and a distinct liking for some of them. In this chapter we shall be concerned primarily with the effect on Crabbe's verse-tales of contact with the work of this first generation of the Romantic poets. (There is no evidence to suggest that Crabbe ever read Shelley or Keats, and although from 1815 on he undoubtedly read some of Byron's poems he does not seem to have been very favorably disposed towards them.)

Very much the most important response by Crabbe to the challenging impact of new Romantic ideas is to be found in "The Lover's Journey," which formed tale 10 in *Tales* (1812). In this tale Crabbe deals, from his own point of view, with a key Romantic theme, namely, the extent to which the perception of natural beauty is dependent upon the frame of mind of the beholder, so much so that in the extreme view the external object may even be said to be actually created by the perceiving mind. The most extended and also highly characteristic enunciation of this theme, which Crabbe might have encountered prior to the composition of "The Lover's Journey," is to be found in stanza 4 of Coleridge's "Dejection: An Ode," a poem that first appeared in the *Morning Post*, 4 October 1802, though it was not published in book form until 1817.[4] This stanza reads:

> O Lady! we receive but what we give,
> And in our life alone does Nature live:
> Ours is her wedding-garment, ours her shroud!
>   And would we aught behold, of higher worth,
> Than that inanimate cold world allowed
> To the poor loveless ever-anxious crowd,
>   Ah! from the soul itself must issue forth
> A light, a glory, a fair luminous cloud
>   Enveloping the Earth—
> And from the soul itself must there be sent
>   A sweet and potent voice, of its own birth,
> Of all sweet sounds the life and element!

Despite his unequivocal acceptance of subjectivity in all human perception, Crabbe's opening statement in "The Lover's Journey" provides a striking contrast to Coleridge in tone:

It is the Soul that sees; the outward eyes
Present the object, but the Mind descries;
And thence delight, disgust, or cool indiff'rence rise;
When minds are joyful, then we look around,
And what is seen is all on fairy ground;
Again they sicken, and on every view
Cast their own dull and melancholy hue;
Or, if absorb'd by their peculiar cares,
The vacant eye on viewless matter glares,
Our feelings still upon our views attend,
And their own natures to the object lend;
Sorrow and joy are in their influence sure,
Long as the passion reigns th'effects endure;
But Love in minds his various changes makes,
And clothes each object with the change he takes;
His light and shade on every view he throws,
And on each object what he feels, bestows.

(1–17)

It is evident that Crabbe's way of putting it assumes tacitly that the object is there, fully there, whether the mind perceives it or not; and that his metaphors firmly though unobtrusively assign the subjective vision to a decidedly lower level of reality. The mind "casts," "throws" or "bestows" something on the object, it "lends" or "clothes"; and if we look more closely, we shall note that each of these verbs takes an additional stress through the position it occupies in the line. Already we are aware of a suggestion that what the soul sees is in some sense illusory, and the suggestion is kept alive by the poet's method of presenting the succeeding narrative.

The lover sets out on a visit to his loved one, riding at first through unenticing stretches of bleak countryside—"a barren heath" that gives way to the "meagre herbage" of "a common pasture wild and wide" and is followed in turn by the sterile vegetation of a salt marsh; yet his feelings of joy and anticipation lead him to see all this as delightful and even beautiful. Arriving at his beloved's house, he finds that she has left a message asking him to follow her elsewhere, so he completes his journey through a green, fertile, and well-kept valley—but now his disappointment and vexation cause him to detest the lushness that surrounds him

I hate these long green lanes; there's nothing seen
In this vile country but eternal green;

> Woods! waters! meadows! Will they never end?
> 'Tis a vile prospect: —Gone to see a friend! —

(260–63)

At each stage we are given first a superbly vivid and detailed objective description of the natural scene and then the lover's idealizing or denigrating vision of it; the effect of this contrast is to convince us that the subjective viewpoint is inescapably unreliable and delusory. For good measure the tale ends with the lover retracing the whole of his journey, but this time his mood is such that he does not even notice the countryside he passes through. During the first stage his "Laura" is with him, and since his mind is preoccupied with her presence his eye does no more than "rove o'er the fleeting views." Subsequently, when alone, his mind is "absent" (dwelling on recollections of the immediate past) and consequently his "vacant eye" merely "wanders o'er viewless scenes."

What we are left with (a far cry from Coleridge) is thus a sense of the unreliability of the individual subjective vision as compared with the objective reality, a reality that has achieved an unquestioned authority for us through the wonderfully realized concreteness of the poet's presentation of it. For both Coleridge and Wordsworth "joy" is a unique, quasi-religious concept that links poetic inspiration with spiritual grace; Coleridge's rapturous celebration of it in stanza 5 of "Dejection: An Ode" describes it as "this beautiful and beauty-making power" given only "to the pure, and in their purest hour" and capable of "wedding Nature to us," while for Wordsworth in "Tintern Abbey" it is "the deep power of joy" that enables us to "see into the life of things" (lines 48–49). For Crabbe, on the other hand, joy is only one among a number of mental conditions that may affect our perceptions, and there is surely a note of dry skepticism in both the phraseology and the movement of the couplet:

> When minds are joyful, then we look around,
> And what is seen is all on fairy ground.

Characteristically enough, however, Crabbe adds a further moral dimension to his treatment of the Romantic theme. During the first (enthusiastically elevated) part of his journey the lover comes upon a sordid Gypsy encampment, and the poet's condemnation of the vicious and ill-regulated way of life of this "vagabond and useless tribe"[5] is tempered only by the compassion with which he foresees their inevitable end. After describing the "brown boys" already adept at begging, the "light laugh and roguish leer" of their already-corrupted twelve-year-old sister, the slatternliness of the wife, and the "steady falsehood" of expression worn by the fortune-telling mother, the passage concludes:

> Last in the group, the worn-out Grandsire sits
> Neglected, lost and living but by fits;
> Useless, despis'd, his worthless labours done,
> And half protected by the vicious Son,
> Who half supports him, he with heavy glance
> Views the young ruffians who around him dance;
> And, by the sadness in his face, appears
> To trace the progress of their future years;
> Through what strange course of misery, vice, deceit,
> Must wildly wander each unpractis'd cheat;
> What shame and grief, what punishment and pain,
> Sport of fierce passions, must each child sustain—
> Ere they like him approach their latter end,
> Without a hope, a comfort, or a friend!
>
> But this *Orlando* felt not; "Rogues," said he,
> "Doubtless they are, but merry rogues they be. . . ."
>
> (182–97)

Clearly the lover's idealizing vision has here betrayed him into a dangerous insensitivity to the moral aspect of human character and conduct. "Nature" for Crabbe embraces the whole of the created universe, including mankind; the truth that it offers for our contemplation is inseparable from the objective and universal moral law, and it is folly to allow our feelings to falsify or distort this truth. The point is reiterated with telling force in the second stage of the journey by the fatuity of Orlando's reaction (in his bad-tempered mood) to another human feature of the landscape, this time a wedding. The outstanding interest of this tale lies in its achievement in treating a typically Romantic concept in a way that does full justice to the phenomenon while at the same time "placing" it in a wider and more objective setting; and the penetration of the implicit commentary upon a dominant Romantic theme will bear a good deal of pondering. During the 1980s the Romantic exaltation of individual subjectivity occasioned a good deal of adverse comment from various critics who did not, however, seem to have noticed Crabbe's cautionary stance towards this key aspect of it. Taken as a whole, this tale may suggest that some of the energy and tension of Crabbe's mature poetry comes from his readiness to expose himself, sensitively yet not uncritically, to the new currents of feeling that were stirring in England around the turn of the century.

Another area in which Crabbe invites comparison with first-genera-
tion Romantic poets is his readiness to accept madness as a fit topic for
poetic treatment. In one aspect Crabbe is doing no more than use for his
own purposes a conventional type-figure already familiar to readers of pre-
Romantic poetry, that of the young woman who is deserted by her lover
and loses her reason as a result—as, for instance, in Cowper's "craz'd Kate"
in book 1 of *The Task*, and in several of the "magazine poems" of the 1790s.
Wordsworth built on this tradition in "The Mad Mother" and "The Thorn"
in *Lyrical Ballads*, and the same may be said of Crabbe's presentation of
Lucy the Miller's daughter in part 2 of *The Parish Register*, while only a slightly
different twist is given to the theme in two later variants, the case of Jane in
"The Sisters" (book 8, *Tales of the Hall*), and that of "Rachel" (tale 4, *Posthumous Tales*). Madness in Crabbe, however, covers a much wider range of
cases than these. If we leave out of account the fleeting reference, at the
close of letter 6 of *The Borough*, to the futility of lawyer Swallow's villainies
since in the end "his heir was mad," there are five other characters (all
male) whom Crabbe portrays as insane—Robin Dingley in *The Parish Register*, part 3, 503–80; Sir Eustace Grey in *Poems* (1807); Peter Grimes, in
letter 22 of *The Borough;* John, the borough-bailiff's youngest son, in "The
Patron" (tale 5 in *Tales* [1812]); and Edward Shore in tale 11 of *Tales* (1812).[6]
These highly varied depictions of insanity owe their existence not so much
to any literary prototypes as to the combination of circumstances that
led to a steadily increasing public concern over, and interest in, the
question of madness and its treatment during the second half of the
eighteenth century.

During this period there was a movement away from the earlier eighteenth-century outlook that combined superstition, apathy and moral dis-
approbation, and toward a more enlightened approach to legislation and a
more sympathetic attitude in treatment.[7] During Crabbe's formative years
the most important single event in this connection was the way in which
George III's madness became a matter of public knowledge and contro-
versy from 1788 onwards, with the result that there slowly developed a
more concerned and informed attitude towards insanity, and in particular
a separation of this attitude from that of moral disapproval.[8] Admittedly
there was a continuance well into the nineteenth century of physical treatments based on medieval humoral pathology, and these were reinforced,
from the late eighteenth century onward, by additional physical treatments,
invariably unpleasant, such as John Wesley's electrical treatment or Joseph
Mason Cox's "swing." However, the efficacy of such treatments was seriously questioned by John Ferriar in his *Medical Histories and Reflections* (1795),[9]
where the writer urged the need for clinical observation pure and simple,

and recommended "a system of discipline, mild, but exact, which makes the patient sensible of restraint, without exciting pain or terror." This "system of mildness and conciliation" became the basic philosophy underlying the regime at the York Retreat founded by the Quaker William Tuke in 1796. It seems likely that Crabbe would have kept himself informed of such developments in thinking about the causes and treatment of insanity, partly because of his own early medical training but even more so because, after the death of their third son William in 1796, his wife was attacked by a "nervous disorder" from which she never made a full recovery. This nervous disorder seems to have been some form of manic-depressive condition; and it seems possible that Crabbe's close firsthand observation of his wife's deranged mental state was at least partly responsible for his inclination to portray madness in his poems and also for the acute psychological insight that distinguishes some of these portrayals. At any rate, of the nine portrayals of madness mentioned above, seven were written during the closing decade of his wife's life, and only two (Jane in *Tales of the Hall*, book 8, and Rachel in *Posthumous Tales*, tale 4) were written after her death.

Of these characterizations (among others) Bareham writes:

> The difference between Crabbe and many of his contemporaries lies not in the quantity of verse he allots to the theme of derangement (although this is considerable), but much more in quality of insight, the near-clinical and yet highly imaginative treatment which he affords the topic.[10]

If we limit ourselves specifically to the studies of madness, some qualification seems to be necessary before we can endorse this generalization. In part 3 of *The Parish Register* the history of Robin Dingley is affectingly told, but there is little analysis of the cause of his madness (Crabbe is content to write merely that: "so high was Hope:—the Failure touched his Brain"), and no hint of a relationship between the form his madness took (a compulsion to "ramble") and the disappointment that triggered it. Similarly, in "The Patron" (tale 5 in *Tales* [1812]), where disappointed hopes are again the precipitating cause, there is only a brief and perfunctory treatment of how and why John's "reason fail'd" (lines 595–602); it is perhaps worth noticing, though, that in his case "all agreed / From rest and kindness must the care proceed" (lines 640–41), an example of the "system of mildness and conciliation" practiced in the treatment of madness at the York Retreat. Both Dingley and John have gone mad (to follow Bareham's way of putting it) "because of things . . . that have been done to them"; Crabbe's fascination with guilt feelings and the workings of conscience leads him to give more extended attention to those characters who go mad because of things they themselves have done, and we need here to revert to the case of Sir Eustace Grey.

In this instance Sir Eustace's madness is seen by the poet (as well as by Sir Eustace himself) as merited retribution for sin. In his prosperous early days when

> blest with Children, Friend and Wife
> Blest far beyond the vulgar Lot
>
> (108–9)

he had been culpably neglectful of his own spiritual concerns. As he himself puts it (and though the voice is that of a madman, his testimony on this occasion cannot be discounted):

> But my vile Heart had sinful Spot,
>   And Heaven beheld its deep'ning Stain,
> Eternal Justice I forgot,
>   And Mercy, sought not to obtain.
>
> (112–15)

Slightly more uncertain may be the status accorded by the poet to Sir Eustace's belief that during his madness he was "the Slave" of two demons ("Two Fiends of Darkness"), since we cannot forget that the idea of demoniac possession as a cause of madness was still widely current in the eighteenth century; however, the physician's interpolation at this point,

> Peace, peace, my Friend; these Subjects fly;
>   Collect thy Thoughts—go calmly on—
>
> (156–57)

presumably indicates that this statement is to be regarded as part of the madman's raving. More damaging to the poem is the extent to which the nobleman's extended hallucinatory visions take on a life of their own that bears singularly little relationship to the events that precipitated his madness. This life bears instead a striking resemblance to the visions experienced by opium addicts and very probably experienced by Crabbe himself, since he took a small, medically prescribed dose of opium constantly from the early 1790s right up to the end of his life. Edward FitzGerald was one of the first to notice this, for he wrote an ms. note on page 269 of his copy of the 1834 edition: "This Dream of madness anticipates De Quincey's Opium; and very likely arose from the same cause." Despite its remarkable vividness, the poem is, in fact, made up of discordant elements that have not been wholly reconciled, and it cannot really be claimed that it shows "near-clinical imaginative insight" into the insane condition.

For Edward Shore (tale 11, *Tales* [1812]) the predisposing condition for his madness is his failure to reconcile his earlier high estimate of his own "conscious worth" with the shameful fact of his seduction of his best friend's wife. "Griev'd but not contrite," he is unable genuinely to repent, and Crabbe identifies this inability with his rejection of the Christian faith, a faith that would have helped him to find a way through the distress that weighs him down. The precipitating incident (the "deciding stroke" that "on his reason like a torrent broke") seems arbitrarily chosen, but if we once accept this, it must be admitted that the course his madness follows is portrayed with remarkable forcefulness:

> In dreadful stillness he appear'd awhile,
> With vacant horror and a ghastly smile;
> Then rose at once into the frantic rage,
> That force controll'd not, nor could love assuage.
>
> Friends now appear'd, but in the Man was seen
> The angry maniac, with vindictive mien;
> Too late their pity gave to care and skill
> The hurried mind and ever-wandering will;
> Unnotic'd pass'd all time, and not a ray
> Of reason broke on his benighted way;
> But now he spurn'd the straw in pure disdain
> And now laugh'd loudly at the clinking chain.
>
> Then as its wrath subsided, by degrees
> The mind sank slowly to infantine ease;
> To playful folly, and to causeless joy,
> Speech without aim, and without end, employ;
> He drew fantastic figures on the wall,
> And gave some wild relation of them all;
> With brutal shape he join'd the human face,
> And idiot smiles approv'd the motley race.
>
> Harmless at length th'unhappy man was found,
> The spirit settled, but the reason drown'd;
> And all the dreadful tempest died away,
> To the dull stillness of the misty day.

                                            (413–34)

The convincing sequence of carefully observed detail here does indeed deserve to be described as near-clinical, though its power is essentially that of poetic insight.

Undoubtedly, however, it is his characterization of Peter Grimes that is mainly responsible for Crabbe's justified reputation as a portrayer of madness, and here there is not a great deal to add to our earlier discussion of the tale. As with Edward Shore, it is the mental conflicts induced by an inability to repent (in this case to repent for truly atrocious crimes) that give rise to Peter's madness, and Crabbe's highly impressive achievement is that of convincing us that such a hardened and unfeeling wretch could be so worked upon by guilt and terror as to lose his reason. The psychological insight that makes this plausible is deployed through a varied sequence of techniques. Initially we are given a powerful objective presentation of the isolation, frustration, and near-starvation to which he has been reduced by public abhorrence of his crimes, and the effect of this is strongly reinforced by the poet's vivid physical evocation of the bleak landscape within which these privations have to be suffered. There follows a direct and concise account of the condition to which these sufferings have reduced him:

> Cold nervous Tremblings shook his sturdy Frame,
> And strange Disease—he couldn't say the name;
> Wild were his dreams, and oft he rose in fright,
> Wak'd by his view of Horrors in the Night, —
> Horrors that would the sternest Minds amaze,
> Horrors that Daemons might be proud to raise:
> And though he felt forsaken, griev'd at heart,
> To think he liv'd from all Mankind apart;
> Yet if a Man approach'd, in terrors would he start.
>
> (223–31)

A switch is made next to the external description of his behavior as observed by the summer visitors:

> At certain stations he would view the Stream,
> As if he stood bewilder'd in a Dream,
> Or that some Power had chain'd him for a time,
> To feel a Curse or meditate on Crime.
>
> (243–47)

This leads to further visits from the townsfolk, and the "new terror" that finally unhinges him is induced by the question some of them ask: "Wretch, dost thou repent?" The final section of the tale takes the form of Peter's rambling account of his delusion, an account that, through its lacunae and distortions, makes clear that he is still far from attaining a genuine state of repentance. The penetration of Crabbe's portrayal should make this tale obligatory reading for all who have met the character only in the sentimentalized travesty that formed the libretto for Britten's celebrated opera.

These representations of madness occurred in parallel with the treatment of madness by the first generation of Romantic poets and not as a consequence of it or as a reaction to it. They are an independent manifestation of Crabbe's own interest in the subject—an interest that was probably at one and the same time medical, social, and personal in its genesis. It is only in "Rachel" (tale 4 in *Posthumous Tales*), a tale originally written with a view to incorporating it in *Tales of the Hall*, that we encounter a study of madness in which the influence of the Romantic movement is apparent. Huchon pointed out[11] that Crabbe's starting point for this tale was Cowper's portrayal of "Craz'd Kate" in book 1 of *The Task*, lines 534–56, part of the evidence being that in the ms. belonging to the Dyce Collection there follows after line 66 the couplet:

> Rachel is craz'd, but she is not like Kate:
> The cause the same, yet hers the harder fate.

In fact the cause in the two cases, though similar, is not precisely identical. Kate "fell in love / With one who left her, went to sea and died"; and her madness was a reaction to "the doleful tidings of his death." Rachel's sailor, David, was captured at sea, and in his captivity forgot about her. Believing him dead, she receives from her Methodistical "religious neighbours" the kind of instruction that is harmful to her unsettled mind, since she is told that the doctrine of predestination makes it sinful of her to pray for David's soul. Despite this she retains a precarious sanity until the night when she is visited in her hut by (as she believes) a ghostly visitant:

> Not man! but something—if it should appear,
> That once was man—that something did she fear.
>
> No causeless terror! —In that moon's clear light
> It came, and seem'd a parley to invite;
> It was no hollow voice—no brushing by
> Of a strange being, who escapes the eye —
> No cold or thrilling touch, that will but last
> While we can think, and then for ever past.
> But this sad face—though not the same, she knew
> Enough the same, to prove the vision true —

> Look'd full upon her! —starting in affright
> She fled, her wildness doubling at the sight;

The "apparition" that thus finally destroyed her reason was David himself, who was in reality still alive and "who that day / Had left his ship at anchor in the bay." Crabbe has in fact elaborated Cowper's straightforwardly pathetic character sketch by the addition of two elements. The first is peculiar to his preoccupation with the perniciousness of Calvinistic preaching, while the second (the effect of a believed ghostly visitation upon an unstable mind) seems to be attributable to a memory of the Scottish ballad "Auld Robin Gray."[12] The resulting tale is powerful and highly concentrated, but distinctly melodramatic.

Crabbe also set out quite deliberately to incorporate some stories of ghosts into *Tales of the Hall*, probably with a view to bringing this work more into accord with the taste of the day. Thus in a letter to Elizabeth Charter (undated but from internal evidence clearly attributable to the spring of 1816) Crabbe wrote: "By the Way can you give me any short stories, especially of Ghosts and Apparitions, but they must be singular and brief or I cannot versify and they will be untractable if long. . . ."[13] Neither of the two tales that Crabbe finally included show him at the top of his form, but they deserve some attention here as examples of an attempt to accommodate himself to current fashion. In book 20 ("The Cathedral-Walk") the tale itself is set in the context of a prolonged introduction in which a group of neighbors meet one "autumnal evening" in the remains of an "old Hall" telling each other ghost stories and debating whether or not all such tales are "groundless and absurd." Following this, an "ancient lady" recounts an experience of her own as an "antidote to fear." Early in life she had had "a generous lover who was worthy found," but before their marriage could take place he died.

> Him nursed I dying, and we freely spoke
> Of what might follow the expected stroke;
> We talk'd of spirits, of their unknown powers,
> And dar'd to dwell on what the fate of ours;
> But the dread promise to appear again,
> Could it be done, I sought not to obtain;
> But yet we were presuming, —"Could it be,"
> He said, "O Emma! I would come to thee!"

                                                        (217–24)

After her fiancé's death she went to live with her widower uncle, the Dean, and spent much of her time alone in the "cathedral's gloom" indulging herself by imagining that she felt her lover's spirit at her side. One night, after praying to be vouchsafed a sight of him, she fell asleep, then woke to see "a figure," "a distant shade," which she followed and began to address in eloquent terms as her dead lover, only to have it turn and confront her with a "hideous form" and "horrid shape" that dissipated her exalted mood by shouting savagely: "Bah! —bother! —blarney! What is this about?" Her otherworldly shade she recognizes as in reality a "knavish fool" who had been attempting to steal from a tomb in the cathedral, and she is able to escape from him only by an adroit ruse. The teller of the tale is careful to stress that this is merely her own story. She refrains from generalizing from it as to "what can or cannot be"; but it is clear that the drift of the book as whole is towards a cautious skepticism. On the one hand, the tale expands and reinforces the warning Crabbe had offered in book 2 of *The Borough* to Sally, who had nursed her sailor lover Thomas in his final illness and who was inclined, after his death, to frequent his gravestone and to be "by fancy led / To hold mysterious converse with the dead." On the other hand it falls in with the common practice of such gothic writers as Mrs. Radcliffe in that it excites the reader with an account of supernatural events that are then provided with a natural and rational explanation.

The other tale, "Lady Barbara; or, The Ghost" (book 16), is much longer and differs from "The Cathedral-Walk" in that a source can confidently be cited for it. In his preface to *Tales of the Hall* the poet acknowledged that he owed this tale "to the kindness of a fair friend," while in the 1834 edition his son states, "This tale was suggested to Mr Crabbe by a Wiltshire friend; in which county the story is almost a popular one." It was W. Aldis Wright who first pointed out[14] the close resemblance between Crabbe's tale and "the Tyrone ghost story" as recounted in *The Diary of a Lady of Quality*.[15] The similarities are indeed far too close to be accidental; and, as a comparison with the summary in the endnote will show, Crabbe seems in fact to have followed the details of his presumed source with a faithfulness that is quite uncharacteristic of his usual practice.

The book opens with a discussion between the two brothers as to whether a ghost might come "to turn a guilty mind from wrong to right"; and if it did so, whether it would be heeded. George then relates Lady Barbara's history as confided by her to a friend before she died. Widowed at a very early age, and both beautiful and wealthy, Lady Barbara had retired to live in the country, where she had helped the rector and his wife to bring up their family and doted particularly on their baby son George. When he had grown up George showed himself a spirited youth with little appetite for his studies at college or for following his father's profession. Instead he determined to go to war as a soldier, but found that he was passionately in love with the still-lovely Lady Barbara. She resisted his court-ship of her, ostensibly on the ground of the disparity of age between them, though she also hinted at another motive that reinforced the refusal that "Reason's voice" dictated to her. Eventually, in response to his importunity, she told the following story.

Her father, a deist, brought up Lady Barbara and her brother Richard as unbelievers. However, after his death they found themselves dissatisfied; and in a state of doubt they swore, at Richard's prompting, a solemn oath that whichever of them died first would return from the grave with news as to the truth or otherwise of the Christian faith. Lady Barbara married, and the brother and sister parted. Then one night Richard's ghost appeared to her, assured her that "the word reveal'd is true," prophesied that she would soon be a widow, and warned her that on no account must she marry again:

> Shouldst thou again that hand in fondness give,
> What life of misery art thou doom'd to live!
>
> (617–18)

At the same time, he explained that she remained free to choose:

> Free is thy will—th'event I cannot see,
> Distinctly cannot, but thy will is free.
>
> (631–32)

She demanded some sign that this was not merely a dream, and the genu-ineness of the vision was attested for her by the icy grip of his fingers on her wrist; when she woke up the following morning, she found a small mark or speck on her skin at the very point where the ghost touched her, and this mark she kept concealed under a bracelet. Four days later she learned that Richard had died on the very night when his spirit had appeared to her.

Though impressed at first by this narrative, George's compunction did not last; and as he prepared to set off to war he selfishly persisted in making one final plea to her; and this time her "failing will / And erring judge-ment" betrayed her. The resulting "life of misery" is more graphically imag-ined and described than any other section of the tale:

> What years of torment from that frailty came;
> That husband-son! —I will my fault review;
> What did he not that men or monsters do?
> His day of love, a brief autumnal day,
> Ev'n in its dawning hasten'd to decay;

Doom'd from our odious union to behold
How cold he grew, and then how worse than cold;
Eager he sought me, eagerly to shun,
Kneeling he woo'd me, but he scorn'd me won;
The tears he caused served only to provoke
His wicked insult o'er the heart he broke;
My fond compliance served him for a jest,
And sharpen'd scorn—"I ought to be distress'd;
Why did I not with my chaste ghost comply!"
And with upbraiding scorn he told me why;
O! there was grossness in his soul; his mind
Could not be raised, nor soften'd, nor refined.

(926–42)

As can be seen, there is more than a hint here of Crabbe's most mature pungency. The total impact of the tale is a little ambivalent, however. Certainly Crabbe's closing lines are in keeping with the rational eighteenth-century caution he often displays:

If our discretion tells us how to live,
We need no ghost a helping hand to give;
But, if discretion cannot us restrain,
It then appears a ghost would come in vain.

(965–68)

Nevertheless, we cannot forget that the ghost's warning was proved correct, any more than we can shrug off Lady Barbara's continuing conviction, right up to the day of her death, that her vision had indeed been a supernatural visitation. In fact, despite the handicap of a plot that verges at times upon the ridiculous, Crabbe manages to clothe the tale as a whole with an aura of conviction that compels from the reader (willingly or not) a certain "suspension of disbelief"—an achievement that is in itself a mark of the tale's distinct Romantic affiliations.

A further Romantic theme that Crabbe touches on in some of his later works is that of childhood. Here, however, we need to tread warily and make certain distinctions. For a characteristic Romantic sensibility (and in particular for Blake and Wordsworth) the experience of the child possessed a very special value, largely because of its freshness and spontaneity, and because of the innocence that shapes its vision of the world. There is none of this sense of the uniqueness of childhood experience to be detected when Crabbe writes about children in, for instance, "Schools" (letter 14 of *The*

Borough), in "Boys at School" (book 3 of *Tales of the Hall*) or even in the more
personal posthumously published "Infancy—A Fragment." Here the
behavior and feelings of children are treated as on exactly the same level
as those belonging to later periods of life, as equally susceptible to analysis,
moral judgment, and psychological generalization. Indeed, part of the point
of "Boys at School" is the way in which the child's virtues and defects are
found, usually though not invariably, to be detectable under different outward forms in later life. In "Silford Hall; or, The Happy Day" (tale 1 in
Posthumous Tales), on the other hand, there is a distinctly turn-of-the-century
flavor to Crabbe's evocation of the boy's intuitions and feelings; and the
social and moral generalizations with which the poet at one time intended
to round off the tale have in the final version been suppressed. What we
have instead is an extended celebration of the mingled "delight" and "awe"
with which the boy, "entranced," contemplates everything he sees during
his tour of the great house. In his portrayal of Peter, Crabbe strikes at times
a distinctly Wordsworthian note:

> The lark that soaring sings his notes of joy,
> Was not more lively than th'awaken'd boy.
> Yet oft with this a softening sadness dwelt,
> While, feeling thus, he marvell'd why he felt.
> "I am not sorry," said the Boy, "but still,
> The tear will drop—I wonder why it will!"

> (158–66)

The "specialness" of the day for him is marked at the outset by the special
preparations made for the occasion by his "fond and anxious mother," by
the shilling given to him by his father, and by the pony on which he is to
ride as he sets out on his journey to Silford Hall in order to collect from the
bailiff a small debt. His errand completed, the boy is in danger of missing
his opportunity to view the wonders of the house and its grounds; but the
housekeeper, Madam Johnson, happens to see him and kindly takes him
under her wing. In the escorted tour that follows we are constantly made
aware of the contrast between this "learned lady's" sophisticated knowing-
ness and the essential innocence and also perceptiveness of the child's vision; indeed, at one point in their visit to the art gallery, the embarrassment
with which Peter turns away from some of the scarcely decent paintings
strikes home to the lady's conscience, arousing in her "one reflecting, self-
reproving sigh." A number of small incidents are portrayed with Crabbe's
characteristic skill, but what is remarkable about the poem is the way in

which the narrative element is subjugated to the overriding intention of evoking with the utmost vividness the boy's feeling-experience of this memorable "Happy Day."

Somewhat similar elements of feeling are identifiable in the second half of book 4 of *Tales of the Hall* ("Adventures of Richard"), where Richard recalls for his elder brother his seaport childhood and the effect on his mind of seaman's tales heard, and tragedies observed, of life lost at sea. Again a distinctly Wordsworthian note appears at times:

> I loved to walk where none had walk'd before,
> About the rocks that ran along the shore;
> Or far beyond the sight of men to stray,
> And take my pleasure when I lost my way;
>
> (447–50)

> I loved to stop at every creek and bay
> Made by the river in its winding way,
> And call to memory—not by marks they bare,
> But by the thoughts that were created there.
>
> (459–62)

Since the emphasis falls now on the influence upon the boy's moral development of his human contacts and of his commerce with scenes of nature, it is passages in *The Prelude* that one's mind turns towards, though owing to its long delay in publication this work was never, of course, available as a model for Crabbe.

Going beyond the theme of childhood, however, there is a succeeding episode in the frame narrative (book 6 of *Tales of the Hall*, "Adventures of Richard Concluded") that seems distinctly to bear the imprint of Wordsworth's influence. In terms of narrative content we are shown Richard as a young man, convalescent from a serious illness, in love with the rector's daughter Matilda but only brought to declare his love by a fit of baseless jealousy. He believes her to be receiving the attentions of a handsome young soldier (in reality the husband of her school friend). In the context, however, the narrative element has become of only minimal importance. Instead, the emphasis falls on the evocation of the lover's feelings: first "the sober certainty of waking bliss," then "the guideless rage" of jealousy, and finally the enchantment of Matilda's presence and "that delight when love's dear hope is crowned." While the design of evoking a state of feeling has not been wholly emancipated from a narrative framework (as it increasingly came to be for Wordsworth), the poetic intention is nevertheless closely

comparable to that of such a Wordsworth poem as "Strange fits of passion," as
we can see from the concluding lines of the book:

> Now in the morn of our return how strange
> Was this new feeling, this delicious change;
> That sweet delirium, when I gazed in fear,
> That all would yet be lost and disappear.
>
> Such was the blessing that I sought for pain,
> In some degree to be myself again;
> And when we met a shepherd old and lame,
> Cold and diseased, it seem'd my blood to tame;
> And I was thankful for the moral sight,
> That soberised the vast and wild delight.

(378–87)

This surely represents a remarkable extension of Crabbe's usual range.
In his essay entitled "The Last Augustan," Ian Gregor wrote:

> while Romantic predilections may have sometimes influenced [Crabbe] in
> his choice of themes, they are peripheral interests, and his tone and attitude
> remains true to the Augustan hub of nature and Good Sense.[16]

There is a good deal of truth in this, but it requires some further elaboration and qualification. Certainly the themes touched on in this chapter—
the subjectivity of human perception, madness and other disordered states
of consciousness, the fascination of the supernatural, the heightened sensibility of childhood—have long been recognized as characteristic preoccupations of the English Romantic poets. What is more controversial is whether
behind these disparate manifestations of the Romantic spirit there is an
underlying coherence that can be identified and explained without doing
violence to the innate complexity and multiplicity of Romanticism. In the
past two decades the efforts to find (or construct) such a coherence have
been many and varied. Nevertheless, for the illumination of Crabbe's closing phase of poetic utterance I still find the most persuasive to be the line of
thought developed by M. H. Abrams in his 1971 study, *Natural Supernaturalism: Tradition and Revolution in Romantic Literature*.

Abrams sees as central to the genesis of Romantic poetry the cataclysmic sociopolitical stirrings of the age, and in particular those of the French
Revolution, that were experienced by the leading European poets and philosophers as an apocalyptic explosion of millennial hopefulness followed by
an agonized reaction of disillusionment and despair. According to Abrams

the millennial expectations that so excited Coleridge, Wordsworth, and Southey in the 1790s should be seen as a culminating transformation of the long biblical and Christian tradition that fixed its sights upon a sudden, sweeping and radical change of a kind promised with the coming of a Messiah and later postponed to his Second Coming.

> For Wordsworth and his contemporaries, too, the millennium didn't come. The millennial pattern of thinking, however, persisted with this difference: the external means was replaced by an internal means for transforming the world. Such a substitution had a precedent early in the Christian era when, the assurance of an immediate Second Coming having been disappointed, Biblical exegetes postponed the literal millennium to an indefinite future and interpreted the prophecies of an earthly kingdom as metaphors for a present and entirely spiritual change in the true believer. . . . Romantic literature, however, differs from these theological precedents in that its recourse is from one secular means of renovating the world to another. To put the matter with the sharpness of drastic simplification: faith in an apocalypse by revelation had been replaced by faith in an apocalypse by revolution, and this now gave way to faith in an apocalypse by imagination or cognition.[17]

The crucial topic for Romantic poetry is thus the internal transmutations that can be evoked or observed when the poet directs his attention inwards— or, as Wordsworth puts it in the preface to *The Excursion,*

> such fear and awe
> As fall upon us often when we look
> Into our Minds, into the Mind of Man—
> My haunt, and the main region of my song.

And although Abrams expounds with great subtlety the extent to which more traditional patterns and values persisted (reformulated) within what had become essentially a secularized system of thought, he leaves us in no doubt that the primary Romantic concern was with the transaction between the human mind and nature in a two-term system where in effect the Creator had been relegated to the sidelines.[18] The most characteristic Romantic poem celebrates an emergence from spiritual crisis by means of a transformation of consciousness that unites man with nature, subject with object, in a revitalized awareness—a regained affinity with the universe that was symbolized for Wordsworth and Coleridge in terms of a new vision brought about by the imagination or by "joy." (For Shelley the redemptive force was "love," which he described as "the bond and sanction which connects not only man with man but with everything which exists.")

This preoccupation with a new and transmuted mode of sight was a common element underlying many differing manifestations of the Romantic spirit.

Abrams discusses three "supplementary ways in which the eye, altering, was said to yield, at least momentarily, a re-created world." The first way was to recover for one's vision the freshness of sensation that had been lost as a result of custom and familiarity, and this power of giving "the charm of novelty to things of every day" was both the hallmark of poetic genius and the quality that above all else Coleridge honored in the poetry of his friend Wordsworth. It was in Coleridge's view the "lethargy of custom" that had to be overcome in order to liberate the "wonder" in the "familiar," and the criterion for such freshness of sensation is "the child's sense of wonder and novelty"; hence the reverence accorded by all the first generation of the Romantics to the child's unspoilt vision.

The second way in which vision could be transformed was by courting exposure to sudden and transient illuminated "moments," of the kind that play a major structural role in *The Prelude* and that make up the whole of many of Wordsworth's best-known shorter poems. Two particularly revelatory moments of this kind were given by Wordsworth the label "spots of time"; but as he himself observed, such moments are "scatter'd everywhere" in his life and work, and they also occur quite frequently in the poetry of Coleridge, Shelley, and Keats.

The third way of transmuting everyday vision into imaginative seeing is through what Abrams terms a perceptual transvaluation, in which what is ordinarily commonplace, lowly, and mean becomes endowed with sublimity and grandeur. This kind of radical elevation in the status of the object or the person viewed is persistently observable in Wordsworth's poetry, where the recurrent concern is to celebrate and dignify mundane objects ("the meanest flower that blows"), ordinary scenes, and humble people. Coleridge in chapter 4 of *Biographia Literaria* testified to his early admiration for Wordsworth's gift of "spreading the tone, the *atmosphere*, and with it the depth and height of the ideal world around forms, incidents and situations, of which for the common view, custom had bedimmed all the lustre."

Crabbe's later poetry offers little evidence of the second and third ways of seeing outlined by Abrams. We shall search in vain for visionary "moments" or "spots of time"; and although Crabbe's subject matter does still quite frequently take into its purview scenes and personages that were currently regarded as mean, low, and unpoetic, he certainly does not try to cast over them any "atmosphere" of the "ideal world." Indeed, in his preface to *Tales* (1812) he readily takes to himself Grant's disparaging phrase "without an atmosphere," and it may be suggested that it was this refusal to dignify scenes of humble life with an idealizing "atmosphere" that is at the root of Wordsworth's disapproval of what he called Crabbe's "unpoetical mode of considering human nature and society."[19]

Thus it is only in relation to Abrams's first "transformed way of seeing," the concern with freshness of sensation, that Crabbe's work shows any very significant absorption of the Romantic ambience; and here it is the child's vision that evokes from him the greatest liveliness of realization. In his studies of madness he follows for the most part his own course, subject to the same influences as the other poets of his time[20] and differing from them mainly in his greater concern for psychological truthfulness. His treatment of the supernatural remains, on balance, cautiously skeptical. In his direct confrontation in "The Lover's Journey" with the central Romantic theme of the intimate interplay between the human eye and the beauty of the natural landscape, what he offers is essentially a rejection of the Romantic position. The fact is that Crabbe belonged to an older generation than that of the Romantic poets, so that his fundamental outlook and values had been fully formed before the cataclysmic events that impinged upon them so forcefully. Though mildly favorable towards the beginnings of the French Revolution he had no millennial expectations of it, and consequently felt no impulsion to compensate for disappointed hopes by constructing an internal mode of renovating the world.

Nevertheless, Crabbe's response to the Romantic challenge should not be dismissed as wholly peripheral. "The Lover's Journey" is rightly to be seen as a masterpiece in its combination of sensitive appreciation of the Romantic stance with a severely critical adverse judgment on its implications. Moreover, in several books in *Tales of the Hall* and in two of the *Posthumous Tales* we have found evidence of a somewhat more sympathetic attitude towards certain Romantic preoccupations; and the work thus influenced is by no means negligible. Indeed, it adds an attractive additional dimension to Crabbe's already varied range of human concern.

Crabbe's amiable readiness, in his old age, to fit in with and accommodate himself to the sensibility of the age goes hand in hand with a certain relaxation of artistic grasp, a certain diffuseness of scale and design in the shaping of the tale as a whole, and a certain dilution of those qualities that we value most in the finest work of his mature period. Conversely, we may suspect that, in the best of the work published in the volumes of 1807, 1810, and 1812, some of the characteristic energy and vitality is attributable to a tension arising from the underlying conflict between Crabbe's predominantly Augustan values and the new currents of feeling that increasingly forced themselves upon his attention.

9

Crabbe and Genre

The concept of genre has enjoyed increased attention in recent years, and certain features of Crabbe's work prompt some consideration of its relevance here. Broadly speaking, there seem to be two main types of approach to the question of genre. One (favored by theorists with a leaning towards scientism) would seek to elaborate genre-models by abstract a priori analysis. The other (surely more promising) starts from a study of current and past usage of the term in appropriate cultural and historical contexts, and comes thereby to the view that genres are best seen as institutionalized conventions that function by setting up for readers likely "horizons of expectation" and for writers provisional "models for writing." And although some theorists have been inclined to see the development or modification of genres as something that takes place on its own somewhat insulated plane (so that a new genre comes "quite simply from other genres . . . by inversion, by displacement, by combination") the trend latterly (under the influence, to some extent, of Bakhtin) has been to hold that new genres arise, in part at least, because of their power to embody certain issues and problems that have arisen in the broader social and historical context.[1]

During the earlier half of the eighteenth century the recognized poetic "kinds" (derived originally from classical literary theory but much augmented in number during the Middle Ages) were widely regarded as a fixed typology, to be accepted unquestioningly and without any serious attempt to examine the nature of the distinctions between them. In this period the "rules" that carried such weighty authority were usually specified not in general terms but according to "kind"; and it was often implied that the table of genres was closed, and no new "kinds" could be admitted. In practice, however, hybrids of existing types did arise and came to be not merely tolerated, but even widely acclaimed, an influential example being the combination of natural description, philosophy, and narrative in James Thomson's poem *The Seasons*. Moreover such authoritative figures as Pope and Dr. Johnson were insistent that innovation that subverts the "rules" can justify itself if successful in achieving its ends.

Nevertheless, there lingered on well into the third quarter of the century a marked deference towards both the hierarchy of "kinds" and the standards of poetical decorum implicit within it, and this is still clearly perceptible in Crabbe's poems of the 1780s. Thus his earliest London-published poem, *The Candidate* (1780), was a "Poetical Epistle" with a quotation from one of Horace's epistles prefaced to it; while *The Library* and *The Newspaper* both fall into the recognized category of the verse essay. *The Village*, too, though by far the most original of these early poems, owes its existence to a continued awareness of the pastoral as a "kind" that it was worthwhile for a poet to react against. Even as late as *The Borough* Crabbe showed a continuing slightly uneasy awareness of those "kinds" whose claims he no longer attempted to meet except by way of an occasional modest token. Thus in letter 11 he approaches the "low" topic of inns by a mildly facetious invocation of the muse whose province is mock-epic or burlesque ; while in letter 19 the opening 120 lines of the tale of the parish clerk Jachin are narrated in language appropriate to mock-heroic, after which Crabbe dismisses "the playful Muse" on the grounds that the theme is now too serious to be continued in the same vein. However the sway of the poetic "kinds" was already in decline by the time of Dr. Johnson's death in 1784, and it is fair to suppose that the increasingly relaxed pressure from critical opinion over the two succeeding decades was one of the factors that enabled Crabbe, in his fifties, to invent a type of verse-tale for which there were no close precedents.

In generic terms Crabbe's tales in verse can be viewed on one level as an amalgam of discursive features drawn from several unrelated genres— versification and language from Pope's *Moral Essays,* narrative content from eighteenth-century novels or biographies, humble or workaday settings and personae from the early poems of Wordsworth or Southey. Crabbe was, of course, a voracious novel-reader, and we know also that around the turn of the century he actually completed three prose novels, which he destroyed as a consequence of his wife's adverse criticism. It seems clear too that through incessant practice (he had formed the habit of writing an average of thirty lines every day) the heroic couplet had become his easiest and most natural form of expression, and consequently the ineluctable medium for his developing narrative bent. And the circumstances that led him toward choosing subject matter that in his earlier days would have been regarded as unacceptably "low" for poetic treatment have already been examined (see chapters 2 and 3 above). What can be said, however, about the patterns of expectation this hybrid genre would set up in its potential readers?

In all probability most of Crabbe's contemporary audience could be counted on to negotiate without difficulty his formal and slightly old-fashioned diction and his tightly organized patterns of meter and rhyme, balance and antithesis, since Pope was still one of the most widely read of all the English poets. (Indeed, several more decades would have to elapse before the full effect was seen of the protracted slide in Pope's reputation foreshadowed by Joseph Warton's characterization of him in 1756 as a man of wit and sense rather than as a true poet.) Thus there can be no mistaking the satisfaction with which the *Quarterly Review* in October 1825 proclaimed itself reassured by the appearance of "three voluminous editions of Pope within the present century"; and there is much similar evidence to support Sir Leslie Stephen's castigation of the common belief that the eighteenth century ended with the year 1800. (In reality, he argued, "it lasted in the upper currents of opinion till at least 1832.")

All the same, the potential reading public at the start of the nineteenth century had altered considerably from that of the high Augustan era. It had certainly grown vastly in absolute terms, and perhaps a little, too, as a proportion of the greatly increased population.[2] Even more to the point was the change in its social composition. This came to extend beyond the gentry and the professions to include the class of tradesmen and artisans—now the dividing line between the reading and the nonreading public. But it was among the stratum just above them, the commercial middle class, that the habit of reading had become most firmly entrenched as a leisure pastime; concentrated mainly in the cities and towns, they were among the most active patrons of the circulating libraries and the most assiduous readers of the newly proliferating genre of the novel. Given this changed social mix, the new reading public was unlikely to jib at the presence in Crabbe's verse-tales of characters, occupations, and settings that half a century earlier would undoubtedly have been objected to as either too "low and vulgar" or too commonplace for treatment in poetry.

However, the expectations they brought to narrative would almost certainly derive more from the novel than from poetry,[3] since the early narrative experiments of Wordsworth (in *Lyrical Ballads*) and Southey (in his *Eclogues*), though possibly offering Crabbe himself some stimulus as a "model for writing," had enjoyed only a modest success in terms of circulation. And the novels published in the 1790s split into two rather diverse subgenres. The most widely read and eagerly discussed were the gothic novels, which had to a large extent absorbed and reformulated many of the features distinctive, in preceding decades, of the novel of sensibility. These gothic romances were, of course, represented at their best by Mrs. Radcliffe's *Mysteries of Udolpho* (whose extravagant plotting Crabbe deplored in letter

20 of *The Borough*). Contrasting with them was the ideological novel, which discussed social, political, and moral issues either from a Jacobin stand-point (Bage, Holcroft, Inchbald, Godwin) or from an answering anti-Jacobin stance (Isaac d'Israeli, Elizabeth Hamilton). Now, it is true that, as Crabbe himself conceded, in Mrs. Radcliffe's famous novel "the characters [are] well-drawn, and the manners described from real life," yet it can hardly be supposed that these qualities were the main attraction that drew so many readers to her works or to those of her imitators. In poetry, continuity with this subgenre was maintained (with some modifications) in the metrical romances of Scott, Campbell, Moore, and the later Southey—a tradition of escapist, incident-packed tales located either in the past, as in *The Lay of the Last Minstrel*, or in remote exotic settings, as in Campbell's *Gertrude of Wyoming* or Moore's *Lalla Rookh*. In parallel to this it may be thought that the ideological novels, preoccupied as they were with the moral dimension to human conduct, set up "horizons of expectation" rather closer to Crabbe's concerns in his tales, though there is certainly a gulf between his distinctly nonpartisan approach to social issues and their patently political orienta-tion. But even if we stress rather more Crabbe's indebtedness (by no means tenuous) to earlier novelists such as Fielding, Richardson, or Mackenzie, it must be admitted that there remains a wide gap between the typical novel's more leisurely development of characters and plot-complication and Crabbe's concentration of focus in each tale upon a rather small area of human motivation and decision.

Perhaps it is dissatisfaction at this gap that has led some writers on Crabbe to seek out, rather too eagerly, precursors for his tales in an eigh-teenth-century poetic tradition whose existence most literary historians have doubted. The consensus view is that of Kroeber : "The Augustans . . . told few tales in poetry. To the great Augustans narrative was a vehicle for satire and wit."[4] (The few generally agreed exceptions—translations, fables, mock-heroic—hardly seem relevant in this context.) Sigworth, in an otherwise useful book, suggests that Crabbe was influenced by an "unbroken tradi-tion" of versified tales reaching back as far as Swift's "Phillis."[5] This is strain-ing the record too far. There *are* occasional miscellaneous narrative pieces by the more important writers—Swift, Gay, Pope, Prior, Goldsmith, even William Whitehead—that Crabbe is likely to have known, and some other isolated ones by very minor writers that he almost certainly did not; but in this pursuit of a conjectural influence conceived in terms of literary form alone, Sigworth loses sight of a genre relationship that was formative in a much deeper sense.

The influence on Crabbe of the eighteenth-century Progress or "prog-ress piece" is not, of course, a new discovery. Yet the implications of this relationship have never been explored at all fully, perhaps because the Progress as a genre has been conceived in unduly crude didactic terms—as a "tragical tract in artistic form, showing in definite stages the punishment, or self-punishment, of a vice or a foible" (Elton)[6] or "a mechanical form . . . [that] . . . enumerates in defined stages the course of punishments attendant upon a particular vice" (Kroeber).[7] However, Elton and Kroeber (and, more recently, New) also quite rightly observed that Crabbe probably owed more to Hogarth's paintings than to any antecedent literary source, and this recognition of the relevant genre as one that crosses the boundaries between verbal and visual art should prompt a reassessment of its most significant characteristics.

For Hogarth, the master-practitioner, the Progress consists of a series of discrete scenes, each carefully composed and realized, each to be valued for the richness of its own detail, yet also in combination with its neighbors carrying implicit within it a story line whose downward social or moral movement exists above all as a vehicle for wide-ranging social satire. Thus *A Harlot's Progress* is "about" Mary Hackabout, a country girl who arrives in London to become successively a Jew's mistress, a common prostitute, a prisoner in Bridewell, and a victim of syphilis; at her coffin the only genuine mourners are her small son and a noseless brothel servant. Essentially, however, the point of this didactic narrative is to enable Hogarth to mount a comprehensive satire on society itself—a society that permits (or even compels) such events to happen. This society is embodied in the engravings by Mother Needham, the procuress; Colonel Charteris, the well-known rake and rapist; and the two quack doctors who peddle their "cures" for venereal disease. In *A Rake's Progress* too, the main thrust of Hogarth's satire is directed not so much against the hapless Rakewell himself as against the whole of society in its manifold dishonesties, follies, debaucheries, corruptions, and brutalities. As Paulson has pointed out, this aspect of Hogarth's art stands out with particular clarity in the third state of Plate 8, "Retouched by the author 1763," where a seal has been added to the wall of the madhouse in the shape of the reverse side of a halfpenny with "Britannia" and "1763" visible on it. The figure of Britannia has her hair flying loose behind her head as if she, too, were mad: "Bedlam, Hogarth suggests, is England as of 1763."[8]

The influence of this on Crabbe is most clearly apparent in letter 15 of *The Borough*, where, as Elton put it, "the decline of Clelia is demonstrated at halting-points of ten years, which affect us like a Hogarthian series."[9] Moreover, if we read this letter in conjunction with its neighbors (those on Blaney and Benbow), remembering that these three characters represent an undeserving and irresponsible social grouping that has been awarded specially favored charitable support by the influential Sir Denys Brand, we may conclude that Crabbe, too, is here using the Progress to effect a wide-ranging condemnation of society and its values. (The tone of the attack is certainly more restrained than Hogarth's, but perhaps that befits the provincial rather than metropolitan nature of the target.) On the other hand, if we take each separate letter on its own, Crabbe's main purpose may seem to have modulated from social satire to didacticism—a moral didacticism whose judgments are harsh and hortatory. We do not know enough about the "horizons of expectation" of Crabbe's contemporary readership to tell us in which light they would most readily have approached these tales, though comments in some of the early reviews might suggest the second alternative as the more probable.[10]

In genre terms, however, what Crabbe took from Hogarth most durably was a structural pattern for narrative that proved remarkably versatile. Thus a similar short series of vivid "scenes" is used effectively not only for the compassionate didacticism of Jachin's "degress," but also, with rather greater subtlety, for the more complex ethical and artistic purposes of *Peter Grimes*. And subsequently in almost all the tales in the 1812 volume, even though the narrative pattern has moved far away from the constricting one of social or moral decline, we can still trace the same basic narrative strategy: an expository introduction or statement of theme, followed by up to half a dozen concretely realized "scenes"—brief snapshots taken in sequence at points within the underlying action, and chosen to point up, in conjunction with others in the series, whatever contrast, parallel, or causal relationship is most relevant to the theme in hand. In these poems of Crabbe's full maturity, however, the overriding goal of the narrative structure is no longer either satire or didacticism, but rather an attempt to explore the full complexity of the moral issues involved. Remarkably enough, the short string of "scenes" serves a variety of new themes and purposes extremely well, and also provides Crabbe's verse-tales with one of the small number of distinctive formal features that qualify them for consideration as a subgenre, or even perhaps as a putative genre that no other writer happened to take up.

It is not easy to explain why this genre or subgenre failed to establish itself, beyond a reminder that it had arisen out of a constellation of highly specific cultural and historical circumstances. One such circumstance must have been the growing preoccupation of the middle-class reading public with the nature and importance of the individual self, particularly as seen in a context of family life and the domestic affections—a preoccupation that has often been regarded as highly characteristic of the Romantic period.[11] In the form that Crabbe developed for it, the tale was particularly well adapted to engage such issues, while at the same time maintaining that concern with the moral dimension of human behavior which was a persisting legacy from the Augustan tradition. Crabbe's popularity in the opening decades of the nineteenth century must have owed a good deal to these considerations (one remembers Jane Austen's enthusiastic tribute to him), and on these grounds it might have been expected to last longer than it in fact did. But a number of the other favoring circumstances were dispersed even earlier than Crabbe's death in 1832, and of them two seem worth particular mention. In the first place, in the wake of the eventual success of Wordsworth's project to simplify and purify poetic language, the highly stylized couplets that had given the genre some of its characteristic edge came to seem unacceptably stilted and artificial. And at the same time the accepted subject matter of poetry was changing too, in ways that favored the expression of intense individual emotion rather than the deliberative examination of human and social interrelationships. Secondly, as a result in part of the prominence given to "scenes" rendered visually, Crabbe's narrative patterns favored an objective, even at times external, approach to characterization. Though there is frequent invitation to empathize with his characters, the limited span of the tales gives little opportunity for that prolonged empathy with an individual protagonist that is usually called "identification." Yet from the time of Richardson and Fielding onward this had been an important element in the novel's attraction for its readers, and after the Brontës it became virtually indispensable. In these respects, it may be suggested, the genre Crabbe had invented was no longer capable of meeting the expectations either of poetry readers or of novel readers. The "horizon of expectation" had evidently moved on.

On its record to date, it may seem doubtful whether genre study can tell us much of value about the originality of the great writer (Blake, Wordsworth, Lawrence) who blazes new trails for human sensibility. But Crabbe, of course, was not gifted with this kind of greatness; his originality lay in his success in making a new synthesis of already existing elements—elements drawn from various genres but deployed by him with an added sensitivity, perceptiveness, and shrewdness. And in his case genre study has something to contribute to our understanding of the development of this synthesis. It may also perhaps be able to offer some hints as to why his verse-tales, though widely appreciated in his own lifetime, have been so much neglected and undervalued during the century and a half since his death.

10

Crabbe, "Realism," and Poetic Truth

As long ago as 1948 Ortega y Gasset described "realism" as an "involved term" that he had always been careful to "use in quotation marks to render it suspect." Despite this caution I have several times found myself using, albeit reluctantly, the adjective "realistic" to characterize certain aspects of Crabbe's verse-tales. Some discussion of this term in relation to Crabbe's work may therefore seem advisable.

Of course, a good deal of the recent (mainly poststructuralist) animus against "realism" both as a critical term and as an authorial practice stems originally from Roland Barthes's influential 1966 essay "L'effet du réel."[1] Barthes, starting out from an example drawn from Flaubert's *Un Coeur simple*, asserted that in "modern realism" (as contrasted with the *vraisemblance* of classical poetic theory) "the "real" [i.e., the "concrete detail"] is assumed not to need any independent justification, that it is powerful enough to negate any notion of "function," that it can be integrated into a structure, and that the *having-been-there* of things is a sufficient reason for speaking of them." On this criterion the hallmark of a "realist" writer would seem to be the presence in his descriptions of lumps of undigested or nonsignificant "reality."

Since Barthes unhesitatingly assigns "modern realism" to a specific historical period, with Flaubert as its archetypal champion, his account of realism can have little relevance to Crabbe's actual practice. In the English language, too, although "realism" had long been in use as a technical term in philosophy, it was not until the mid-nineteenth century that it was first used to denote fidelity of representation in literature and visual art.[2] This fact is in itself enough to cast doubt on the hindsight that would designate Crabbe as a "realist." Such claims have not infrequently been made, nevertheless. The earliest that I have been able to trace is Leslie Stephen's observation in 1874 that "Crabbe, like all realistic writers must be studied at full length. . . . His scenery is as realistic as a photograph. . . ."[3]

163

Now, although the use of the "realistic" label is undoubtedly anachronistic, this does draw attention to a specific feature of Crabbe's descriptive writing that has been much commented on, though often in rather misleading terms. Even in the poet's own lifetime we can find precedents for the suspicion, voiced again quite recently, that Crabbe's writing is "nonfiction in all but name": for example, Hazlitt's complaint that "literal fidelity serves him in place of invention" and Wordsworth's slightly sour observation that "nineteen out of twenty of his pictures are mere matter of fact."[4] Such responses may be seen as an unwitting tribute to Crabbe's ability to evoke in his readers, through an accumulation of meticulous detail, a compelling *illusion* of precisely visualized reality. For there can be no serious doubt that the details in question have been drawn from a variety of different sources, including both firsthand observation and remembered reading,[5] and that the artistic achievement is a matter of selecting and fusing together "minute particulars" so that the resulting description is fully meshed in with the emotional and intellectual requirements of the story and discourse as they develop. An obvious example that comes to mind is the masterly description of the river scene that daily confronted Peter Grimes from the boat on which, ostracized by his fellow townspeople, he was "by himself compelled to live each day"; this is, as it happens, tied with exceptional closeness to a particular stretch of the River Alde, yet it is unmistakably there not for topographic but for emotional and thematic effect. Even more telling for the point under discussion is the description of the Kindreds' room in "The Frank Courtship," where every single detail mentioned plays its part in defining for us the character of the family living in it—prosperous, austere, devout, orderly, self-satisfied.

> Fix'd were their habits; they arose betimes,
> Then pray'd their hour, and sang their party-rhymes;
> Their meals were plenteous, regular and plain,
> The trade of *Jonas* brought him constant gain;
> Vender of Hops and Malt, of Coals and Corn —
> And like his father, he was merchant born:
> Neat was their house; each table, chair, and stool,
> Stood in its place, or moving mov'd by rule;
> No lively print or picture grac'd the room;
> A plain brown paper lent it decent gloom;
> But here the eye, in glancing round, survey'd
> A small Recess that seem'd for china made;
> Such pleasing pictures seem'd this pencil'd ware,
> That few would search for nobler objects there—

Yet, turn'd by chosen friends, and there appear'd
His stern, strong features, whom they all rever'd;
For there in lofty air was seen to stand,
The bold Protector of the conquer'd land;
Drawn in that look with which he wept and swore,
Turn'd out the members and made fast the door,
Ridding the House of every knave and drone,
Forc'd, though it griev'd his soul, to rule alone.
The stern still smile each Friend approving gave,
Then turn'd the view, and all again were grave.

                                                        (41–64)

This is a good example of the single-minded economy with which Crabbe regularly tailors his descriptions to fit very precisely the artistic purposes he has in hand. At the same time the verbal evocation of the scene produces such a vivid illusion of reality that more than one reader has been moved to comment about the clinching detail of Cromwell's concealed portrait that this did not seem "like something Crabbe had invented."[6] There is, interestingly enough, a footnote by Crabbe's son in the 1834 edition of the *Poetical Works* that vouches for the authenticity of this episode as follows: "Such was the actual consolation of a small knot of Presbyterians [*sic*] in a country town, about sixty years ago." Perhaps, though, this testimony adds less to our knowledge than we might at first suppose: since the son was not born until 1785, he cannot be doing more than retail his father's version of the incident as told to his family some years later, and it is in any case unclear whether this version was based on anything more than hearsay. Concern about the historical status of this "referent" for a fictional "signified" is in any case clearly misplaced. If we read the passage with due attention, we realize that the meticulous detail is carefully defining for us the complacent conviction of their own worth that lies behind the austere manners of the "saints" and that the treasured portrait of the Protector Cromwell ("Forc'd, though it griev'd his soul, to rule alone") is there essentially as a means of bringing out the connection between this attitude of self-satisfied righteousness and the father's overbearing domestic tyranny. In this instance, then, as indeed in almost all Crabbe's descriptive writing, the "concrete detail" can be shown to be thoroughly functional and to be deployed not in the manner of "modern realism," but according to the principles and purposes of what Barthes referred to as the *vraisemblance* of classical poetic theory.

However, to confine the discussion to Crabbe's descriptions of places would obviously be a mistake, since far more central to an understanding of his poetic procedures is his depiction of people—in which, understandably enough, description of physical appearance plays only a part. Here as else-where what must not be underestimated is the enduring strength of his Augustan roots, not only in his handling of verse forms and textures, but also in the values and purposes that they serve. In general, of course, the assumption that literature should teach useful lessons that are widely appli-cable had led eighteenth-century writers and critics to prefer those charac-ters and situations that could be seen to be "general" rather than "particu-lar." Hence Dr. Johnson's dictum: "Nothing can please many and please long, but just representations of general nature." What he meant by "gen-eral" is made plain by his further comment that whereas "in the writings of other poets a character is too often an individual," in those of Shakespeare (whom he found pre-eminent in this respect) "it is commonly a species."

For the most part Crabbe's characters are certainly not "types" in any derogatory sense; in fact, they are likely to strike us at first as highly de-tailed, particularized, and individual. Nevertheless, there can be no doubt that they are at the same time quite deliberately representative on two lev-els. In the first place, they are presented as socially typical. Thus the squire in "Advice" combines in his own person all the traits held to be common in members of his particular social group. Indeed, this tale "Advice", taken as a whole, encapsulates in a quite remarkable way a whole phase of English social history. All the salient aspects are there, and each is given its due weight—the manners, morals and outlook of the eighteenth-century squire, the relationship between the church and the landowning class, the impact of the Evangelical movement, and even the eventual outcome of the con-flict. It is no doubt a perception of this quality in Crabbe that has led social historians to take more interest in his work than many literary critics have done. But Crabbe's characters are also put forward as representative on a second and more fundamental level. They exemplify deep-rooted traits in human nature, so that the moral issues and conflicts that they embody have a wider and more enduring significance than that belonging to one par-ticular time and place. Crabbe himself, one feels, would hardly have thought it extravagant to call them universal and timeless, any more than he would have felt inclined to question, for instance, the explicit assertion by Fielding—one of his favorite authors—of the constancy and universality of human nature in the person of the lawyer in *Joseph Andrews* who "is not only alive, but hath been so these four thousand years." Certainly in the case of "Advice" we can readily think of parallels in the modern world to the dilemma of the young priest caught between his devotion to his ideals and his preference for a comfortable existence untroubled by conflict with the powers that be, yet sufficiently sensitive to be made uncomfortable by the excesses of some of his own party.

As was pointed out earlier, in virtually all his poetry Crabbe sets out to "instruct by pleasing," and with characteristically Augustan confidence in divine providence, believes he can do so by "imitating" a nature that embraces the whole of the created universe, including mankind, and that has inherent in its workings an objective and universal moral law. There are, nevertheless, changes over the years in his conception of the "instructive truth" that he seeks to convey. In his early and highly generalized antipastoral poem *The Village*, the "Truth" that is to "paint the Cot . . . as bards will not" had been an abstract personification. In his mature poetry from *The Parish Register* on, however, Crabbe clearly sets himself the task not only of representing in each character some universal aspect of human nature but also of achieving a more local typicality. This development, foreshadowed in *The Village* by the two brief outline sketches of the apothecary and the parish priest, was now fleshed out with a much greater wealth of detail, detail selected in such a way as to epitomize the members of a specific group or class recognizably present in the England of the poet's day. This increased resort to "minute particulars" (which had been tolerated only in a modest subsidiary role by the Augustan critical theory of Johnson and Reynolds) is undoubtedly innovatory for its period, but it cannot rightly be seen as an early manifestation of nineteenth-century "realism." In his preface to *Tales* (1812), Crabbe does certainly insist that "a fair representation of existing character" is a proper activity for a "true poet"; but he is here engaged in rebutting claims of exclusive poetic status for the kind of writing (about enchanters, spirits, and monsters) that lifts its readers "above the grossness of actual being." Moreover, his argument is that, whether characters and occurrences are "actually copied from life" or invented by a "creative fancy," it is only through the poet's art (his judicious management of "the manner in which the poem is conducted") that they can have the requisite "effect of realities" in the reader's mind. In the light of this authorial credo the attempt to track down original sources or "referents" for specific items (such as the portrait of Cromwell in "The Frank Courtship") can have little relevance to Crabbe's poetic intentions and is not likely to prove very illuminating in regard to his actual poetic practice, either.

It is true, of course, that, when asked, Crabbe willingly agreed that "really existing creatures" had formed the originals for almost all his characters;[7] and in the intimacy of the family circle he was evidently prepared to name a number of them. In his son's notes (those appended to the 1834 edition of the poems, together with those written down in 1854 or 1855 at the request of Edward FitzGerald) we find asserted the real-life originals for some twenty-five characters in *The Parish Register*, *The Borough* and *Tales* (1812). However, comparison between the son's information and the poet's verse portraits strongly suggests that Crabbe's poetic art was less closely tied to "existing character" than he himself believed, and that in many cases the real-life character can have served as no more than an initial stimulus. Thus the "infidel poacher" in part 1 of *The Parish Register* is said to have been

> a blacksmith at Leiston, near Aldborough, whom the author visited in his capacity of surgeon in 1779, and whose hardened character made a strong impression on his mind. Losing his hand by amputation, he exclaimed with a sneer, "I suppose, Dr Crabbe, I shall get it again at the resurrection!"

One can well see that this seasoned skepticism may have set the imagination to work to produce the sardonic closing lines of his character sketch:

> By night as business urg'd, he sought the Wood,
> The ditch was deep, the rain had caus'd a flood;
> The foot-bridge fail'd, he plung'd beneath the Deep,
> And slept, if truth were his, th'eternal sleep.
>
> (*The Parish Register*, 1.820–23)

But the transformation has been a far-reaching one.

Other instances compel doubt as to the truth of Crabbe's own (indubitably honest) conviction that "he seldom takes anything from books, but all from what he sees and hears."[8] Thus in part 3 of *The Parish Register* the poet's son confidently identified the active and overbearing Widow Goe with Mrs. Tovell, the aunt of the poet's wife. Consider, however, the telling and memorable lines that record the Widow Goe's last words:

> Bless me! I die and not a Warning giv'n,—
> With *much* to do on Earth and ALL for Heav'n!
> No Reparation for my Soul's Affairs,
> No Leave petition'd for the Barn's Repairs;
> Accounts perplex'd, my Interest yet unpaid,
> My Mind unsettled and my Will unmade;—
> A Lawyer haste, and in your way, a Priest;
> And let me die in one good Work at least.
>
> (*The Parish Register*, 3.175–82)

It is hard to doubt that here Crabbe has also been influenced by (and has indeed improved upon) Richardson's account of the dying Widow Sinclair:

> "And here, she said—Heaven grant me patience! (clenching and unclenching her hands)—am I to die thus miserable—of a broken leg in my old age! Self-

do! Self-undone! No time for my affairs! No time to repent! and in a few hours . . . etc. (*Clarissa*, vol. 4, letter 138)

There are enough detectable examples of a similar confluence of a real-life with a literary source to suggest that at this "socially typical" level of characterization much of Crabbe's particularized descriptive detail must have been taken partly from observation and partly from remembered reading. But in any case what he both aims at and achieves is undoubtedly (in Roland Barthes's way of putting it) *vraisemblance* (whose implicit motto is "Esto . . . Let there be, suppose. . . ") and not "realism" (or "discourse which accepts statements whose only justification is their referent").

The mention of Richardson's great masterpiece provides an opportunity to return the question of Crabbe's "realism" to the context in which it properly belongs—namely, that of the eighteenth-century English novel, the establishment of which was clearly a prior condition for the development of Crabbe's narrative art. The contention that the distinguishing feature of the novel is its "formal realism" (or, in an alternative formulation, its "realism of presentation") was put forward with great persuasiveness by Ian Watt as long ago as 1957 in *The Rise of the Novel;* and the case argued there has stood the test of time remarkably well. As recently as 1987 Michael McKeon wrote that Watt's book had been "for many years now . . . the most successful attempt to explain the origins of the English novel," and then continued: "Watt specifies the novel's distinctive 'narrative procedures' with subtlety and precision: the repudiation of traditional plots and figurative eloquence; the particularization of character and background, of naming, temporality, causation, and physical environment."[9] Perhaps this summary of the argument should be supplemented by Watt's own way of putting it:

Formal realism is . . . the narrative embodiment of a premise . . . which is implicit in the novel form in general: the premise, or primary convention, that the novel is a full and authentic report of human experience, and is therefore under an obligation to satisfy its reader with such details as the individuality of the actors concerned, the particulars of the times and places of their actions, details which are presented through a more largely referential use of language than is common in other literary forms.[10]

Now it should be evident that most of the features pointed to in this (retrospective) attribution of "realism" to the eighteenth-century novel are present to some considerable extent in Crabbe's tales. We have already discussed at some length the particularity whereby Crabbe seeks to present his tales as "an authentic account of the actual experience of individuals"—even down to the use of proper names (usually ones actually current in the East Anglia of his day) to establish the individual identity of his personae. There can be little doubt that if "formal realism" is a characteristic of the novels of Defoe, Fielding, and Richardson, the term can properly be applied in the same sense to Crabbe's narratives.

On the other hand, it should be mentioned that some recent critics (most notably Michael McKeon) suggest that Watt painted too sharp a contrast between the "formal realism" of the nascent novel and the tradition of romance that it came to replace. Although Defoe, Richardson, and (especially) Fielding "explicitly subvert the idea and ethos of romance, they nevertheless draw upon many of its stock situations and conventions," and some of these romance elements are ones that could be seen as transmutations of long-lasting archetypal patterns.[11] Thus in Defoe we have the eventual triumph of the younger son, in Richardson the servant whose virtuous conduct leads to her becoming a lady, in Fielding the foundling who turns out to be of genteel birth. We find ourselves asking, therefore, whether in Crabbe's tales there are similar overarching romance or archetypal elements alongside the formal realism of presentation. As far as our author's best work (the *Tales* of 1812) is concerned, such elements are not at all obvious, and the question is not an easy one to answer.

However, the genuinely problematic aspect of the relationship between Crabbe's poetry and its context relates neither to the provenance of the plots nor to the provenance of specific details, but rather to the degree of congruence we can plausibly suppose to exist between the characters and communities as portrayed in their entirety, and the underlying social reality they seem clearly designed to epitomize. Here we can perhaps identify two main areas of difficulty.

In the first place, we need to take into account the extraordinary diversity of the rural England of Crabbe's day. Not only was it a thinly populated countryside of small villages isolated by appallingly bad roads from contact with a wider world; it was also (as the study of local records has revealed over the past half-century) a country with an almost inconceivable variety of differences between its village communities—differences of size, geographical location, past history of land settlement, crop cultivation, land use, traditional custom, and so forth. Yet until his removal to Trowbridge in 1814 Crabbe, despite having traveled more widely than most of his fellow clergymen, had had intimate experience, apart from his native town of Aldborough and the nearby town of Woodbridge, of only three small parishes in Leicestershire and four in Suffolk. His personal experience would not have told him what a hard task he was setting himself when he aimed, as his use of the definite article in his titles certainly implies, at "the common idea and central form" (in Sir Joshua Reynolds's phrase) underlying the varied individual forms that go under the heading of village, parish, and borough.

In respect of certain rather unimportant features of rural life (most notably those that are countable, such as the church bells, schools, and inns studied by W. K. Thomas)[12] we are now in a better position than Crabbe was to check the representative quality of his fictional institutions or personae. For such aspects Crabbe's communities seem to fall well within the bounds of the possible: thus there *were* churches (though not at Aldborough) with as many as ten bells, some bells *were* engraved with intriguing Latin mottoes, and so on. A more interesting (and contrary) example is provided by the parish workhouse, which Crabbe's readers might suppose an unvarying feature of every village, dreaded alike by the "hoary Swain" in *The Village* and by the "Noble Peasant" Isaac Ashford in *The Parish Register*. In fact, however, the official returns of expenditure on poor relief for the year 1802–3 show that less than a third of the nearly fifteen hundred parishes possessed a workhouse, and that these workhouses maintained less than one-twelfth of all those receiving poor relief at some time during that year. Conversely, the parliamentary enclosure of open fields and commons that affected many villages between 1740 and 1832, particularly in the Midlands, has been thought by most historians to have had far-reaching social and economic consequences. Yet there is no instance of any such event being recorded in Crabbe's verse.[13] This may in part be due to the fact that in the Midland parish he knew best, Muston in Leicestershire, enclosure had taken place by agreement early in the seventeenth century. But even though he had no direct experience of the process, parliamentary enclosures did take place in other Leicestershire parishes not far away, and he must have heard these talked about.[14]

The second source of difficulty is that Crabbe's lifetime covered a period of unprecedentedly rapid economic and social change, very little of which is shown at all explicitly in his poetry. It is true that the most dramatic developments, particularly in regard to growth of industry, large towns, and population, took place in the north of England and the West Midlands, so that if *The Parish Register* gives the impression of a stable countryside in which change takes place only slowly, if at all, this may have been more tenable in relation to those counties in which Crabbe had lived up till then. Nevertheless, in the portrayal of his world there is in general an absence of that sense of historic time that is an important element in our modern consciousness.

Two examples may be given here. In book 3 of *The Parish Register* the displacement in her old age of the village midwife Leah Cousins by the science-minded Dr. Glibb is rendered with admirable and convincing concreteness; yet few modern readers can have recognized it as an instance of a change in social practice to which an approximate historic date can be assigned. External evidence reveals from the mid-eighteenth century onward a widespread shift from untrained female midwives to male doctors equipped with new techniques, such as the use of forceps; and the details Crabbe uses in his fictional anecdote cannnot be faulted historically. Leah is a typical old-style midwife, virtually untrained, relying for help therefore on Heaven (to which she "prays in danger's view"), and licensed (if at all) by the bishop of the diocese on the basis of her moral character; while Doctor Glibb, although the poet is discreetly inexplicit about the "art" he delights to use to win his way against Nature and "act in her despite," is recognizably a follower of Dr. William Smellie, whose three-volume *Treatise on the Theory and Practice of Midwifery* enjoyed great success when it was published between 1752 and 1764. The charges bandied against each other by Crabbe's two contestants reflect quite closely, moreover, the bitter antagonism of the debate between male and female midwives in the 1750s and 1760s. For all that, there is a distinctly ahistorical tone to the poet's use of this material, and indeed his closing reference to "this our changing world" seems almost to relegate it to the category of yet one more instance of the eternal mutability of fashion.

Our second example concerns the illegitimacy rate. It is widely acknowledged that around the end of the eighteenth century betrayed and forsaken young women made their appearance with exceptional frequency both in English life and in literature, and indeed recent studies have concluded that the bastardy rate as a percentage of baptisms rose from around 3 percent in the 1750s to a consistent 5 percent or above between 1785 and 1814.[15] The incidence of "yielding maids" in Crabbe's poetry does not therefore seem to be historically inappropriate (although his two most celebrated portrayals in the genre, Phoebe Dawson and Lucy the Miller's daughter, are certainly both exceptionally touching and exceptionally memorable). Moreover, their circumstances do for the most part typify precisely those in which most illegitimacies are now believed to have arisen—circumstances, that is, very similar to those of first births in marriages, in that "bastards tended to be born of persons of an age and condition to marry each other, but who were prevented. . . ."[16] It is noticeable, however, that Crabbe does not give any place in his account to those *changing* features of rural life that social historians now postulate as having intensified the force of the "temptation" from which the poet (in the Phoebe Dawson passage) repeatedly urges youth to "refrain." By the end of the eighteenth century there was a

marked reduction in the average age at which men, and even more so
women, contracted their first marriage. This is thought to have been caused
in large part by the diminution of female work in agriculture, the effect of
enclosure in ending prudential motives for delaying marriage, and the decline of farm service.[17] These pressures leading to earlier marriage must
also have led to an increase in the proportion of young people engaging in
courtship, and at the same time to an increase in the number thereby incur-
ring a risk of prenuptial pregnancy or single motherhood. This is not of
course to suggest that Crabbe *ought* to have mentioned factors of this kind;
but at the same time there is surely a certain significance in the fact that he
presents the conflict between temptation and prudent self-restraint as an
ageless one, with the only possible response being reiterated (and largely
fruitless) moral exhortation.

If at this point we return to "Advice," we shall do so with an enhanced
awareness (owed in part at least to developments in historical sociology
over recent decades) of how difficult it must always be to evaluate the degree of congruence between a writer's imagined world and the world it
purports to represent.[18] It seems beyond question that, in this fine example
of his mature verse-tales, the representation of a socially typical moral conflict formed a significant part of Crabbe's goal. Surely Crabbe himself,
moreover, would have agreed unhesitatingly with my comment above that
the Squire (who is after all quite a close reworking of the ironically commended "good Squire Asgill" in letter 16 of *The Borough*) combines in his
own person all the traits held to be common in members of his particular
social group. (And would not his contemporary readers have thought the
same?) Yet how, we have to ask, could it have been possible for Crabbe to
know? Even if we leave out of account those village communities that never
had a resident squire (perhaps a fifth of the total number in England according to a recent estimate), it is clearly inconceivable that he should have
had enough direct experience of village squires to validate a judgment (which
must in the last analysis be numerical) as to just what could rightly be regarded as "typical" of them as a class. Nor indeed would a social historian
today see much prospect of unearthing reliable evidence for or against the
"typicality" of those traits that the poet has chosen to use in his portrayal.
Thus while individual instances could perhaps be found of hard-drinking
and sexually licentious squires, including some whose proclivities brought
them into open conflict with the rector of the parish, this would not resolve
the question of whether they were as preponderant in real life as the fiction
of the period often implied.

Of course, at a time when about half the livings in England and Wales
were in the gift of one of the landowning families, moral conflict between

parish incumbent and squire as patron would doubtless be found no more surprising than its opposite—the moral subservience that also became, after Fielding's Parson Supple, a fictional stereotype. As it happens, the conflict in "Advice" can be located in historic time with a degree of particularity unusual in Crabbe. The "patriot's zeal," for example, with which the squire claims to have persisted in churchgoing in face of the old rector's denunciation of him from the pulpit, irresistibly recalls the account in *The Annual Register* for 1793 of the unwonted queues of carriages outside churches, by means of which "the upper ranks of society" manifested their hostility to "the irreligious and profligate doctrines" of the French Revolution, while the resemblances between James's Evangelical preacher and the Cambridge clergyman Charles Simeon also strongly suggest a date in the mid-1790s. But these details (far from being there for any effect of adventitious "realism") are surely highly functional. By fixing the action at a time when the Evangelical campaign against moral laxity (launched a decade earlier by Wilberforce) was reaching its floodtide, they intensify the emotional charge attaching to the clash between old squire and young priest, and at the same time give it a more representative significance. Yet for the modern reader the social reality underlying the poem remains in some sense ungraspable, nor can he confidently reconstruct the response of Crabbe's contemporary readership to the particulars he has built into his narrative (the squire's hopeful advice about sermons, for instance, or the young preacher's overzealous performance in the pulpit), or establish from external evidence the extent to which they may have sensed in such particulars a social typicality that worked to secure in them a suspension of disbelief.

In the absence of any external source of validation the historical sociologist seeking to assess literary evidence as a source of accurate information may feel he has little to go upon other than the commonsense principle of credibility, and this seems in effect to reduce itself to an intuitive judgment, essentially ahistorical, about "truth to [an unchanging] human nature."[19] There is more than one way, however, in which intuition may be swayed, and even controlled, by poetic art; and the literary critic with a similar set of interests might want to ask not only, Do these characters ring true to human nature? but also, Do they seem to be living human beings rather than mere conventionalized types? In the case of Crabbe rather more of his characters than one at first realizes turn out to be variants on standard patterns available to him in the pages of eighteenth-century novels and therefore open to the suspicion of "representing" what his contemporary public was willing to believe rather than what actually was. Nevertheless, his repertoire covers a wide range: from the wholly stereotyped (the rapacious lawyer Swallow in letter 6 of *The Borough*) through the type-figure to which the poet has added some small but telling detail that lends a touch of individuality (the curate in letter 3, poor, learned and polyphiloprogenitive, harassed by debts and duns, and distinctive only in the compassionate concern for his ailing wife that has stranded him in his seaside backwater) right down to the highly individualized portrayal in which the type has been transformed into a sentient, breathing human being through the accumulation of concisely phrased detail, often neatly ironic (Andrew Collett or the Widow Goe in *The Parish Register*).

In characterization of this latter kind there is a recognizable continuity with Augustan poetic theory as modified in the later decades of the eighteenth century under the influence of such writers as Kames and Blair, and set out in more popularizing form by Craig in an essay in the *Lounger* in 1786 commending "this last improvement . . . in the representation of human characters; when not only their general features, under certain great classes, are exhibited, but when writers descend to, and are able at the same time to point out the smaller discriminations into which those general classes subdivide themselves and appear in different men. . . . " In "Advice" the credibility we readily accord to Crabbe's characterization is accounted for, in part at least, by the weight given, in each of the two protagonists, to traits that run counter to type. In the reprobate squire we recognize as a convincing notation of human complexity the mind sufficiently "conscious of its own excess" to feel at the opening of the poem the unspoken reproach of his neighbors and capable therefore, at the close, of uneasy longing for a wholehearted effort of reform that he knows himself to be too weak to accomplish. Similarly, his young nephew, though self-righteously "zealous still," feels both distress at the discord he has created within a once-harmonious parish, and well-bred embarrassment at the vulgar and self-conceited enthusiasm of his more ardent followers. Is it truth to human nature ("wholly or partly permanent") that we are responding to, or the creation of individual human beings? And does an author's success on either the level of general human nature or the level of particularized individuality engender the belief, perhaps illusory, that what has been represented must at the same time be accepted as socially typical? Whether or not these questions seem answerable, we can doubtless agree that these "levels" are too closely intertwined to be seen as anything more than an occasionally useful heuristic device.

Indeed, the outcome of this rather lengthy discussion can only be a renewed emphasis on the complexity of the issues raised. It may be worth recalling that Roman Jakobson, writing nearly half a century earlier than Barthes, delivered a scathing attack upon those who fail to "distinguish among the variety of concepts latent in the term 'realism'," and had himself set out as many as five separate meanings for the word.[20] One of the more interesting of his suggestions concerns the extent to which, in their quest for verisimilitude ("maximum faithfulness to life"), writers have regularly felt a need to eschew the "stale" or "petrified" verbal formulations of their predecessors in order to focus upon other features, previously scarcely noticed, that they have come to regard as more capable of capturing the "real" quality of existence. This can be seen as an anticipation of what Wimsatt and Brooks later characterized as the "negative definition" of realism, where the term is used to denote a reaction against artistic conventions or tendencies thought to be *un*real in their purport.[21] It is in this (limited) sense of a reaction against the *un*realism of idealizing conventions that the critics' attempts to apply the term "realist" to Crabbe may seem most wholly understandable; indeed, in this light we may even think justifiable the rather free use that has been made of the words "real" and "reality" as applied to his writings. It was in fact Crabbe himself who in the opening lines of *The Village* announced an intention to paint "the real picture of the poor," thereby repudiating the deceptively "pleasing scenes" of pastoral in favor of depicting "the real ills" of rural life as he knew them; and the word seems to have struck a chord of recognition in the minds of many of his early readers, for they frequently refer (sometimes with a sense of outrage) to his heavy preoccupation with unpleasant or even ugly "realities." Hazlitt, for instance, complained in 1821 that Crabbe's "song" was "one sad reality, one unraised, unvaried note of unavailing woe"; and Crabb Robinson in an 1835 diary entry echoed what had clearly become a critical commonplace in his comment that Crabbe "could faithfully portray what he saw" yet "had an eye only for the sad realities of life." While Crabbe certainly did not flinch from portraying unpleasant and even sordid aspects of the life around him, such comments clearly exaggerate to an absurd degree the amount of gloom to be found in his poetic world. This represents yet another—and even more limited—sense for the term "realism," however. What is objected to is not the accretion of "real" detail for its own sake, but the unacceptably somber principle upon which the detail has been selected and organized for thematic effect.

There remains one further, somewhat nebulous, general question that it may be worth trying to formulate more precisely. Is it not possible that in *all* fiction, of whatever period or school, the elaboration of detail in descriptions has the function (over and above any thematic relevance) of authenticating the text as a whole—of enlisting the reader's confidence in the veracity of the author in large matters as well as in small? It is easy enough to find examples of this kind of motivation in writers who belong to what is loosely

termed the realist tradition. James Gould Cozzens, for instance, in correct-
ing for a second edition the text of his novel about an American air force
base in World War II, *Guard of Honor*, made numerous meticulous revisions
to details about instrumentation and flying technique, all in the service of
achieving greater accuracy. Since few of his readers could have been qualified to notice errors of this type, his conscientiousness may be seen by some
as amounting almost to a pathological obsession; it should perhaps be seen
rather as an extreme case of an author's compulsion to convey to his readers an impression of authenticity, a sense that he can be believed all along
the line because he knows what he is talking about.

Is this "authentication effect" confined to physical details only, though?
In the sphere of characterization, do not storytellers regularly rely on getting right in small matters the feelings and reactions of characters, so that
they may be more readily believed over issues that are more important in
terms of plot or theme? (For that matter, do not writers of thoroughly nonre-
alistic fictions—H. G. Wells in his scientific romances, for instance—often
seek to induce us to believe the impossible by way of convincing notations
about more mundane events?) Nor are examples of such procedures to be
found only in more recent times. Attend, for instance, to Samuel Richardson
justifying to his readers his decision to narrate his novel *Clarissa* in the form
of letters :

> The minute particulars of events, the sentiments and conversations of
> the parties, are, upon this plan, exhibited with all the warmth and spirit that
> the passion supposed to be predominant at the very time could produce, and
> with all the distinguishing characteristics which memory can supply in a his-
> tory of recent transactions.

And in a similar way he defends the great length of the novel.

> To all which we may add, that there was frequently a necessity to be very
> circumstantial and minute, in order to preserve and maintain that air of
> probability, which is necessary to be maintained in a story designed to repre-
> sent real life; and which is rendered extremely busy and active by the plots
> and contrivances formed and carried on by one of the principal characters.[22]

Here, in an author unquestionably devoted to the pursuit not of "realism"
but of the *vraisemblance* associated with "poetic truth," is an overt awareness
of the value of minute particularity, in regard both to external events and to
internal feelings, as a means of creating an air of probability that can persuade the reader to swallow what might otherwise be hard to believe. Although

he did not formulate it explicitly, it seems evident that Crabbe's approach to the use of detail in the depiction of the world around him has similarities with that of Richardson (with whose novels he was unmistakably well-acquainted). In *Tales* (1812) at least (as opposed to some parts of *The Borough* with their occasional tendency to overelaboration), his primary concern was always to select particulars for their thematic relevance; yet the cumulative effect of so much tightly packed and keenly observed detail may be thought to be at the same time highly effectual in insinuating an aura of authenticity that can disarm any inclination toward incredulity. Even so, our final judgment must surely be that, however convincing the illusion it evokes in the reader, the "concrete detail" in the best of Crabbe's poetry is far from being "justified only by its conformity to 'reality'." On the contrary it is, almost invariably, fully integrated into a narrative structure whose thrust is unmistakably directed not towards "realism" in Barthes's sense but toward the more time-honored goal of "poetic truth."

11

Crabbe and Indeterminacy

One of the most influential intellectual movements of the 1970s and 1980s was that generated by Jacques Derrida's claim that any text, when rigorously questioned, inevitably "disseminates" into semantic indeterminacy—a deadlock between incompatible meanings that the reader has no certain grounds for choosing between. Derrida himself is, of course, a philosopher whose subtle and complex argument relates to all human language and not specifically to literature, but his theory has been used by his followers to generate deconstructionist readings of a great many poems, including, as a matter of fact, one of Crabbe's 1812 *Tales*. Since Crabbe is a poet whose determinate meanings have usually been thought to be peculiarly (indeed almost blamably) translucent, it is only right to examine carefully how far, and by what precise means, they can now be dispersed into indeterminacy.

Language, Derrida argues, has no indubitable founding element in a world outside language. Instead it derives both its shape and its meaning from its own internal structures, and these are for him all we can know with certainty. Each unit in the structure takes its signification through its perceived difference from other such units, and this meaning, acquired by virtue of its position in a system of linguistic contrasts, can never have any certainty of reference to the nonlinguistic universe. Hence the often-quoted "axial proposition" around which *Of Grammatology* is constructed: "There is nothing outside of the text [*il n'y a pas de hors-texte;* lit., "there is no outside-text]."[1]

The archetypal model for subsequent deconstructive procedures was provided by Derrida's method of dealing with the text of a previously little-known work by Rousseau, the *Essay on the Origin of Language*. Here for a series of selected passages Derrida presents, first, a reading obtained through "all the instruments of traditional criticism"—instruments that, he acknowledges, serve as an "indispensable guardrail" protecting the text from wild comments by critics who might otherwise think it legitimate "to say almost anything." He next moves on to his second phase, a deeper "critical reading" purporting to uncover an ungovernable "excess" of meaning that repeatedly contradicts what the writer "wishes to say" and that in the end inevitably "disseminates" the intended meaning into semantic indeterminacy, a deadlock between incompatible meanings which the reader has no certain grounds for deciding between. The way he proceeds through this second stage is difficult to describe briefly, and for the present purpose I shall confine myself to mentioning his perversely literal-minded avoidance of the contextual indications that tell us how a metaphor is to be read and his corresponding insistence that every conceivable meaning must be regarded as present on every occasion.[2]

In his impressively opaque prose Derrida details a vast number of examples as a basis for the claim that in the *Essay* as a whole Rousseau "says what he does not wish to say, describes what he does not wish to conclude." Moreover Rousseau is not alone in being caught in this linguistic trap, since according to Derrida "all meaning and therefore all discourse is caught there."[3] Thus it comes about that any text, when rigorously questioned, is bound to leave the deconstructive reader enmeshed in the same blank, mind-boggling contradictions—what Derrida terms *aporia*.

Although in general Derrida's writings have attracted little attention from Anglo-American philosophers, their influence on literary criticism has been far-reaching, and the variegated nature of this influence has been well-captured in a comment by M. H. Abrams:

> What we tend to blanket as deconstructive criticism is in fact highly diverse, ranging from an echoing of distinctive Derridean terms—"presence," "absence," "difference," "effacement," "aporia"—in the process of largely traditional explication, through foregrounding the explicit or implied occurrence in a work of a Derridean theme (especially the theme of writing, or inscription, or decoding), to a radical use of Derridean strategies to explode into dissemination both the integrity and the significance of the literary text that it undertakes to explicate.[4]

Professor Abrams follows this up with a brilliant analysis of J. Hillis Miller's reading of Wordsworth's "A Slumber Did My Spirit Seal," chosen as a characteristic example of the more radical type of deconstructive interpretation. As it happens, Hillis Miller is also responsible for the only extended deconstructive reading that I have tracked down of a poem by Crabbe.

"The Parting Hour" in *Tales* (1812) is a somewhat uncharacteristic story, clearly suggested, as the footnote to the 1834 edition of the poems informs us, by the real-life experiences of the poet's younger brother.

Mr Crabbe's fourth brother, William, taking to a seafaring life, was made prisoner by the Spaniards: he was carried to Mexico where he became a silversmith, married and prospered, until his increasing riches attracted a charge of Protestantism; the consequence of which was much persecution. He at last was obliged to abandon Mexico, his property, and his family; and was discovered, in the year 1803, by an Aldborough sailor, on the coast of Honduras, where again he seems to have found some success in business.

The main events of the tale follow quite closely the vicissitudes that befell Crabbe's brother, except that whereas in actual life William Crabbe never returned to England and the Aldborough sailor's casual interview with him in 1803 was the last his family ever heard of him, the tale is focused above all on its protagonist's return home after forty years of wandering. After a poignant vignette showing the distressful old age they share together when finally reunited, the opening section of the poem describes with gentle tenderness the early history of Allen Booth and Judith Fleming, whose relationship as childhood sweethearts ripens into a love that has little immediate prospect of fulfilment in marriage. The "parting hour" of the title is that in which Allen, impatient to overcome the obstacles in their path, sets sail for "a Western Isle" to join a rich and childless kinsman who needs a helper in his business.

The theme of the poem has been set out in generalized terms in the first fourteen lines, and, uncharacteristically for Crabbe, it is not one that adumbrates a specifically moral issue. The generalization to be illustrated, if we take the words at their face value, is the slowness with which time effects its changes upon a man; they are so slow that if we see him continually we don't notice the change, but if we are separated from him for a lengthy period the difference is strikingly revealed when we see him again. The dominant feeling of the poem is consequently one of pathos—a pathos reinforced by the narrative time sequence that jumps forty years from the vividly realized "parting hour" to the moment when Allen ("A worn-out man, with wither'd limbs and lame") sets foot again upon his native shore. The lost bewilderment that ensues for him is equally vividly realized; and the remainder of the poem is given over to his subsequent chance encounter with Judith, which leads to a revival of their old feeling for each other and is followed by his progressive revelation to her of the complicated vicissitudes that have intervened.

Hillis Miller's deconstructive reading of the poem[5] starts out, however, from a different understanding of the opening generalization, which is therefore quoted here in full :

> Minutely trace man's life; year after year,
> Through all his days let all his deeds appear,
> And then, though some may in that life be strange,
> Yet there appears no vast or sudden change:
> The links that bind those various deeds are seen,
> And no mysterious void is left between.
> But let these binding links be all destroy'd ,
> All that through years he suffer'd or enjoy'd;
> Let that vast gap be made, and then behold —
> This was the youth, and he is thus when old;
> Then we at once the work of Time survey,
> And in an instant see a life's decay;
> Pain mixt with pity in our bosoms rise,
> And sorrow takes new sadness from surprise.

(1–14)

For most readers this will surely evoke the memory of an experience from their own living—the experience of losing sight of some relative, friend or neighbor, and then encountering him or her again after a long interval. Ease of geographical mobility has perhaps made such experiences too widespread nowadays for them to excite much explicit comment; on Crabbe, who spent much of his adult life away from his native Aldborough yet never relinquished his roots there and never ceased returning to it, their impact seems to have struck deep. Not only did he rework the theme in a rather different way in "Procrastination," but he also used it as the basis for a series of sixteen tales with the general title "The Farewell and Return" that were left unfinished at his death. To a deconstructionist, however, predisposed to the conviction that words can never have reference to anything except other words, the message is a different one. J. Hillis Miller finds in these lines a "narrative theory proposed by Crabbe" in which there is "a double claim: the claim that any human life, however strange, hangs together, and the claim that any human life is therefore narratable." This reinterpretation is accomplished by two stratagems. First, he silently substitutes for Crabbe's word "trace" the similar but subtly different word "re-trace," so that the narrative can be represented as a *recapitulation* of Allen's life history in search of the "causal continuity" that will "make sense" of it and give it "a beginning, middle, and end." Secondly, he seeks to reanimate, however implausibly, associations sometimes present in the word "trace"—a word that, as Crabbe actually uses it, would be felt by most readers to be a dying metaphor, if not indeed a wholly dead one. Here, however, is what it suits Miller to find in it:

"Minutely traced": the figure is of one image superimposed on an earlier image and following it over again, like marked tracing paper over a previously made design, tracking it again with the utmost care as one follows the spoor of a beast.

Of the two sets of associations put forward here, that of a hunter following a spoor does at least have a minimal relevance to the context, though the connotation of a determined hunt after an elusive quarry finds no support from elsewhere in the passage. (If the man's life is "followed"—observed, noticed consecutively—without interruption, then, as Crabbe states quite unambiguously, the links binding his actions together will be plain to see.) The second image, however, that of a piece of tracing paper, seems to be a wholly gratuitous irrelevance, introduced solely to insinuate that Crabbe is in some sense not just telling Allen's story but repeating an earlier version of it ("tracking it again," "superimposing" one image on an earlier image) and thereby to induce the kind of mental confusion in which credence might be given to Miller's bizarre contention that the subject of Crabbe's poem is not human life but a narrative theory.

In his discussion of Hillis Miller's deconstruction of "A Slumber Did My Spirit Seal" M. H. Abrams pays incidental tribute to the sensitivity of Miller's "deft and lucid exposition" of his initial determinate or "guardrail" reading of Wordsworth's poem—the reading that precedes and forms a basis for the subsequent deconstructive interpretation. This quality is less conspicuously present in Miller's basal construing of the Crabbe tale, where there are, indeed, some surprising misreadings or misunderstandings. Thus there is remarkably little warrant in the text for his description of "The Parting Hour" as "a poem about [sic] thwarted or inhibited sexual desire," and even less for his assertion that what prevents Allen from marrying the woman he loves is "some vaguely Oedipal taboo opposed by the parents on both sides against their marriage . . . a bar that is, metaphorically at least, that of consanguinity." The fact is that in Crabbe's poem the only hint of parental disapproval occurs when Allen's mother fretfully attributes to Judith a frivolous preoccupation with "dress and amusements," and this accusation the poet explicitly discounts as due to "a mother's jealous love." Apart from this there is no mention at all of opposition to the match from either set of parents, whether vaguely or metaphorically oedipal or otherwise; and the obstacles that face the young couple are the economic and sociocultural ones that were commonly experienced by the young in all unprosperous families of the period. As Crabbe puts it (unmistakably enough, one might think):

The Lovers waited till the time should come,
When they together could possess a home:
In either house were men and maids unwed,
Hopes to be sooth'd, and tempers to be led.

(74–77)

It is fairly well known that in the context of late-eighteenth-century rural life the normal expectation was that young people would not marry until the man had both the competency to support a family and the firm prospect of a separate dwelling to shelter them; custom prescribed also that the limited opportunities should go to siblings in order of seniority (and Allen was, like Crabbe's brother William, a fourth son). A radical failure to appreciate the nature of this social context seems to be implicit in Miller's comments that Allen and Judith "cannot marry until he has a fortune" and that "it was lack of money which drove Allen away from England in the first place." While it is no doubt true that a couple would have been thought imprudent if they married without having some savings set aside, this way of putting it is grossly to exaggerate the importance of purely monetary considerations, whilst ignoring the limitations imposed by a widespread scarcity of cottages to live in.[6]

Some similar inability to enter imaginatively into a historical situation very different from that of the modern American city-dweller seems to lie behind Miller's puzzlement over why Allen Booth "married someone else, abjured his faith, failed to come back sooner." Crabbe does in fact specify circumstances and reasons powerful enough in themselves to rebuff such questioning: there were wars in which Allen became embroiled, he was captured by the Spaniards, carried across the Atlantic Ocean, had to work as a slave in the mines, when freed despaired of ever "escaping the land," later twice tried unsuccessfully to sail to England, was seized by the press gang for service in more wars, lost a limb in bloody fighting in the Indian seas, and so on. What is clearly missing from Miller's interpretation of all this is a feeling for the difficulties and dangers of travel in those days and for the consequent almost unimaginable immensity of distances that we now treat lightly. If we remember the anxiety that Sir Thomas Bertram's family felt (in *Mansfield Park*) over the hazards of his journey to and from the West Indies, we shall not be surprised that a mere Allen Booth found it dauntingly difficult to accomplish his return home from similar parts of the world. Viewed in this light, what Miller terms Allen's "betrayal of his Judith and of his community by marrying a Spanish Catholic maiden" calls for a more tolerant assessment—which is indeed what Crabbe accords to it. But then Crabbe would, without doubt, have found wholly incomprehensible Miller's comment that this marriage "only reaffirms the betrayal which occurred when he [Allen] parted from Judith in the first place." In the tale there is certainly no element of "betrayal" in Allen's departure, jointly agreed upon, in pursuit of the "prospect" that the young couple saw as their sole hope for an early marriage.

The unrelenting moral censoriousness that Miller brings to this poem leads him astray again in his interpretation of the aged man's musings over the "grievous events" that have constituted his "past distress." Whereas Crabbe's tone at this point too is compassionate and nonjudgmental, Miller offers as his summary: "Allen tells his story repeatedly in a hopeless attempt to get it right, to justify himself in his eyes and hers." Then in headlong pursuit of his preoccupation with this tale as an exercise in narrative theory, he continues: "The key term for this narration is the word 'relate'. It is a word for connection, for telling, and for family tie." Here we meet again the deconstructionist's penchant for insisting that *all* the alternative meanings of a word must be counted as present in any single occasion of its use, whatever the context may tell us to the contrary. Undoubtedly the word "relate" *can* be used in its two other senses, but any reader with extended experience of Crabbe's verbal habits will be reasonably certain that here it is used quite simply as a synonym for "tell." Certainly the four instances of "relate" that Miller cites are paralleled within this very passage by three uses of "tell" and one of "describe."

No less far-fetched is Miller's proclaimed detection of a "signal" of "temporal incoherence" in what he describes as "the shift back and forth between the past tense and the historical present" so that Allen's "relation vibrates between the two tenses." In actual fact the two past tenses of "relate" that Miller cites are surrounded in the text by four synonymous past tenses. The sequence of Allen's "relation," then, goes as follows: "First he related" (line 313); "He told" (line 365); "He next related" (line 372); "And then he told" (line 396); "He told" (line 408); "He then described" (line 426). It is only in reporting the start and conclusion of Allen's relation that the historic present appears, so that "vibration" hardly seems the appropriate word to use. These two linguistic features, the lexical and the syntactic, are alleged to reveal a failure in Crabbe's intention to "connect the past to the present by a minute tracing of the intervening events"; but the attempted demonstration of this is too strained and relies too much on distortion to be at all convincing.

More worthy of serious consideration than Miller's assault upon Crabbe's supposed "narrative theory" is his suggestion that "The Parting Hour" deconstructs "almost in spite of itself" that "cherished certainty of humanist literary study . . . the continuity of the self." For although Miller is demonstrably off-center in his belief that Crabbe's central theme in this poem is "the claim that any human life, however strange, hangs together," it can hardly be doubted that some such view of human affairs would have been found acceptable by Crabbe and perhaps even regarded by him as axiomatic. And Miller certainly succeeds in bringing into the foreground of attention various gaps or discontinuities in the life of Allen Booth that are implied by Crabbe's narrative but not openly confronted in it; their significance remains, however, matter for a more cautious debate than he is himself inclined toward.

Miller's principal contention is that "far from doing what he promises at the beginning, showing the continuity of a life, all Crabbe's storyteller's efforts only make the 'mysterious void[s] . . .between' more evident. His narration presents discontinuous vignettes rather than a continuous chain of events." In making this charge Miller relies on imputing to Crabbe an intention and point of view that he summarizes as follows:

> Though a given life may in one way or another be odd, if it is narrated with an *absolute* fidelity to detail it will hang together like the unbroken links of a chain. . . . On the other hand, if there is *any* failure *at all* in this tracing, the life will appear not strange but *utterly* mysterious, unfathomable. It will be broken by the *abyss* of a blank. (My italics)

The melodramatic language of this does not sound much like Crabbe's customary measured tones, and in fact Miller's stark alternatives are the complete obverse of Crabbe's carefully presented moderation, according to which the instantaneous vision of "a life's decay" appears *only* if the "binding links" (between the youth and the aged man) are *all* destroyed ("The Parting Hour," lines 7–12, quoted above). But the contrast between these two views of the human situation puts into better perspective the polarities regularly proclaimed by the deconstructionists—those ungovernable opposites said to lead so inescapably to the mind-boggling self-contradictions that constitute *aporia*. In this case the all-or-nothing opposites are continuity versus discontinuity in the self; but of course in Crabbe's poem (as in the reality of ordinary living as human beings experience it) continuity of selfhood is not an absolute. For Allen Booth in old age there is present and operative within him *both* the memory of his anxious yet still-hopeful "parting hour" with Judith *and* that of his "best days" with his Spanish wife and children. The irony of the fact that the dream from which he wakens relates to his lost Spanish family and is known by Judith to do so is not some "narrative failure," which if critically examined will disseminate into undecidability. On the contrary, it represents a deliberate intention on the poet's

part to encapsulate in a concluding episode the complexity of human existence disclosed by the tale as a whole—an intention very much in line with
that of so many of the other tales in the 1812 volume, though here perhaps
less securely grounded in what has gone before than in the very best of
them.

It must seem doubtful, however, whether irony, with its invaluable capacity for holding together disparate aspects of experience, is something
that most deconstructionists, locked in their principle of single-mindedness,
are either capable or desirous of engaging with. It may be noteworthy that
deconstructive literary criticism has tended to concentrate particularly on
Romantic or post-Romantic poets in whose work irony seldom plays a very
important role.[7] From this point of view we should perhaps be grateful to
Hillis Miller for bringing out the extent to which the *un*characteristic qualities in this particular tale are ones that it shares with the poetry of Crabbe's
Romantic or pre-Romantic contemporaries—and that open it up in part to
deconstructive analysis. But in relation to the qualities most typical of
Crabbe's verse-tales—those where the determinate meaning is unusually
translucent and the associations called up are defined and controlled with a
precision more usually found in good prose than in major poetry—it has
still to be shown that deconstructive procedures can convincingly "explode
into dissemination both the integrity and the significance" of these poems.

12

Crabbe and Ideology

In a fairly recent book by Roger Sales[1] offering a politically radical account of the English Romantic period, the pages on Crabbe pillory him as "an overseer of the country poor" and consequently the self-constituted spokesman for "officialdom." Admittedly, the author does not claim that Crabbe was ever *actually* a parish overseer; the chapter is merely engaged in exploiting an overextended metaphor borrowed from Hazlitt's slightly shabby rhetoric about Crabbe in his *Lectures on the English Poets*. Nevertheless, Sales's argument can without unfairness serve as a pertinent example of a certain trend in Marxist literary theory—namely, the assumption that a poet's vision of life can invariably be shown to be a direct expression of his class position in the social hierarchy of his time. To see this as an oversimplification is not, of course, to question that a writer's perception of the world around him is inevitably shaped by his experience as a member of a particular human grouping with its own historic relationship to socioeconomic realities. The view taken by Engels, however, was that only *ultimately*, in the "mutual interaction of all the elements [in history]," is "the superstructure" determined by "the economic base"—and this can perhaps serve as a suitable starting point for a consideration of that slippery term "ideology" and its role in literature.

An ideology has sometimes been defined as a systematic matrix of ideas and attitudes, held in common by many if not all of the members of a particular limited social group or class, and making its appeal to them because it sees both society and the world at large in terms that correspond to their own interests. This touches only glancingly on the questionable validity of ideological beliefs, but it does suggest why it is commonly assumed that ideas that are held ideologically are in some sense inadequate, partial, or distorted—why Engels, for instance, in an often-quoted phrase, described ideology as "false consciousness." For Marx himself, however, the inadequacy of an ideology is caused not by gullibility or by a failure of observation; it is due rather to failure to penetrate below the deceptive surface of perceived forms to the underlying social relations concealed by them. Thus a viable Marxist definition should perhaps include the claim that an ideology is necessarily limited because it is content to accept a surface view of reality— a position that is, after all, in accord with the widely accepted sense in which the term "ideological" invariably involves some limiting connotation.[2]

The question here is how much Crabbe's portrayal of the life around him was influenced (and perhaps either cramped or distorted) by ideological factors—that is to say, by his own social experience as a country clergyman who had risen from poverty to comparative affluence, in part through his own industry, in part through the benevolence of an aristocratic patron. It will be recalled that the decades from 1790 to 1810, during which his mature style was formed, are usually represented as a period of political turmoil and widespread social unrest. Certainly in the 1790s the initially sympathetic response to the French Revolution was followed, after the events of 1793, by some years of near-hysterical right-wing reaction and even repression; and the years around and after the turn of the century were marked in some areas by movements of protest at the rural poverty that either resulted from, or was made more acute by, the economic effects of the wars against France. Yet there is singularly little trace of these events in Crabbe's poetry. Indeed, virtually the only overt reference to contemporary political disputes occurs in "The Dumb Orators" (tale 1 in *Tales* [1812]), a neat and witty satire at the expense of public speakers who delight in the sound of their own voice. This tale, as we have seen, holds the balance impressively level between the apoplectically reactionary Tory squire, Justice Bolt, and the fanatical Deist and Radical, Hammond. Crabbe's son tells us (we should not otherwise have known) that his father had "hailed the beginning of the French Revolution" (a circumstance that led to a mistaken rumor traveling from Suffolk to his parish in Leicestershire that he was a Jacobin) but later "execrated its close," and that he came to be a convinced supporter of the war against Napoleon even though he had disapproved of its origin when it was directed against the young French Republic. The *Life*, in fact, presents Crabbe, plausibly enough, as a man of moderate views whose passions "were never violently enlisted in any political cause whatever"; and it certainly does seem to be the case that he was never easily stirred to written expression by sociopolitical topics.

Crabbe's inveterate commitment to the principle of moderation is perhaps an instance of individual temperament (confirmed by individual experience) coalescing with the dictates of an insistent group ideology. The virtues of hard work, thrift, prudence, and the cautious avoidance of extremes were certainly highly esteemed not by this poet alone but also by large sections of that middle class (tradesmen, shopkeepers, merchants, professional people) which formed both an increasingly large proportion of the rapidly growing population and a majority of the enlarged reading public. Crabbe's commendation of the middle way is seen at it most attractive in his portrayal, in *The Parish Register*, book 1, of the small-holder Robert and his wife Susan, whose sedate happiness (formed of "health, quiet, comfort") is sandwiched on the page between Lucy the Miller's daughter's "stolen moments of disturb'd delight" and the improvident fecklessness of the village harlot. The combination of self-reliant industriousness and "guiding nice frugality" that enables this "decent couple" to be "each pay-day, ready with their rent" is conveyed with a convincing concreteness. A similar emphasis on the way "toil, care and patience bless th'abstemious few" is apparent, in the introduction to the poem, in the more extended description of "the Cot . . . where thrives th'industrious Swain," though here the effect is marred a little by the poet's slightly condescending attitude to the "careful peasant," particularly in the references to his amusements and his taste in wall decorations or books.

It is when Crabbe turns from "dwellings simply neat" to his contrasted depiction of the "infected Row" inhabited by the "thoughtless herd" whose moral shortcomings lead them to be pursued by "fear, shame and want" that we sense the possible presence of ideological distortion or exaggeration. It is not merely that the concentration of so *much* "Vice" and "Misery" in so small a compass seems a little overdone; we find ourselves questioning also the justice of Crabbe's confident diagnosis of the underlying causes :

> Whence all these woes?—From want of virtuous will,
> Of honest shame, of time-improving skill;
> From want of care t'employ the vacant hour,
> And want of every kind but want of power.
> (*The Parish Register*, 1.226–29)

It would be naïve to deny that the failings that Crabbe enumerates with telling detail can and often do lead to a condition of sordid misery; but there is surely something suspiciously simplistic here about the inevitability with which vice and virtue are said to reap their just rewards. One is reminded of the self-complacent moral preaching addressed to the poor by certain middle-class writers of the period, one characteristic (though surprisingly readable) example of which, Elizabeth Hamilton's 1808 novel *The Cottagers of Glenburnie*, the poet had on the shelves of his library at Trowbridge. As a general rule Crabbe's moral universe is not quite so starkly black and white as this; although it is true that there are indications of a rather similar censoriousness in the parallel description (in letter 18 of *The Borough*) of the "long-boarded building" indiscriminately let out to an assorted collection of "the Poor" by an eccentric and ill-humored theorist or "system-builder."

> In this vast Room, each Place by habit fix'd,
> Are Sexes, Families, and Ages mixt, —
> To Union forc'd by Crime, by Fear, by Need,
> And all in Morals and in Modes agreed; —
> Some ruin'd Men, who from Mankind remove;
> Some ruin'd Females, who yet talk of Love;
> And some grown old in Idleness—the prey
> To vicious Spleen, still railing through the Day;
> And Need, and Misery, Vice and Danger bind
> In sad alliance each degraded Mind.
>
> (344–45)

It may be noted, however, that "Need" is allowed here to share with "Vice" and "Crime" (not to mention "Spleen") some of the responsibility for the degradation of these inmates. The animus is less insistent, but the tone still suggests the pursed lips of disapproving middle-class morality.

In general, class-based prejudices are not strongly in evidence in Crabbe's portrayal of society's treatment of the poor and needy, one of the social issues to which he reverts quite frequently. The spirit is some way removed from that of the penny-pinching and hard-hearted overseer anxious above all to keep down the parish poor-rate. It may be thought unsurprising that he should pay particular attention to the problem of poor relief, since it is now generally agreed that the framework of laws and policies developed over some two hundred years had proved crucially unable to cope with the unemployment and hardship caused by the agricultural crisis of the 1790s. Remarkably enough, however, the able-bodied of working age figure hardly at all as recipients of relief in Crabbe's account of it.[3] The only notable exception to this generalization is one that has been used to mount a damaging attack upon the objectivity of the poet's social observation. The lines in question occur near the end of the opening section of *The Parish Register*, after Crabbe has delineated, on the one hand, the dwellings of the frugal and industrious poor and, on the other, those of the idle and improvident:

> Such are our Peasants, those to whom we yield
> Praise with relief, the Fathers of the Field;
> And these who take from our reluctant hands
> What *Burn* advises or the Bench commands.
>
> (*The Parish Register*, 1.269–72)

It seems likely that there is a reference here to what is usually known as the Speenhamland system of poor relief, whereby the wages of farmworkers were supplemented by allowances paid out of the parish poor-rate to compensate for the abnormally high price of bread. The probability of such an allusion is increased by the evidence unearthed by W. K. Thomas that in the late 1790s this system was in operation in a number of Suffolk parishes adjacent to Aldeburgh, including Great Glemham where Crabbe himself was resident curate from 1796 to 1801.[4] Thus in 1799–1800 in Great Glemham thirteen able-bodied laborers appear to have received parish aid at the rate of two guineas a year for each child to enable them to keep their families from falling below subsistence level—a practice that no doubt was much applauded by the well-off farmers who would have dominated the vestry and valued the encouragement thereby given to keep down the wages of their employees. The point of Crabbe's lines is, then, to maintain a distinction between the industrious and able-bodied who were lucky enough to have employment (those deserving "Fathers of the Field" who were gladly granted supplementary aid to help feed their children) and the more doubtfully worthy recipients (the malingerers? the work-shy?) to whom the vestry doled out only the minimum prescribed by the magistrates or recommended in Richard Burn's authoritative volume *The Justice of the Peace*. But it seems clear that in thus presenting with implicit approval a system that has attracted much condemnation from social historians, Crabbe was ignoring the feelings of those laborers who were reduced by it to dependent pauperdom and was in effect aligning himself with the viewpoint of the farmer-employers. (This alignment may have come the more naturally to him in that his own prosperity was in large part dependent on his status as a tithe-owner.) He was, in fact, allowing an ideological predisposition to distort his version of social reality.

Why should a humane and devout cleric, such as Crabbe undoubtedly was, have been in this instance so blind to the indignity forced on the poor by the Speenhamland system? There is no doubt something to be said for W. K. Thomas's contention that what influenced the poet here was his attachment to the concept of charity as an imperative duty enjoined on every good Christian so that charity was thought of as a natural action to be accepted as such both by the donor and by the recipient. (This attitude, still widespread around the turn of the century, found notoriously crude expression in Wordsworth's poem "The Old Cumberland Beggar." In the historical context one could not of course expect Crabbe to be readily open to the searing truth contained in Blake's lines:

> Pity would be no more
> If we did not make somebody poor

But it might have been hoped that he would have been sympathetic at least to the comment of his own admired patron Charles James Fox that "it was not fitting in a free country that the great body of the people should depend on the charity of the rich.")

Something should perhaps be attributed also to Crabbe's deep if slightly old-fashioned sense of the village as a community bound together by ties of human relationship and not by the values of monetary exchange (or the "cash nexus"). We may speculate that from this point of view the vestry's granting of supplementary aid was seen as meeting an obligation imposed on the community as a whole—and seen as such to an extent that excluded from notice the employer's equally obligatory Christian duty to pay his workers a living wage. It is probable moreover that, initially at least, the precipitating circumstances were seen (and not by Crabbe alone) as a temporary emergency caused by factors outside anyone's control. These considerations cannot, however, excuse the obtrusion on this occasion of a certain moral obtuseness that tends to weaken our confidence in the poet as an impartial observer of the social scene.

Apart from this instance, the parish poor with whom Crabbe concerns himself consist mainly of those too old to work, orphans, widows, deserted wives, unwed mothers, and those crippled by illness or mental defect. For all such unfortunates Crabbe is, on humane grounds, a strong advocate of outdoor relief wherever this is possible—a "weekly Dole" that enables them to continue to live in their own homes, follow their own chosen way of life, however idiosyncratic, and maintain contact with the relatives and neighbors they are used to and attached to.[5] For those who cannot be provided for in this way, he recommends, in *The Borough*, that they be looked after in a parish poorhouse in their own locality:

> Others together dwell,—but when they come
> To the low Roof, they see a kind of Home,
> A social People whom they've ever known,
> With their own Thoughts and Manners like their own.
>
> (letter 18, 7–10)

It is to be hoped that the building supporting this "low Roof" was more substantial and well-maintained than the dilapidated one whose walls of mud Crabbe had inveighed against twenty-seven years earlier in *The Village;* but in part his changed attitude to the parish poorhouse is due to his detestation of the large union poorhouses that were set up by groups of parishes in the wake of Gilbert's Act of 1782. Crabbe does not dispute that in the "Pauper-Palace" with its "Giant-Building" the poor are well-provided for in physical terms, with "airy Rooms and decent Beds," or that its administration is in the hands of well-meaning guardians who differ from the typical "lordly" parish overseer by being ready to listen sympathetically to complaints. He does, however, contend that so large an institution cannot but have a prisonlike atmosphere, being necessarily governed by inflexible "general Rules," and that, worst of all, through its topographical remoteness it cuts the inmates off permanently from relatives and friends and from all their familiar roots in their own small society.

> Here the good Pauper, losing all the Praise
> By worthy Deeds acquir'd in better days,
> Breathes a few Months, then to his Chamber led,
> Expires, while Strangers prattle round his Bed.
>
> (211–14)

Unless this is to be read as an oblique reference to it, Crabbe does not anywhere mention that an important motive for thus centralizing poor relief was to reduce the cost to the parish rates.

Crabbe concludes his section on the poorhouse with a contrast between the compassionate care given by the hunter to his broken-down old horse and the failure of the community to do the same for the no less deserving human laborer in his old age. This surely provides the clue to the intensity of his feeling about the ingratitude he detects in the poor law's treatment of the aged and infirm. In Crabbe's usage the term "peasant" invariably connotes not a countryman who cultivates his own patch of soil but a wage-laborer who works on another man's farm. In the earlier decades of the eighteenth century both farms and village communities had been small so that the human relations involved in care for the unfortunate were intimate and personal; the parish and its overseers in dispensing relief were felt to be (and indeed were) disbursing on behalf of employers upon whom the aged laborer had a recognized and rightful claim. As both population and the size of farms increased in the latter half of the century, relationships became more impersonal and often also (the evidence suggests) more harsh and unfeeling—so that "churl" or "tyrant of the parish" have become for Crabbe almost ritual synonyms for "parish overseer."[6] Clearly Crabbe feels nostalgia for the lost warmth of communal responsibilities; and the resulting complex of attitudes can be interestingly studied in the entry on the "Noble Peasant," Isaac Ashford, in part 3 of *The Parish Register*.

We may put the entry in context by referring to the note by Crabbe's son in the 1834 edition of the poems, which tells us that Ashford's prototype was "honest John Jasper, the parish-clerk at Glemham" from whom the poet took not only Ashford's "manly independence of mind and integrity of conduct" but also the significant detail that his "only complaint was a dread of a workhouse when his ability to labour should be over." It seems possible that Crabbe has also taken something from *Cheap Repository Tract No. 19*, "The Shepherd of Salisbury Plain," first published in 1795, in which Hannah More presents an aged and virtuously religious shepherd whose merits are delineated with a somewhat nauseating profusion of circumstantiality. Those traits that bear some relation to Isaac Ashford are his propensity to be pleased with whatever God thinks fit for him and his insistence on always comparing his lot with those worse off than himself. On the death of the parish clerk the shepherd is installed as his successor—a detail paralleled in Crabbe by his Clerk's expressed view that in the event of his death "Ashford might succeed." Another point of interest is that in the tract the shepherd alarms his interlocutor by accusing himself of pride, though it turns out that it is his wife's virtues he takes pride in and not his own. One is forced to wonder whether it can be wholly coincidental that Crabbe devoted fifteen lines to defining rather carefully the precise nature of the wholly justified pride that Ashford admits to ("In fact, a noble virtue, misnamed pride"). It is true that the tone of Crabbe's character sketch is some way removed from the sickly moralizing of Hannah More; but one could almost suspect that the poet, consciously or not, has here set out to "do over again according to Nature" the standardized character of the "noble Peasant." If so, it must be admitted that while he has got rid of the sentimentality, he has not entirely avoided an element of idealization, of stereotyping, and of excessively overt didacticism. Indeed the sole feature that breathes life into this portrait is the one taken directly from life—Ashford's dread of the workhouse, developed by Crabbe into a cogently expressed social protest at a system that contracts out the upkeep of the parish's paupers to a heartless profiteer.

> 'Twas then a Spark of—say not Discontent—
> Struck on his Mind and thus he gave it vent: —
>   "Kind are your Laws, ('tis not to be denied,)
> That in yon House, for ruin'd Age, provide,
> And they are just;—when young, we give you all,
> And for Assistance in our Weakness call. —
> Why then this proud Reluctance to be fed,
> To join your Poor and eat the Parish-Bread?
> But yet I linger, loath with him to feed,
> Who gains his Plenty by the Sons of Need;
> He who, by Contract, all your Paupers took,
> And gauges Stomachs with an anxious Look:

On some old Master I could well depend;
See him with joy and thank him as a Friend;
But ill on him, who doles the Day's supply,
And counts our Chances, who at Night may die:
Yet help me Heav'n! and let me not complain
Of what befalls me, but the fate sustain."

(*The Parish Register*, II, 469–86)

Ironically, Ashford cheats this fate at the last moment by having the good fortune to drop dead at his own cottage gate. There is surely evident, however, in this entry as a whole a certain degree of conflict between Crabbe's impulse towards radical social criticism and the image (insistent throughout but enshrined above all in the entry's concluding line) of the grateful peasant as a "wise good Man contented to be poor." This image is surely highly suspect as a "reflection" of social reality, because it is so exactly the one that conventional middle-class ideology would hope to find in the lower orders.

Crabbe was certainly acquainted with other publications by Hannah More; there was a copy of *Coelebs in Search of a Wife* in his library at Trowbridge. We have no firm evidence that he had read the *Cheap Repository Tracts*, but he could hardly fail to have done so in view of their extremely wide circulation. (Hannah More's own claim was that they "were bought by the gentry and middling classes full as much as by the common people"). These "antidotes to Tom Paine" (Mrs. Piozzi's phrase) had been explicitly designed as "strong counteraction" to the way in which, in the 1790s, "speculative infidelity" had been brought down, in penny-book form, to "the pockets and capacities of the poor." They conscientiously copied in their format, in their illustrations and in their simple language the hawker's popular stories and ballads, and were sold at a halfpenny, a penny, and one-and-a-half pence apiece. Their content, however, is unrelentingly moralistic and didactic, with a special emphasis on those Christian virtues (meekness, humility, obedience, resignation) that could be expected to keep "the common people" in their proper place, dutiful and uncomplaining.

There are two other entries in *The Parish Register* that have a recognizable counterpart in a *Cheap Repository Tract*. The first is that of Gerard Ablett (part 1, lines 469–509), who after being blessed with six births (the last one twins) in six years of marriage is finding that the "playful branches" looked forward to with enthusiasm at the wedding ceremony are now so numerous as to "disturb his peace," strain his abilities as provider of bread, and generally "keep the sunshine of good-humour out." The poet's response to this is to point out that Ablett's economic worries will soon evaporate as his daughters get married "unportioned" and his sons leave home to become laborers and each lord of his own cot. By contrast, his master, at present a prosperous farmer, will face increasing financial demands from his sons and daughters as they grow up and require dowries or farm establishments of their own. His wife will urgently demand a chaise, and

> The smart young Cornet who, with so much grace,
> Rode in the ranks and betted at the race,
> While the vext parent rails at deeds so rash,
> Shall d—n his luck, and stretch his hand for cash.

(502–5)

The conclusion is:

> Sad troubles, Gerard! now pertain to thee,
> When thy rich master seems from trouble free;
> But 'tis one fate at different times assign'd,
> And thou shalt lose the care that he must find.

(506–9)

In theme this is certainly reminiscent of *Cheap Repository Tract No. 45*, "Sorrowful Sam; or, The Two Blacksmiths," first published in 1795, the burden of which, presented with characteristically canting and insensitive crudity, is that the rich man has as much to endure as the poor and is no happier. An attentive reading suggests that Crabbe has here taken a current commonplace moralizing theme and made of it something gently ironic and slyly original. Ablett's current hardships are real and inescapable, but his "rich master's" future cares will be in part a retribution merited by his unseemly social pretensions; with his fine steed and high living he is "a farmer proud beyond a farmer's pride."

The third character sketch with a counterpart in *Cheap Repository Tracts* is that of the unnamed "rustic Infidel" at the end of part 1 (lines 787–823). Here the obvious parallel is with "Black Giles the Poacher," also published in 1796. In this very crudely characterized tale the stress falls upon the varied villainies of Giles, his wife Tawny Rachel, and their thieving children (these make a practice of stealing apples). Giles is opposed to the church and the parson, but on quite general antisocial grounds rather than upon principled ones claiming authority from Tom Paine. He breaks his thigh in falling from a rotten high brick wall that he had climbed in order to steal a fruit-net, and dies a few days later in agony, unable to repent, yet thinking "there must be some truth in religion." By contrast Crabbe's firsthand acquaintance with the "blacksmith in Leiston" on which we know him to have drawn enabled him to bring to his portrayal touches of both realism and wit that are notably absent from Hannah More's lampoon. In part, of course, the difference between the two pieces is one of audience. Hannah More was preaching (as she believed) to the uneducated and potentially disaffected poor who needed to have the truths of religion bludgeoned into them. Crabbe, by contrast, assumes readers who are unquestionably at one with him in their civilized assumption of revealed religion, of the rights of property, and of the unassailable rightness of the established order. He is, of course, no friend to deistic doctrines, nor for that matter to radical ones, but the tone tends on the whole towards one of good-humored contempt, bespeaking a confidence in his own outlook and assured beliefs that is impressively untroubled by the upheavals of the American and French Revolutions.

> Each Village Inn has heard the ruffian boast,
> That he believ'd "in neither God nor Ghost;
> That when the sod upon the Sinner press'd,
> He, like the Saint, had everlasting rest;
> That never Priest believ'd his Doctrines true,
> But would, for profit, own himself a Jew,
> Or worship Wood and Stone, as honest Heathen do;
> That fools alone on future Worlds rely,
> And all who die for Faith, deserve to die."
>   These Maxims,—part th'Attorney's Clerk profess'd,
> His own transcendent genius found the rest.
>
> (793–803)

So relaxed, indeed, does he feel that he can even afford a sly joke at the expense of the pious matrons who half expect "this bad man" to betray his devilish nature by the overt signs of horns or a cloven hoof. It may be noted that the boldness and even the courage of the "ruffian" pass unquestioned, that the infidel has been allowed to speak for himself in an authentic-sounding idiom, and that even the jeer, later in the passage, at Tom Paine[7] (unfair though it may be) is endued with an engaging wit by its telling formalism. Indeed, the neatness with which, in this entry as a whole, the somewhat un-Augustan content is fitted without any sense of strain into the confines of the heroic couplet contributes greatly to our sense of a temperate urbanity and moderation, a striking contrast to the rancorous spleen of Hannah More and her anti-Jacobin stable companions.

Good temper and moderation are not, however, qualities that Crabbe always finds it possible to maintain in face of atheistic or deistic views. This can be seen at its most obvious in "The Learned Boy," tale 21 in *Tales* (1812). This starts out with a character sketch of Farmer Jones, recently widowed and left with three daughters and a son to bring up. We are clearly intended to see him as an estimable character ("an honest man. . . and true"); and his credentials are established even more unmistakably by the firmness and adroitness with which he fends off the various spinsters and widows who aspire to fill his late wife's place, and by his success in bringing up his daughters capably and marrying them off satisfactorily. However, he makes the mistake of allowing the boy to be petted and spoiled by his grand-mother. She guides the boy into sharing her own "pious folly"—evidently a superstitious and unreasoning form of religion, possibly of a slightly Methodistical bent. Stephen himself is a "feeble boy," timid and brainless; but when sent to the village school he does show application:

> He thought not much indeed—but what depends
> On pains and care was at his fingers' ends.
>
> (152–53)

Recognizing that his son will never make a farmer, Jones decides that he might be turned into a clerk, and therefore sends him off to a London cousin who is able to find a place for him, "easy but humble." After a time Stephen is taken in hand by one of the older clerks in the office who, though despising the lad as a "booby," nevertheless undertakes to educate him, advising him on his choice of clothes, initiating him into theatergoing and other dubious entertainments, and choosing his books for him. His new mentor explains his plan as follows:

> we will now select
> Some works to please you, others to direct:
> Tales and Romances shall your fancy feed,
> And reasoners form your morals and your creed.
>
> (299–302)

Though nervous at first, Stephen soon shows himself an apt pupil and learns his new lessons all too thoroughly. In due course the kinsman, having sur-reptitiously sampled Stephen's library and been shocked by its contents, writes to the father to report that, "though steady at his desk," the lad has become "a rake and coxcomb" in his leisure hours. Farmer Jones peremp-torily summons home the reluctant Stephen, who cautiously remains mute with his father but reveals his new way of thinking more freely to his dismayed grandmother. Meantime the father has examined his son's "choice volumes" (and made a bonfire of them) and secretly hidden himself where he can overhear the conversation between Stephen and the grandam. When the point is reached where the boy rudely expresses to her his defiance of his father, Farmer Jones emerges from his hiding place and savagely whips his son. The tale ends with a protracted defense and indeed glorification of this "cure."

The literary source for this culminating incident was detected with remarkable promptitude, since the *Monthly Review* (no. 69, December 1812) in its review of *Tales* commented, quite justly, that this tale was "borrowed from the 108th number of the *Tatler*.[8] There is an unattractive smugness of tone about the *Tatler* anecdote; but in the form in which Crabbe has adapted it, the incident has lost all trace of such urbanity as Addison contrived to clothe it with. There is indeed a note of sadistic relish in the lines describing the beating itself:

> In vain; stroke after stroke,
> On side and shoulder, quick as mill-wheels broke;
> Quick as the patient's pulse, who trembling cried,
> And still the Parent with a stroke replied;
> Till all the medicine he prepar'd was dealt,
> And every bone the precious influence felt;
> Till all the panting flesh was red and raw,
> And every thought was turn'd to fear and awe;
>
> (509–16)

Distasteful too is the way in which throughout the poem there is a heartless, narking, jeering at the feeblemindedness of Stephen, as though this could serve as a justification for his brutal chastisement. The jarring note is compounded by the way the father hides in order to spy upon his son, and then (though already described as "with power and vengeance fraught") is finally provoked to violence by the personal indignity of Stephen's disrespectful reference to him.

In allowing himself to indulge in this unwonted coarseness of feeling, Crabbe must have been influenced in part by Addison's precedent, but at the same time there can be no doubt about the strength of the venomous feelings he harbors towards godless "reasoners." A similar animus is in evidence, but in a more controlled way, in another of the 1812 tales, "Edward Shore" (tale 20), where the protagonist is a young man who falls into moral danger not because he is dim-witted but because he sees himself as a genius and therefore above any need for the "tried faith" that keeps ordinary folk virtuous. In his case the ultimate fate is madness brought on by the "remorse, confusion, dread" that follows his yielding to sexual temptation in company with the young wife of an elderly friend whose advocacy of "reasoning" has laid the foundation for his downfall. There can be no question as to the author's abhorrence of the views advanced by this skeptic ("Deist and Atheist call'd, for few agreed / What were his notions, principles, or creed"); yet he is dealt with very fairly in his role as trusting husband— almost too fairly for the tale's main poetic purpose, since although, like Shore, he has no Christian faith to sustain him, he nevertheless remains strong-minded, benevolent, and even magnanimous in face of adversity. (Ironically, what finally upsets the precarious balance of Shore's mind is his discovery that the anonymous benefactor who has rescued him from a debtors' prison was in reality the friend he had wronged.) In general Crabbe regularly insists upon the complementary functions of faith and works, so that in recording here a sharp divergence between beliefs and conduct he may seem to be abandoning (temporarily at least) his more customary doctrinal position. However, the fair-minded readiness to recognize and record the existence of contrary instances is better seen as an outcome of the essential moderation of his own Christian religion—a moderation that was certainly deeply rooted in his personal temperament but that seems also to have been characteristic of the dominant ideology of his social group.

The intimate relationship between Crabbe's religious and social preoccupations comes to the fore when we consider one of the most powerful of the tales from *The Borough*, the one entitled "Ellen Orford" (letter 20). In declared contrast to the highly colored agonies and afflictions portrayed in the novels of the period (those "flow'ry Pages of sublime Distress"), Crabbe presents Ellen's narrative as an account of "how we truly live," her sorrows being ones that are "Too often seen" in real human experience but "seldom in a Book." As she looks back, an aged blind pauper, over a long life crowded with event, the story she tells is, in fact, almost unremittingly bleak —a bleakness thrown into even greater relief by her initial meek acceptance that "we should humbly take what Heav'n bestows" and by her concluding assertion of cheerful Christian faith in God's benevolence. After her long succession of misfortunes it may seem to a modern reader extraordinary, indeed almost passing comprehension, that her closing words should be:

> And as my Mind looks cheerful to my End,
> I love Mankind and call my God my Friend.

(336–37)

Yet Crabbe gets surprisingly near to compelling our belief even in this. How is this achieved?

Among Ellen's many vicissitudes there are included some in regard to which it would have been highly unreasonable for her to take any blame to herself. This clearly applies to those early years of "Sorrow much and little Cheer" that she herself describes as "a common case"—her own father having died and her mother having made an unhappy second marriage, she had been fully engaged up to her twentieth year in exacting "domestic Care" looking after her numerous siblings. Yet these are woes that she views retrospectively as a visitation designed for the good of her soul ("Thus for my Age's good, my Youth was tried")—a rather extreme religious self-abasement that does indeed strain credulity. In the next phase of her hard life, when she allows herself to be deceived and seduced by a wealthy young man who gets her with child and then abandons her, she is guilty of serious moral transgression, as she fully recognizes:

> still the Sorrow grew
> Because I felt that I deserv'd it too,
> And begg'd my infant Stranger to forgive
> The Mother's Shame, which in herself must live.
>
> (177–80)

It is easy to see how this sense of guilt might be intensified when the illegitimate daughter turns out to be an "Idiot-Maid," so that on this occasion Ellen's unquestioning submission to the fresh "Wound" seems perfectly credible. (The only protest she ever makes relates to the dual standard whereby society is so indulgent to the seducer—he marries a "blooming bride" of his own class—and so severe on his victim, who is expelled from her family and has to live in a hovel in poverty and disgrace.) A few years later, prompted by "reason" though not by her "heart," she accepts an offer of marriage from "the sober master of a decent trade" who is prepared to overlook her "errors"; they have five sons, but the marriage turns out badly, partly through poverty, but even more because the husband turns deludedly to Calvinist preachers "of things foredoomed and of Election-grace" and finds that the all-important "mysterious Call" they speak of never comes to him. In the end he hangs himself out of despair, and the family is split up; the healthy boys are put out as pauper apprentices, while Ellen, her "Idiot-Maid," and one ailing son subsist on parish relief. Throughout all this her sense of guilt and unworthiness is seen to persist. Her husband's despair is explicitly related back, in part, to her own earlier disgrace:

> he now revil'd
> My former Conduct, — he reproach'd my Child:
> He talk'd of Bastard Slips, and curs'd his Bed. . .
>
> (245–47)

And in the subsequent fate of her children (one of the sons is hanged for an unspecified crime) there is a certain suggestion, never quite formulated, of a link with her former "errors," both in allowing herself to be seduced and in forming a loveless marriage. But her unquestioning "Reliance" upon the "Heavenly Parent" is to be tested even more severely :

> My Idiot-Girl, so simply gay before,
> Now wept in pain; some Wretch had found a time,
> Deprav'd and wicked, for that Coward-crime;
> I had indeed my doubt, but I supprest
> The thought that day and night disturb'd my rest;
> She and that sick-pale Brother — but why strive
> To keep the Terrors of that time alive?
>
> "The Hour arriv'd, the new, th'undreaded Pain
> That came with violence and yet came in vain.
> I saw her die: her Brother too is dead;
> Nor own'd such Crime — what is it that I dread?
>
> (309–19)

The vague and ill-defined moral unease still felt after a long lapse of time ("what is it that I dread?") suggests on Ellen's part a self-questioning not merely about the facts of the case but also about the nature and degree of her own responsibility for them. It may suggest also, on the part of the author, a creative insight into the psychological relationships implicit in his narrative that is more acute and penetrating than anything that has surfaced overtly. Noticeable here also is the unflinching readiness to deal frankly with even the most sordid aspects of human behavior. In the tale as a whole this combines with the quiet, factual, uncomplaining tone of the first-person narrative to draw the reader into complicity with an attitude towards divine providence that our twentieth-century consciousness would normally find distinctly alien. Left on her own, Ellen finds "a blest Subsistence" in keeping a school where she teaches her charges to "bless the Power who gave / Pains to correct us, and Remorse to save." The final visitation of blindness that prevents her from continuing to earn her own living will seem to most modern readers a gratuitous unkindness of fate; but, as throughout the long previous sequence of calamities, Ellen retains all the dutiful resignation expected of a good Christian, determinedly counting her blessings:

> Those Eyes which long the Light of Heaven enjoy'd,
> Were not by Pain, by Agony destroy'd:
> My Senses fail not all; I speak, I pray,
> By Night my Rest, my Food I take by Day. . . .

(332–35)

Perhaps it is not surprising that a modern critic such as Jerome J. McGann should find this tale "peculiarly shocking," particularly when he takes Ellen's phrase "a common case" to apply not to her early years only but to her life's events as a whole, and consequently to show that her "terrible story" is "typical of people who live in certain social and economic circumstances."[9] But should the tale be taken as "typical" in quite this sense? Certainly Ellen's misfortunes embrace much that is characteristic of what has to be endured by the underprivileged in a class society (and perhaps in any society). But as we have seen, she also experiences others that are essentially independent of low socioeconomic status; being largely unpredictable, they are either the result of individual human folly and wickedness, or they are among those that, in the nature of our human lot, descend upon rich and poor alike. It is this mix of trials and tribulations that reconciles us to a doctrinal stance that, if crudely presented by a Hannah More, would be rejected out of hand. The fact remains, however, that the ideological suspicion provoked by this tale cannot take hold unless it is *only* the poor and powerless who are exhorted to welcome the corrective pains and sorrows; and my own judgment is that "Ellen Orford" escapes that charge, even if only by a hair's breadth.

In the instances discussed in this chapter there has been a recurrent emphasis on the virtue of resignation to the divine will, and in particular to acceptance that misfortunes are sent not to punish us but rather to "correct" our errant feelings and to "guide" us towards the proper Christian humility needed to ensure salvation and eternal life in the hereafter. In fairness it should be noted, however, that the role thus predicated for unhappiness and misery is not confined in Crabbe's exemplars to the poor or indeed to any particular social grouping. Thus the grief felt by the prosperous Farmer Frankford when his wife dies suddenly "in the Strength of Life" leads to the comment :

> Oh sacred Sorrow! by whom Souls are tried,
> Sent not to punish Mortals but to guide;

and this is followed immediately by Crabbe's application of the same principle to his own spiritual self-discipline:

> If Thou art mine, (and who shall proudly dare,
> To tell his MAKER, he has had his Share?)
> Still let me feel for what thy Pangs are sent,
> And be my Guide and not my Punishment!
>
> (*The Parish Register*, 3.629–34)

Moreover Crabbe's commitment to this austere doctrine is not slavishly unthinking. Witness his lengthy disquisition (part 3, 191–232) on Death's "Infant-train" as exemplified in the case of Gerard's baby son, taken from him after a painful "three Days' Life" spent in "feeble Cries." Here the argument vacillates uneasily between two views: on the one hand, the consolatory view that the baby's "sad sobs and piteous Sighs" have earned him immediate access to "Heav'n's eternal Year" without subjection to the "Years of Want and Grief" still to be endured by his surviving twin-sister; and, on the other hand, the contrasting and incompatible view that all the "Burthens" sent by "Love Divine" as spiritual discipline for "weary men" are not sent unnecessarily and in vain. The avian simile that winds up the passage is arresting but inconclusive:

> Say, will you call the breathless Infant blest,
> Because no Cares the silent Grave molest?
> So would you deem the Nurseling from the Wing
> Untimely thrust and never train'd to sing,
> But far more blest the Bird whose grateful Voice
> Sings its own Joy and makes the Woods rejoice,
> Though, while untaught, e'er yet he charm'd the Ear,
> Hard were his Trials and his Pains severe!

This doesn't really resolve the issues that have been raised.

Nevertheless the passage can stand as representative of ways in which, while starting from within the consensus view of his middle-class peers, Crabbe's scrupulous honesty not infrequently leads him to incorporate into his poetic vision observations that conflict with or even negate the conventional ideological assumptions. Thus in the sphere of social concern we have seen him sharply critical of some of the accepted social institutions of his time, notably the system of poor relief in its more inhuman aspects and the double standard of morality as between men and women. Though his view of the world was undoubtedly influenced by the ideological presuppositions of those around him, he did not accept these inertly or allow himself to be unduly constrained by them; and there can be little doubt that so far as his own experience extended, he was a faithful (if sometimes slightly censorious) chronicler of the lives of the rural poor. On balance, then, Hazlitt's characterization of Crabbe as having in him "too much of the parish beadle, an overseer of the country poor" does seem to have been an unwarranted jibe.

Part III

13

Biographical Speculations

Although contemporary literary theory has increasingly ignored or devalued the role of the author in literary works, the reading public at large has continued to show a lively interest in the individual author's life, his personality, and his psychology. In recent years, for example, there has been a flood of new biographies of distinguished poets, novelists, and dramatists, and these have often achieved massive sales. This appetite for intimate personal revelation cannot find a great deal to feed on in Crabbe's published work. His tales are built upon observation rather than self-analysis or self-display; and although he often enables the reader to enter vividly into the feelings of the characters, the poet's own relation to these characters remains for the most part notably detached and objective. This continues to be the case even where we have reason to believe that he is drawing upon his own life experience in a more than usually direct way. Thus in "The Patron," tale 5 in *Tales* (1812), it cannot be doubted that much of the convincing detail is taken from Crabbe's own experience at Belvoir from 1782 to 1785 as domestic chaplain to the duke of Rutland, or that the inspiration for the poem was fueled by resentment at some of the treatment he received during that period; yet no one could sensibly suppose that the tale is in any sense a direct transcription from his own life. Crabbe clearly made good use of his memories of both country mansion and townhouse (the cold and empty waiting room at the latter is rendered with evident authority); but the aspiring young poet (son of "A Borough-Bailiff, who to law was train'd") is equally clearly not a surrogate for Crabbe's youthful self but a character in his own right. In a similar way, although the route traversed by Orlando in "The Lover's Journey," tale 10 in *Tales* (1812), was unquestionably one well known to Crabbe in his own person, the narrative in this case is carefully detached from personal resonances, the better to concentrate on the poem's more generalized and near-philosophical theme.

There are a few poems and fragments of poems, principally ones published posthumously, that invite a more personal application. And we can turn also to the attractively written *Life*, compiled by his son around the time of the poet's death and first published as part of the 1834 edition of the *Poetical Works*. Although this was toned down and softened in certain respects, partly out of filial devotion, partly in deference to the advice of Moore, Rogers and others, it does within its limits give a credible and lively impression of the poet's personality; and it can be supplemented by reference to some of the poet's letters that have survived. The material is too scanty to be made into a convincing psychobiography, but there is enough of it to provide some interesting personal background relevant to our understanding of the poetry.

As has already been mentioned, the bulk of this poetry has an ambience that is calm, level-headed, and somewhat undemonstrative. The characteristic tone gives the impression of a carefully controlled utterance—controlled not only in its patterning of the versification and its organization of the verbal texture but also in its publicly modulated presentation of facts and feelings. It is here, above all, that we sense a continuance of the Augustan poetic tradition, recalling that, as Ian Watt has phrased it : "The adjective Augustan surely evokes a special way of speaking—precise in syntax, elegant in diction, and very detached in its attitude to the subject, to the audience, and even to the self and its feelings."[1] (Watt goes on to describe the "most characteristic mode" of the Augustan voice as "ironic"; and although in Crabbe's tales irony surfaces only intermittently, the ironic note is seldom far away.) The poetic persona suggested by this "way of speaking" is one that sets out to trace, behind the multifarious idiosyncrasies of human behavior, a rational moral order governing the whole of the created universe; and if there is any sense of strain generated by the difficulties of this enterprise, it shows itself as a rule only in the vitality and energy of Crabbe's narrative and character drawing. Yet the characteristic poetic tension that guarantees his avoidance of shallow complacency must have had its source in some degree of internal conflict; and it is elsewhere than in the tales themselves that we are forced to look for this.

The most obvious starting point is the shortish autobiographical poem entitled "Infancy," written between 1814 and 1816, and first published, posthumously, in the 1834 edition. In its avowed concern with personal reminiscence, these 141 lines, though shaped into heroic couplets, are unlike anything else in Crabbe's poetic output; among other things, they differ in being unusually bleak and gloomy in their outlook upon life. The general proposition set out in the early part of the poem is that the "pleasure" that we all seek is essentially no more than relief from pain or discomfort.

For what is Pleasure that we toil to gain?
'Tis but the slow or rapid Flight of Pain.
Set Pleasure by, and there would yet remain,
For every Nerve and Sense, the Sting of Pain:
Set Pain aside, and fear no more the Sting,
And whence your Hopes and Pleasures can ye bring?

                                                                (23–28)

This austere doctrine is illustrated for us first by the observation that the
Lover's "Rapture" results from removal of the "Grief" caused by his
mistress's absence—a causal relationship said (a little cynically) to be proved
by the fact that it soon dissipates once marriage has removed the cause.
Second, there follows Crabbe's more overtly personal testimony that in looking back over his memories he finds that "Grief" both struck early and
remains long in the mind, whereas "Joys" are ephemeral and evanescent
"like phosphoric light / Or Squibs and Crackers on a Gala Night." The
most memorable part of the poem, however, is an extended account of a
single childhood day that Crabbe describes as "Emblematic" of his life—
an oft-repeated pattern which began with ardent anticipation and enjoyment and ended in dissatisfaction and disillusionment.

Sweet was the Morning's Breath, the inland Tide,
And our Boat gliding, where alone could glide
Small Craft and they oft touch'd on either Side.
It was my first-born Joy. I heard them say,
"Let the child go; he will enjoy the day."

                                                                (85–89)

But the enjoyment soon evaporates when the boating party reaches a town,
and the adults, "on themselves intent," forget about their infant companion:

I lost my Way, and my Companions me,
And all, their Comforts and Tranquillity.
Mid-day it was, and as the Sun declin'd,
The early Rapture I no more could find.
The Men drank much, to whet the Appetite,
And growing heavy, drank to make them light;
Then drank to relish Joy, then further to excite.
Their Chearfulness did but a Moment last;
Something fell short or something overpast.
The lads play'd idly with the Helm and Oar

> And nervous Ladies would be set on Shore,
> Till Civil Dudgeon grew and Peace would smile no more.
>
> (100–111)

These few lines of shrewd social observation offer a good example of what Lilian Haddakin justly calls Crabbe's characteristic "sardonic astringency." Immediately following this human discord the climate takes a hand in order to add its own contribution to the day's mortifications.

> Now on the colder Water faintly shone
> The sloping Light—the cheerful Day was gone;
> Frown'd every Cloud, and from the gather'd Frown
> The Thunder burst and Rain came pattering down.
> My torpid Senses now my Fears obey'd
> When the fierce Lightning on the Water play'd.
> Now all the Freshness of the Morning fled,
> My Spirits burden'd and my heart was dead;
> The female Servants show'd a Child their fear
> And Men, full wearied, wanted Strength to chear;
>
> (112–21)

Crabbe now returns to his original proposition about the nature of "Pleasure":

> And when at length the dreaded Storm went past,
> And there was Peace and Quietness at last,
> 'Twas not the Morning's Quiet—it was not
> Pleasures reviv'd but Miseries forgot:
> It was not Joy that now commenc'd her Reign,
> But mere relief from Wretchedness and Pain.
>
> (122–27)

The deep pessimism with which Crabbe extends the pattern of this childhood day to cover that of all his later experience has no parallel in the tales, though it may underlie the more dispirited passages in a few of them.

Crabbe wrote this unpublished and unrevised poem in the aftermath of his wife's death, and some of the concluding lines have an explicit reference to the disappointments of his married life:

> Ev'n Love himself, that Promiser of Bliss,
> Made his best Days of Pleasure end like this:
> He mix'd his Bitters in the Cup of Joy
> Nor gave a Bliss uninjur'd by Alloy.

All Promise they, all Joy as they began!
And these grew less and vanish'd as they ran!
Errors and Evils came in many a Form,
The Mind's Delusion and the Passions' Storm.
The promised Joy that, like the Morning, rose,
Broke on my View, grew clouded in its Close;
Friends who together in the Morning sail'd
Parted ere Noon, and Solitude prevail'd.

The extent to which the evident distress in these lines should be applied specifically to the disappointments of his marriage may not be wholly certain, but they clearly send us to an aspect of Crabbe's experience that must have had a central importance for him. We have little certain knowledge about it, however. In 1783 Crabbe was married to Sarah Elmy after a lengthy engagement during which his future wife had given him much moral support in his hard struggle to become established as a poet. In its beginnings their marriage seems to have been a happy one, but only two out of the seven children born to them survived into adulthood, and after the death in 1793 of an infant son, Mrs. Crabbe began to show signs of a nervous disorder that was to last, with some fluctuations in its severity, until her death in 1813. Crabbe's son limits himself to the following rather tight-lipped account:

[The nervous disorder] proved of an increasing and very lamentable kind; for, during the hotter months of almost every year, she was oppressed by the deepest dejection of spirits I ever witnessed in any one, and this circumstance alone was sufficient to undermine the happiness of so feeling a mind as my father's. Fortunately for both, there were long intervals, in which, if her spirits were a little too high, the relief to herself and others was great indeed. Then she would sing over her old tunes again—and be the frank, cordial, charming woman of earlier days.[2]

For the rest there are some indications in Crabbe's correspondence suggesting that his wife's illness made it difficult for him to keep up the friendly contacts that his naturally sociable disposition inclined him towards; and certainly his domestic difficulties seem to have become known among his friends and acquaintances from about 1803 onwards. Southey wrote to a friend in 1808:

It was not long before his [Crabbe's] wife became deranged, and when all this was told me by one who knew him well, five years ago, he was still almost confined in his own house, anxiously waiting upon this wife in her long and hopeless malady. A sad history! It is no wonder he gives so melancholy a picture of human life.[3]

Other rumors, such as Mitford's report that Mrs. Crabbe had formed a "prodigious" collection of Bath stones, should perhaps be treated more cautiously. For the most authoritative testimony we have to turn to a letter written by Crabbe to Mrs. Alethea Lewis, a friend of long standing, on 25 October 1813, a few weeks after his wife's death.

> She has been dying these ten years: more I believe & I hope I am very thankful that I am the Survivor. . . . I cannot weigh Sorrows in a Ballance or make Comparisons between different Kinds of Affliction, nor do I judge whether I should have suffered most to have parted with my poor Sally, as I did part (if indeed such was parting) or to have seen her pass away with all her Faculties, feelings, senses acute & awake as my own. When I doubt of our parting (a conscious feeling on both sides that we were separating) you will judge of the propriety of such Expressions, for with Respect to Intellect & the more enquiring & reasoning of the Faculties, she, dear Creature, had lost these even years since: The will sometimes made an Effort, but Nature forbad: the mind was veiled, clouded & by Degrees lost. Then too were the Affections wrecked: No I was no more than another! not so much as the Woman who administered to the hourly Calls for small Comforts. The senses remained & even too acute but I hope, I believe there was not pain with the Restlessness which preceded the Evening of the 20th of Septr & for her, there was no Morning after that.
>
> Appetite & Strength had been decaying for 2 or 3 years, but very gradually. . . . Medical Men could do nothing: my poor Mrs Crabbe only lived to the present: we could not speak of the past. We could not hope together for the future: all was centred in the Moment's feeling & when I stood over her & carried my thoughts backward to the Mind that was, the Intelligence that might have been gained, the Improvement, the Communication that we should have made if—but it is not in Men to foresee nor to repine but to submit. God almighty grant me a Spirit of absolute and total Resignation.[4]

This moving firsthand account brings home both the extent and the depth of the anguish caused by his wife's manic-depressive illness, and may suggest that this misfortune must have played a large part in leading him to wrestle in his poetry with those aberrant areas of human experience that his Augustan predecessors had tended to leave out of their reckoning. Perhaps it accounts also for the remarkably compassionate understanding that he extends not only to the mentally deranged but to sinners as well.

Crabbe's son gives a more muted account of his mother's death. "During a long period before her departure," he tells us, "her mind had been somewhat impaired by bodily infirmities; and at last it sank under the severity of the disease." He does, however, provide his own confirmation of the intensity of Crabbe's regret at the disappointments of his marriage by quoting the following comment written in his father's hand upon the outside of an old letter of his wife's : "Nothing can be more sincere than this, nothing more reasonable and affectionate; and yet happiness was denied."

Two days after his wife's death Crabbe was afflicted by an alarming illness, which, his son tells us, "bore a considerable resemblance to acute cholera without sickness." For a time his life was thought to be in danger, but an improvement, followed by a very gradual recovery, was effected by the administration of emetics—a "species of medicine" to which, according to his son, Crabbe had always had "a great aversion." If this laconic comment is taken in conjunction with the lines in part 2 of the early poem *Inebriety* describing in rather unpleasant detail the drunken vomiting of the young fop Fabricio, we may perhaps hazard the conjecture that Crabbe suffered from a somewhat phobic attitude toward vomit, such that the compulsion toward control that we have already noted in his poetic utterance either extended to or was rooted in a neurotic concern about control over bodily function. This guess (it is little more) would certainly be consonant with what little we know about the ailment for which he was prescribed opiates from middle age onwards. His son tells us that Crabbe at first thought the vertigo to which he was subject was "indicative of a tendency to apoplexy"; but after an "alarming attack" that took place in Ipswich around 1790 he was examined by a Dr. Clubbe, whose diagnosis was, "[L]et the digestive organs bear the whole blame: you must take opiates." The biographer continues :

> From that time his health began to amend rapidly, and his constitution was renovated; a rare effect of opium, for that drug almost always inflicts some partial injury, even when it is necessary: but to him it was only salutary—and to a constant but slightly increasing dose of it may be attributed his long and generally healthy life.

From this, and from another comment elsewhere in the biography, we may reasonably infer a psychosomatic illness with its main symptoms affecting the digestive system. Relevant in this connection are his son's comments on the improvement in spirits enjoyed by Crabbe after his removal to Trowbridge in 1814:

> But a physical change that occurred in his constitution, at the time of the severe illness that followed close on my mother's death, had, I believe, a

great share in all these happy symptoms. It always seemed to be his own opinion that at that crisis his system had, by a violent effort, thrown off some weight or obstruction that had been, for many years previously, giving his bodily condition the appearance of a decline,—afflicting him with occasional fits of low fever, and vexatiously disordering his digestive organs. In those days, "life is as tedious as a twice-told tale," was an expression not seldom in his mouth; and he once told me, he felt that he could not possibly live more than six or seven years. But now it seemed that he had recovered not only the enjoyment of sound health, but much of the vigour and spirit of youthful feelings.

It is hard to doubt that the "weight or obstruction" referred to here was the physical correlate of a psychic oppression resulting from the painful and probably conflicting feelings induced by Mrs. Crabbe's illness, and that the crisis that followed her death was a mental as well as a physical one.

Among the more self-revelatory poems that remained unpublished during the poet's lifetime there are a few whose subject matter is dreams. Before discussing them and their possible relation to his opium taking, however, it will be appropriate to refer to a dream that is reported in the biography. The following extract is taken from the entry for 21 July in the journal that Crabbe kept during his 1817 visit to London:

I returned late last night, and my reflections were as cheerful as such company could make them, and not, I am afraid, of the most humiliating kind; yet, for the first time these many nights, I was incommoded by dreams, such as would cure vanity for a time in any mind where they could gain admission. Some of Baxter's mortifying spirits whispered very singular combinations.[5] None, indeed, that actually did happen in the very worst of times, but still with a formidable resemblance. It is doubtless very proper to have the mind thus brought to a sense of its real and possible alliances, and the evils it has encountered, or might have had; but why these images should be given at a time when the thoughts, the waking thoughts, were of so opposite a nature, I cannot account. So it was. Awake I had been with the high, the apparently happy: we were very pleasantly engaged, and my last thoughts were cheerful. Asleep, all was misery and degradation, not my own only, but of those who had been. —That horrible image of servility and baseness— that mercenary and commercial manner! It is the work of imagination, I suppose; but it is very strange.

When taken in conjunction with another recurrent dream in which he was tormented by some lads whom he could not thrash because they were made of leather, this suggests a powerful repressed sense of guilt that can be seen to surface in the ravings of Sir Eustace Grey and in the posthumously published dream poem, "The World of Dreams." On one level Sir Eustace Grey's tribulations are presented as just retribution for his jealous revenge-murder of his unfaithful wife and her young seducer; but on a deeper level he accepts his punishment as merited on account of his earlier lack of Christian faith and devotion:

> I never then my God address'd,
>   In grateful Praise or humble Prayer;
> And if His Word was not my jest!
>   (Dread Thought!) it never was my Care.
> I doubted: Fool I was to doubt!
>
> (96–100)

In his madness his overpowering preoccupation is with himself as a "man of Sin":

> A Soul defil'd with every Stain,
> That man's reflecting Mind can pain.
>
> (327–28)

In "The World of Dreams" too it is the dreamer's "sin" (line 25) that "admits the shadowy throng" of "black Enemies" who are responsible for nightmarish visions.

It has been argued convincingly, first by M. H. Abrams and later by Alethea Hayter,[6] that these two poems (and also the dream fragment "Where am I now?") are constructed around memories drawn from opium-induced dreaming, as manifested in characteristically strange imagery relating to variations in light, rapid movement over vast distances, variations in consciousness of time and space, and so on. As we have noted earlier, the visions of Sir Eustace Grey are not particularly appropriate to his case history, but do very much resemble the visionary experiences recorded by other opium takers. What is to our immediate purpose, however, is the extent to which these alarming sensations are presented as consequent upon a sense of unworthiness and consciousness of sin. In "The World of Dreams" (a vivid and strongly felt poem) the most affecting passage is one in which the dreamer is reunited with the image of his late wife only to have her snatched away again by the malevolent sprites who control his dreaming. The other (unfinished) poem, "Where am I now?," is much less powerful, and its interest relates more to the further light it casts upon Crabbe's mental processes than to any intrinsic poetic merit. These three atypical poems (all written in stanza form and not in heroic couplets) do, however, provide insight into the existence of a turbulent and tension-ridden inner life that could not easily have been guessed at from the reading of Crabbe's most characteristic poems and tales.

As has already been suggested, this characteristic work leaves behind above all the impression of a quest for control—an objective to be attained, first of all, by the controlled understanding and controlled representation of a known world, but also, more centrally, by the confident marshaling of all the evidence for the presence in that world of a just and divinely or- dained moral order. Now there can be little doubt that in this endeavor Crabbe saw himself as engaged simply in conveying "th'instructive truth" about human nature and the human lot, and that consciously he would have experienced no sense of strain about matching his imagined world with the tenets of his Christian faith. Yet the poetic energy that gives con- tinuing life to the best of his verse-narrative does seem to suggest that un- derneath the calm surface there may lurk unacknowledged and unsuspected tensions. In addition to the challenge (already discussed) from new mani- festations in the intellectual and cultural sphere, this chapter has pointed up some indications that in his personal life, too, Crabbe was subject, dur- ing his most productive period, to considerable strains. In the light of our more recently acquired understanding of the way unconscious forces oper- ate in the human mind, we may perhaps speculate that in Crabbe there can be observed at work the archetypal Freudian poet who, like a child at play, "creates a world of his own or, more/truly, rearranges the things of his world and orders it in a new way that pleases him better."[6]

Afterword

The preceding pages have traced some of the most important circumstances that made it possible for Crabbe to create during the sixth decade of his life a radically original art form—the "tale in verse," which can be observed taking its decisive shape in seven of the concluding letters of *The Borough*, which reached its finest flowering in *Tales* (1812), and which continued to generate significant poetic achievement in parts of *Tales of the Hall*. Crabbe's tales in verse are unique in the way that they fuse Augustan versification and largely Augustan values with particularized description and character drawing; in their ability to deal with ordinary people, sometimes of humble station but more often from the middling ranks of society, in ways that catch their individuality yet at the same time treat them as both socially typical and as representatives of general human nature; and in the way their moral preoccupations emerge organically, and usually with little overt didacticism, from the characters and incidents portrayed. The poet's own experience of the people he met in various country parishes and in the small town of Aldborough over several decades clearly contributed a good deal to his ability to transmute life into art in these verse-tales. To a greater extent than he himself seems to have realized, however, his vision of people and events was shaped and codified by his own wide reading and particularly by his reading of eighteenth-century essayists and novelists. Some encouragement to develop this new art form may have come from changes in critical theory between the 1780s and the 1800s, in particular the declining authority of the poetic kinds and an increased tolerance of particularity in description. In addition, some poets around the turn of the century, most notably Wordsworth, Southey, and Bloomfield, had begun to write narrative poems, realistic in tone, about humble characters and ordinary incidents, and this may have fortified Crabbe in his own narrative experiments. The magnitude of the creative leap apparent in his own practice during the first twelve years of the nineteenth century should not, however, be underestimated.

Yet though highly original, these verse narratives were very much in tune with their time, and were much esteemed by the contemporary reading public. We know that Jane Austen "thoroughly enjoyed Crabbe," was disappointed not to have caught a glimpse of him at the theater during a visit to London, and "would sometimes say, in jest, that if she ever married she could fancy being Mrs Crabbe."[1] Pollard rightly sees *Tales* (1812) as the volume that brought Crabbe to "the high water-mark of his popularity," and he endorses Jeffrey's emphasis upon the poet's "stature as an observer of human nature" as the quality that accounts above all for the high esteem accorded to this work by its readers.[2] Gregor, however, pointed to the "sharply contrasting reception given to the *Tales* (1812) and those of 1819" and suggested that this contrast pinpoints "with some accuracy the moment when the decisive shift towards Romanticism took place in public taste." Having reminded us that between 1814 and 1818 there appeared *The Excursion, Waverley, Guy Mannering, Alastor,* "Christabel," "Kubla Khan," *Manfred, Endymion,* and *Childe Harold III and IV,* he added that: "After 1818 Crabbe was unmistakably "a survival" from an age that had passed."[3] Certainly, although *Tales of the Hall* was favorably received by the reviewers, it did not sell as well as Murray had expected, and it is clear that from this point onwards Crabbe's popularity went into a steady decline.

What is remarkable is the almost complete absence of any perceptible influence of Crabbe upon later poets; the verse-tale as he conceived it was born with Crabbe, and with him it also died. John Speirs has argued that Crabbe's achievement was subsumed into the art of the nineteenth-century novel, mainly via the work of Jane Austen, but the evidence for this view is somewhat indirect and not wholly conclusive.

One factor that may have contributed to the nineteenth century's withdrawal of its favor from Crabbe's verse-tales deserves a little further discussion. What I have in mind is the strikingly Augustan objectivity that he regularly displayed towards his personae. As our analyses have repeatedly shown, an ironic stance towards the characters (the main protagonists as well as the lesser personae) is a recurrent feature in almost all his tales. Even where the ironic tone is muted or in abeyance, as in, for instance, "The Parting Hour" (tale 2 in *Tales* [1812]), his attitude to his characters, even if favorable, remains notably detached. The reader is often led to empathize, fully and accurately, with the outlook and feelings of the characters; but it is only very rarely that he becomes emotionally involved with the fate of the protagonists to the degree that is commonly described as "identification." There are two examples in *Tales* (1812) that might be cited as exceptions to this general rule, though in each case the identificatory feelings form only

one strand in a well-plotted tale in which the ignoble characters are portrayed with sharp irony. In "Jessie and Colin" (tale 13) our feelings of sympathetic concern go wholeheartedly along with the newly orphaned Jessie
in her disgust at the petty tyranny that her putative patroness exercises over
her three dependents; and when she rejects the degrading role allotted to
her of household spy, we experience vicarious relief at her ability to return
to the welcoming arms of Colin, the industrious small farmer who had
previously offered himself as a suitor. In a similar way, in "The Confidant"
(tale 16) our feeling sympathies are engaged in no small measure on behalf
of Anna, the virtuous and loving wife whom a former childhood friend is
blackmailing in connection with a youthful sexual transgression; and we
cannot fail to triumph along with her when her husband Stafford, using a
trick borrowed from the Arabian Nights, sends her blackmailer packing.
Although each of these tales must be counted among Crabbe's successes,
the indulgence in identificatory feeling carries with it a certain artistic pen-
alty; in the first the idyllic simplicity of Colin Grey's humble home seems a
trifle idealized, while in the second the considerate and cool-judging character of Anna's husband seems rather too good to be true.

Ironic detachment is less consistently present in Crabbe's portrayal of
his main characters in *Tales of the Hall*, particularly in those parts of this
volume where Romantic influences are detectable. We are certainly led to
identify fairly thoroughly, for instance, with the younger brother Richard in
the frame narrative, while book 7, "The Elder Brother," offers an intriguing and rather more complicated pattern in this respect. It is a self-critical
first-person account of George's prolonged infatuation as a young man with
a girl he encountered only on a single occasion yet identified immediately
as his imaginary ideal woman and spent years of his life vainly searching
for. Eventually, when he has given up hope, he meets her unexpectedly in
sordid circumstances, a "ruin'd girl," faded and tawdry, whom he tries unsuccessfully to reform but whose death is at least comforted, at the last, by
repentance and due spiritual aid. The narrative element is perfunctory and
unconvincing, lacking any of the circumstantial trappings that such a story
would require. The poet's energy has gone essentially into the rendering of
George's psychological state, and there is a certain haunting power about
this uncharacteristic exploration of the hinterland of feeling; yet it has to be
admitted that the stylistic form often seems ill-suited to the purpose in hand.
Crabbe's command of the heroic couplet has as its forte an antithetical
pointedness of ironic presentation in the sphere of socially sanctioned values; with irony largely absent, he lapses all too often into a disconcerting
lack of control over his poetic tone. "The Elder Brother" is a poem of great

interest in which one feels that the poet is more closely identified with his protagonist than the reader can always be; but it will not (perhaps for that very reason) be judged one of his successes.

We have been looking here at exceptional cases, however. In the vast majority of his tales Crabbe makes a decidedly Augustan use of irony and detachment, enabling his readers to empathize with the personae, certainly, but ensuring that our satisfactions are focused mainly upon the cool, objective, carefully balanced evaluative judgments that the author communicates to us, at times overtly, at other times through more indirect formal means. Such judgments are, of course, part of the regular stock-in-trade of the writer of fiction. Yet from Richardson and Fielding onward the identificatory experience had also formed an important element in the appeal of the eighteenth-century novel; it continued (alongside and interwoven with the detached and critical stance of the novelist's own point of view) as a significant part of the attraction of Jane Austen's fiction; and, especially perhaps after the sweeping success of the Brontës' works, it began to assume an even more central emotional importance in the majority of nineteenth-century novels. Its almost complete absence in the best of Crabbe's tales must have seriously limited his appeal, henceforth, to many readers. Certainly during this period his standing, and with it his readership, plunged lower and lower. It is only in the last half-century that his narratives have again begun to enjoy some of the attention they deserve. Surely the time is now ripe for a reassertion of the varied and complex satisfactions that can be gained from reading the verse-tales of this fine and unique poet.

Notes

Preface

1. McGann, *Social Values and Poetic Arts*, ix.

Chapter 1. The Last Augustan?

1. Broman, "Factors in Crabbe's Eminence," 42. An intriguing precursor of this "long-established pattern" is provided by Henry Crabb Robinson, who confided to his diary in December 1835 that he had never read any of Crabbe's works later than *The Village*, an omission that did not hinder him from recording that he took "no pleasure in his unpoetical representations of human life."

2. The reductio ad absurdum of this kind of distortion is to be found in an extraordinary digression by W. Somerset Maugham in the opening pages of his 1919 novel *The Moon and Sixpence:*

> Sometimes a man survives a considerable time from an era in which he had his place into one which is strange to him, and then the curious are offered one of the most singular spectacles in the human comedy. Who now, for instance, thinks of George Crabbe? He was a famous poet in his day, and the world recognised his genius with a unanimity which the greater complexity of modern life has rendered infrequent. He had learnt his craft at the school of Alexander Pope, and he wrote moral stories in rhymed couplets. Then came the French Revolution and the Napoleonic Wars, and the poets sang new songs. Mr Crabbe continued to write moral stories in rhymed couplets. I think he must have read the verses of these young men who were making so great a stir in the world, and I fancy he found it poor stuff. Of course, much of it was. But the odes of Keats and of Wordsworth, a poem or two by Coleridge, a few more by Shelley, discovered the vast realms of the spirit that none had explored before. Mr Crabbe was as dead as mutton, but Mr Crabbe continued to write moral stories in rhymed couplets.

Among the hundreds of thousands of readers of this bestseller, there cannot have been more than a handful who had any inkling of the extent to which, as far as Crabbe is concerned, Mr. Maugham's literary history was complete fantasy.

3. See Haddakin, *Poetry of George Crabbe* ; Chamberlain, *George Crabbe* ; Sigworth, *Nature's Sternest Painter;* New, *George Crabbe's Poetry;* and Bareham, *George Crabbe* .

4. See Johnson, "Meaning of Augustan," 507–22, and Weinbrot, *Augustus Caesar in "Augustan" England.*

5. See Erskine-Hill, "Augustans on Augustanism," 55–83; and Watt, "Two Historical

Aspects," 67–88. For a more recent supporting discussion, see also Meehan, *Liberty and Poetics*, 64–72.

6. Frye, "Varieties of Sensibility," 159–60.

7. Watt, "Two Historical Aspects," 70.

8. For an illuminating and exceptionally well-documented discussion of these issues, see Erskine-Hill, *Social Milieu of Alexander Pope*. An attractive exposition of a similar set of values (though on a more modest territorial scale) can be studied in John Pomfret's admirable poem "The Choice." Written in the year 1700, this appropriately enough appears as the very first item in *The New Oxford Book of Eighteenth-Century Verse*.

9. In 1750–52 Johnson's twice-weekly *Rambler* essays never sold more than five hundred copies in their original form, but their readership was vastly multiplied as a result of their reprinting in the country newspapers. See Wiles, "Middle-Class Literacy," 64; and also Belanger, "Publishers and Writers."

10. In *The Bee* for 24 November 1759.

Chapter 2. Traditional Influences

1. Reynolds, *Literary Works*, 1:341 (Discourse III).

2. As Alexander Knox put it, "those little domestic circumstances which perhaps no poet before him ever thought of making use of." *Flapper*, no. 30 (14 May 1796).

3. See particularly James Hurdis, *The Village Curate* (1788); Thomas Gisborne, *Walks in a Forest* (more especially in the second edition, published in 1796); Richard Polwhele, *Poetic Trifles* (1796); and Robert Bloomfield, *The Farmer's Boy* (1800).

4. Mayo, "Contemporaneity," 495.

5. See Jacobus, *Tradition and Experiment*, 185–86.

6. In the later version included in *English Eclogues* (1799), this note of social protest, which mitigates a little the guilt of her lover's abandonment of her, was suppressed. The emphasis fell more upon Hannah's "sorrow of neglect" and her consequent long suffering and painful thoughts, which led her to pine away and to be unable at the last even to express affection for her infant. It is implied that her death is the outcome of her mental condition, but she maintains her sanity even in her suffering.

7. Letter from James Lecky to Mrs. Leadbeater, dated 21 November 1820, reporting a conversation he had had with Crabbe in October 1820 (quoted in Bareham, *George Crabbe*, 161).

8. Abrams, *Mirror and the Lamp*, 40–41.

9. Reynolds, *Literary Works*, 1:336.

10. See Taylor, "Particular Character," 161–74.

11. Reynolds, *Literary Works*, 1:346 (Discourse IV) and 2:22 (Discourse XI).

12. Ibid., 1:346 (Discourse IV).

13. See, for instance, "A Tale" by John Logan in *Poems* (1781); some shortish verse-tales by John Thelwall in *Poems on Various Subjects*, vol. 1 (1787); James Hurdis's "Elmer and Ophelia" and "The Orphan Twins" in *Poems* (1790), and his *Adriano; or, The First of June*, published separately in in the same year; and G. D. Harley's "Lovelorn Anne," in *Poems* (1796).

Chapter 3. Immediate Precursors

1. See particularly Arthur Sales's introduction to his edition of Crabbe, *The Village* ; Chamberlain, *George Crabbe*, 39; and Thomas, "George Crabbe: Not Quite the Sternest,"

166–75. The argument is summed up in the following footnote in the recent scholarly edition by Dalrymple-Champneys and Pollard: "Parts of *The Village*, particularly 1.172 to the end of Book I, are strongly reminiscent of Langhorne's *Country Justice*, ii.43–66." See Crabbe, *Complete Poetical Works of George Crabbe*, 1:669.

Chapter 4. *Poems* (1807): The Tale in Embryo

1. Since Crabbe did not take up his second residence at Muston until October 1805 and had paid his last visit to Muston as nonresident incumbent in July 1802, it seems unlikely that in his conversations with FitzGerald in 1854–55 Crabbe's son misremembered the year; the great snowstorm should probably be placed in the winter of 1805–6.

2. Cf. letter 77 of *Sir Charles Grandison*, in which Nancy Selby can be found representing "the dreary unconnected life of a single woman in years" in terms of "Poor Mrs Penelope Arby . . . surrounded with parrots and lapdogs."

3. New, *George Crabbe's Poetry*, 62.

4. Ibid., 59.

5. The word *nymph* is used regularly throughout *The Parish Register* without any evident stylistic intention, and usually with no ironic implications; Crabbe seems at this stage to be using this fragment of eighteenth-century poetic diction almost as a matter of habit, and he applies it to virtually any young unmarried woman, though seldom to those of the lowest social class. In a similar way *swain* is used indiscriminately for any young countryman.

Chapter 5. Further Narrative Development in *The Borough*

1. Haddakin, *Poetry of Crabbe*, 95.

2. See Crabbe, *Life*, 173 and 187; the ms. note quoted by Huchon, *George Crabbe*, 207; and the preface to *The Borough* (in Crabbe, *Complete Poetical Works*, 352–53.

3. Sigworth, *Nature's Sternest Painter*, 122.

4. Pope, *Epistles to Several Persons*, epistle 1, 241.

5. New, *George Crabbe's Poetry*, 89.

6. See Pope, *Epistles to Several Persons*, epistle 3, 366–67.

7. See Richardson, *Clarissa*, vol. 2, letter 21.

8. See Forster, *Aspects of the Novel*, 93–94; Chatman, *Story and Discourse*, 45 and 47; and Muir, *Structure of the Novel*, 16.

9. See Rogers, *Augustan Vision*, 31–32.

10. See New, *George Crabbe's Poetry*, 99.

11. The Proceedings of the Sessions of the Peace, and Oyer and Terminer, for the City of London and County of Middlesex on Friday 12th, Saturday 13th, and Monday 15th of January 1733, Case No. 3.

12. Cf. "When husbands or when lap-dogs breathe their last." Pope, *Epistles to Several Persons*, epistle 3, 158.

13. Leavis, *Revaluation*, 128.

Chapter 6. The Goal Achieved: *Tales* (1812)

1. According to the *Memoirs of the First Forty-five years of the life of James Lackington, Bookseller* (1791), Lackington, originally an apprentice shoemaker in Taunton, was converted to Methodism for a time as a young man, lapsed into leading the life of a rake, then reformed

again and married a Methodist wife. As with Crabbe's convert, it was a Methodist who later, in London, helped Lackington set himself up as a bookseller, though part of the background in Lackington's case was that he had already become something of a reader. In the real-life history it was after Lackington's wife had died and he had remarried that he drifted away from the Methodists. Something of the animus they then expressed towards the renegade is recounted in letter 23 of the *Memoirs* in terms that Crabbe seems to have made use of:

> I had no sooner left Mr Wesley's society, and begun to talk a little more like a rational being, but I found that I had incurred the hatred of some, the pity of others, the envy of many, and the displeasure of all Mr Wesley's—old women! . . . Some as they passed by my door in their way to the Foundry would only make a stop, and lift up their hands, turn up the whites of their eyes, shake their heads, groan, and pass on." (lst edition, p. 171)

Lackington's *Memoirs* include a good deal of scurrilous raillery, verging on the pornographic, about the private lives of Methodists, accusations that appear only in very muted form in Crabbe's tale and are restricted to the relatively innocuous "carnal appetite" of gluttony. Later in *The Confessions of J. Lackington, late Bookseller* (London, 1803), Lackington regretted and retracted his accusations, and offered the confessions as a moralizing treatise that recounted his own spiritual progress towards the haven of Methodism, but Crabbe does not show any awareness of the existence of this book. Nor does he show signs of having known about the later phases of Lackington's continuing love-hate relationship with Methodism. In fact, Lackington moved in 1806 to Taunton and set up a Methodist chapel there, but in 1810 he fell into a dispute with the Conference over the conveyancing of this chapel, and this dispute persisted on and off until his death in 1815.

  2. See Stauffer, *Art of Biography*, 161 and 257–61.

  3. *Spectator*, no. 450 (Wednesday, 6 August 1712).

  4. The footnote of Crabbe's son to this tale is so discreet as to convey little information on its own; he writes merely: "It is understood that this tale was suggested by some realities in the history of Mrs Elmy, the mother of the Poet's wife." Huchon, however, uncovered the fact that "James Elmy of Beccles, Tanner" was reported bankrupt in the *Ipswich Journal*, 3 November 1759, and infers that he had "perhaps" behaved in a dishonorable way to his wife. See Huchon, *George Crabbe*, 46. The possible literary source is in chapter 3 of Maria Edgeworth's *Belinda* (London, 1801), where the points of parallelism seem too close to be coincidental. Lady Delacour tells Belinda: "I know nothing of business. So I signed all the papers they brought to me . . . I signed, and I signed, till at last I was with all due civility informed that my signature was no longer worth a farthing. . . . I was made to understand that if Lord Delacour were to die the next day I should live a beggar. . . . My uncle assured me that I had been grossly imposed upon by my lord and his lawyer, and that I had been swindled out of my senses and out of my dower. . . . Love quarrels are easily made up, but of money quarrels there is no end. From the moment these money quarrels commenced, I began to hate Lord Delacour; before I had only despised. You can have no notion to what meanness extravagance reduces men." It will be noted that Paul's wife too uses the word "meanness" to characterize her husband's behavior to her.

  5. Haddakin, *Poetry of George Crabbe*, 112.

  6. Crabbe's son believed this episode to be based upon a real-life incident that Crabbe had known about. "A surgeon of Ipswich had an addition to his family just as he had obtained the consent of a young lady to marry him. The breaking off of the match, by the good principles and delicacy of the intended bride, gave rise to much difference of opinion at the time, and suggested this tale" (footnote in 1834 edition). Without questioning this, it must be

remembered that Arabella's situation is a recurrent one in the fiction of the later part of the eighteenth century, and that the course of action regularly recommended is identical with the one she took. There can be little doubt that, among the various possibilities, Richardson is the writer most likely to have influenced the poet in this tale, since there are unmistakable parallels between Arabella's situation and certain events in the careers of his two heroines, namely Clarissa Harlowe in *Clarissa* (1748) and Miss Harriet Byron in *Sir Charles Grandison* (1754).

The parallels with Clarissa are the more striking. Thus in vol. 1, letter 3, Clarissa, expressing agreement with her family's unwillingness to allow her to accept Mr Lovelace's proposal of marriage on account of his repeated immoralities, writes, "[T]he person who could reject Mr Wyerley's address for the sake of his *free opinions*, must have been inexcusable, had she not rejected another for his *freer practices*." This brings to mind Arabella's treatment of Dr. Campbell and Edward Huntly respectively, particularly when it is explained, in vol. 1, letter 40, that Mr. Wyerley's fault was that of being a "jester upon sacred things," while in vol. 2, letter 39, it emerges that Lovelace had earlier tricked Miss Betterton into absconding, seduced her, left her, and never bothered himself about the bastard child she died bringing into the world while he was abroad. It is noteworthy also that Clarissa, like Arabella, had won universal admiration for her beauty, her accomplishments, and her moral qualities, and that it was indeed her preeminence in these respects (including incidentally her facility in learning languages, including Latin) that brought upon her head the "envy" and "disdain" of her brother and sister. These terms find a suggestive echo in lines 17–18 of "Arabella," where the "wise mammas" who praise Arabella to their daughters excite the opposite response to the one desired. As Crabbe puts it:

> From such applause disdain and anger rise,
> And envy lives where emulation dies.

(17–18)

Miss Harriet Byron has similarly shown an early pre-eminence in both beauty and accomplishments (though her languages were deliberately confined to French and Italian, and did not include Latin). Like both Clarissa and Arabella she rejected suitors on the ground of their "immoralities." It is worth noticing that in letter 6, expanding her reason for rejecting Mr. Greville, Miss Byron writes: "What a dreadful, what a presumptuous risk runs she, who marries a wicked man, even hoping to reclaim him, when she cannot be sure of keeping her own principles!"

As an indication that such issues remained under continual discussion until around the turn of the century it may be worth quoting from Thomas Holcroft's epistolary novel *Anna St Ives* (1792)—which itself derives fairly directly from *Clarissa*. In letter 96 Anna writes about her attempts to reclaim Coke Clifton by promising to marry him. "I have been guilty of a great error. The reformation of a man or woman by projects of marriage is a mistaken pernicious act. Instead of being an act of morality, I am persuaded it is an act of vice. Let us never cease our endeavours to reform the licentious and depraved but let us not marry them."

7. Quoted in Jaeger, *Before Victoria*, 17–18.

Chapter 7. The Downward Slope

1. Quoted in the 1834 edition of Crabbe's *Poetical Works*, chap. 6, 17.
2. As late as December 1818, Crabbe had in mind for his volume the title *Remembrances;*

but he later changed this to *Forty Days*, a title that would have emphasized more strongly the frame narrative. Murray in the end rejected this in favor of the more neutral *Tales of the Hall*.

3. Mr. Stanhope, "a man of great elegance of mind" was "drawn in by a vanity too natural to young men, that of fancying himself preferred, by a woman who had no one recommendation but beauty. . . . He was overcome by her marked attentions so far as to declare himself, without knowing her real disposition. It was some time before his prepossession allowed him to discover that she was weak and ill-informed, selfish and bad-tempered. . . . My friend, with patient affection, struggled for a long time to raise her character, and to enlighten her merit; but finding that she pouted whenever he took up a book . . . the softness of his temper and his habitual indolence at length prevailed. His better judgement sunk in the helpless contest. . . ." (More, *Coelebs in Search of a Wife*, 1:24–25).

4. J. Aikin, *An Essay on the Application of Natural History to Poetry* (1777), 2.
5. See Broadley and Jerrold, *Romance of an Elderly Poet*, 82–83.
6. Quoted in Pollard, *Crabbe*, 235.
7. Ms. note in Crabbe, *Poetical Works* (1834), chap. 7, 275.
8. New, *George Crabbe's Poetry*, 228.
9. Chamberlain, *George Crabbe*, 159.
10. Vol. 1, letter 26.
11. On p. 22.

Chapter 8. Crabbe's Verse-Tales and Romanticism

1. *Life*, chap. 7., 164.
2. In the margin of FitzGerald's copy of the 1834 edition there appears against these lines an ms. note, presumably dictated by Crabbe's son, which reads, "1803 Botany Bay Dialogues," though from its positioning this note is probably intended to refer specifically to "the exceeding simplicity of the language." Southey's *Botany Bay Dialogues* were in fact published in 1794; it may be that the biographer was really thinking of the same poet's *English Eclogues*, which were nearer in their date of publication (1799) to the 1803 of the note.
3. Scott, *Letters*, 3:279n.
4. As authority for both the novelty and the representativeness of this theme in Romantic conceptions of poetry, we may quote M. H. Abrams:

> The analogies for the mind in the writing of both Wordsworth and Coleridge show a radical transformation. Varied as these are, they usually agree in picturing the mind in perception as active rather than inertly receptive, and as contributing to the world in the very process of perceiving the world. (*Mirror and the Lamp*, 58)

Similarly, H. W. Piper writes:

> Nowhere before the last years of the century do we find any sign of what was to be the leading sense of the word Imagination for Wordsworth and Coleridge in 1797, and for Wordsworth for much longer; that is, as meaning a power operative in man's experience of the external world and enabling him to recognise sensibility, purpose and significance in natural objects. Nor is there any substantial anticipation of Coleridge's later and more generalised theory in which the primary and the secondary Imagination were in effect one power, working first to create the external world in its totality and then to create, from that material, fresh creations which would have in them the same life and truth. (*Active Universe*, 16–16)

The genesis of these ideas (which Piper traces above all to the Radical theories of the Unitarian Joseph Priestley and the poet Erasmus Darwin) is not really relevant to our present purpose; but it may be worth commenting a little further on the differing emphases adopted by Wordsworth and Coleridge respectively. For Wordsworth the activity of the perceiving human mind was essentially a reciprocal one, that of achieving communion with the "active principle" that he believed to be alive within all natural objects, whereas for Coleridge the stress came to fall increasingly upon the extreme subjectivism apparent in the "Dejection Ode." Both versions of the theory were, of course, highly influential upon the second generation of Romantic poets as upon their successors.

It is somewhat surprising that although the active nature of perception was a frequent topic of discussion between Wordsworth and Coleridge during the years immediately preceding the turn of the century, very little of their writing on it had been published prior to the appearance of Crabbe's *Tales* in 1812. Thus a highly explicit statement by Wordsworth on the creative power of the senses may be found in a fragment of 1797–98:

> There is creation in the eye
> Nor less in all the other senses; powers
> They are that colour, model, and combine
> The things perceived with such an absolute
> Essential energy that we may say
> That those most godlike faculties of ours
> At one and the same moment are the mind
> And the mind's minister.
>
> [*Poetical Works,* v. 343, fragment 4]

This fragment was not published, however, during Wordsworth's lifetime, let alone before 1812. A considerable amount of relevant material first drafted about the same period eventually achieved publication, in revised form, in 1815 in books 1 and 9 of *The Excursion,* while other allied passages found their way into *The Prelude,* but were not published separately.

Crabbe might well have encountered the glancing reference to the concept in lines 106–8 of "Tintern Abbey"—

> all the mighty world
> Of eye and ear, both what they half create,
> And what perceive

—while there are also a few relevant lines in the 1802 addition to the *Preface to Lyrical Ballads* (see W. Wordsworth, *Wordsworth's Literary Criticism,* 23). Here, as part of the answer to his own question, "What is a Poet?" Wordsworth writes: "a man pleased with his own passions and volitions, and who rejoices more than other men in the spirit of life that is in him; delighting to contemplate similar volitions and passions as manifested in the goings-on of the Universe, and habitually impelled to create them where he does not find them." Apart from these hints, however, we are left with Coleridge's "Dejection: An Ode" as the main published statement against which Crabbe could have been reacting in "The Lover's Journey."

5. As Cowper might have described it. See *The Task,* 1:559.

6. Bareham deliberately associates Crabbe's studies of madness with the wider corpus of "studies of derangement," arguing that

> Madness is too simple a term to connote the range of experience which Crabbe embraces in his work on this subject. He covers an area from mild but persistent indulgence of dream fancies to the full flight of uncoordinated frenzy. (*George Crabbe*, 175)

It is useful to be reminded of the wide-ranging interest Crabbe shows in a multitude of abnormal states of mind; but the objection to Bareham's argument is that Crabbe is always quite clear in his own mind as to where the borderline lies between madness and a state of mind that, though abnormal, remains sane. Thus Lucy the Miller's daughter teeters on the brink of madness but has not yet gone over the edge, though we are certainly left with the impression that her own "dread" of madness may yet be realized. Jane, in "The Sisters," at times moves temporarily over the border into a delusion that she has written a poem that will earn her a fortune, but she can be recalled from her "dream" by the watchful care of her loving sister Lucy. In the case of Jachin, after his disgrace, there is only one phrase ("the strong yearnings of a ruin'd Mind," *The Borough*, 273 [letter 19]) that offers any hint of ambiguity. For the rest, the displaced Parish Clerk, though rightly "dejected and dismay'd," seems to be portrayed as wholly sane in his sufferings and does not therefore deserve to be listed by Bareham alongside Peter Grimes (Bareham, *George Crabbe*, 171) any more than does the condemned felon in *The Borough*, letter 23, whose delusion of escape from his fate comes to him as a dream while he has briefly dropped off to sleep in his cell. Surprisingly, perhaps, it seems to be the case that Crabbe does not regard Abel Keene (also listed by Bareham on the same page) as having actually lost his reason, even though his "melancholy" and his "discontented thoughts" lead him to take his own life. In turning to the Calvinist preacher for spiritual guidance, he has been misled into believing that since he does not hear a "call," God has no mercy to offer him, but though duped he has not turned mad. The same is true of Ellen Orford's husband, who is led by similar spiritual misdirection into such "despair" that he too hangs himself. It seems Crabbe felt that if a man were persuaded into a reasoned belief that "he who feels not the mysterious call, / Lies bound in sin," then in the absence of such a "call" self-destruction would be a rational course of action.

    7. See Jones, *Law, Lunacy and Conscience;* Hunter and Macalpine, *Three Hundred Years of Psychiatry;* 402–690; Porter, *Mind-forged Manacles.*

    8. See Hunter and Macalpine, *Three Hundred Years of Psychiatry,* 509–14.

    9. Ibid., 543–46.

    10. Bareham, *George Crabbe,* 182.

    11. See Huchon, *George Crabbe,* 441 n. 6.

    12. Crabbe could have encountered "Auld Robin Gray" in a version by Lady Anne Lindsay in D. Hird, ed., *Ancient and Modern Scottish Songs,* vol. 2 (1776). In the ballad the young sailor Jamie returns only four weeks after Jennie has married Robin Gray, and she has to endure her lot as best she can:

> I gang like a ghaist, and I carena much to spin;
> I darena think o' Jamie, for that wad be a sin.
> But I will do my best a gude wife aye to be,
> For auld Robin Gray, oh! he is sae kind to me.

Crabbe's Rachel continues to live in solitude for some years before her sweetheart's return upsets the balance of her mind.

    13. See Broadley and Jerrold, *Romance of an Elderly Poet,* 131.

    14. In *Notes and Queries,* 7th ser., vol. 6 (29 December 1888): 506.

    15. Edited by A. Hayward, pp. 43–54. The "Lady of Quality" was Frances Williams

Wynn, who kept a journal from 1797 to 1844, in ten ms. volumes. A. Hayward made a one-volume selection published in 1864. The first of the two versions of the Tyrone ghost story printed by Hayward (the one that has close parallels to "Lady Barbara") is described in the text as "Copy of a copy taken in 1801," so the story must clearly have been in circulation in this form at the time when Crabbe was writing *Tales of the Hall*.

In Wynn's version Lord Tyrone and Lady Beresford were "educated under the same roof, and in the same principles of Deism." After their guardian's death their friends tried to persuade them to "embrace the revealed religion" but succeeded only in unsettling their beliefs. "In this perplexing state of doubt" they made a vow to each other "that whichever died first should (if permitted) appear to the other and declare what religion was most acceptable to the Almighty." After her marriage Lady Beresford woke one night to find sitting by her bedside the ghost of Lord Tyrone, who declared: "I died last Tuesday, at four o'clock, and have been permitted by the Supreme Being to appear to you to assure you that you can be saved." The ghost predicted also that her husband would shortly die and that she would be married again to a man who would make her miserable; when asked whether she could not prevent this, the ghost's answer was: "Undoubtedly you may, you are a free agent, and may prevent this by resisting every temptation of a second marriage." At Lady Beresford's insistence the ghost gave proof of his supernatural status by touching her wrist with a hand that was "cold as marble." When she woke the next morning the discovered a blemish, which she concealed by covering her wrist with some black ribbon. A few years later her husband died and she "shut herself very much up" and "visited no family but that of the clergyman of the village." The son of the family had been, at the time of her first husband's death, "quite a boy"; however, she was in a few years married to him, and he proved a profligate husband who "behaved to her in a most scandalous manner." (This summary omits some further implausible and sensational details that Crabbe did not make use of in his tale.)

It is possible that Crabbe was the more inclined to use this rather lurid story because one element stressed in it was already familiar to him from Mrs. Elizabeth Rowe's *Letters from the Dead to the Living* (1728), a book that had been reprinted more than a dozen times by 1816 and a copy of which we know to have formed part of the poet's library. The twenty letters in prose that make up the volume are written by different imaginary characters after death to their surviving relatives or friends with the general purpose of impressing on them "the notion of the soul's immortality." The first letter in particular is written to the Earl of R— by Clerimont, who had promised to appear to him after death "to give evidence of a future state" but had been forbidden to make himself visible. Subsequent letters contain various warnings from the other world, including one (letter 9) against a passion that is unknowingly incestuous.

16. *Dublin Review* 229 (1955): 47.

17. Abrams, *Natural Supernaturalism*, 334.

18. Cf. Hazlitt's comment on Wordsworth's *Excursion:* "It is as if there were nothing but himself and the universe." Hazlitt, review of *The Excursion*, in P. P. Howe, ed., *Complete Works of Hazlitt*, 4:113.

19. An interesting late example of Crabbe's intransigence in regard to mundane detail occurs in book 7 of *Tales of the Hall*, where the visit leading to the elder brother's chance encounter, after many years of fruitless searching, with the object of his youthful passion is introduced as follows:

> Something one day occurr'd about a bill
> That was not drawn with true mercantile skill,

And I was ask'd and authorised to go
To seek the firm of Clutterbuck and Co.

(470–73)

Despite the scorn that these lines have sometimes evoked it can be argued that there is in the narrative context a legitimate justification for their banality; they are certainly not an inadvertent lapse.

20. Cf. Broman, "Factors in Crabbe's Eminence," 49: "Pertinent to the concerns of the first two decades of the nineteenth century with the passions was an intense curiosity about insanity. This curiosity was reflected in the large number of published treatises on alienation, causes of mental aberration, and the problems of caring for the insane. This interest was also reflected in poetry, where madness was regarded as an excellent means of gaining effects of terror and force. Here, too, Crabbe was a child of his times."

Chapter 9. Crabbe and Genre

1. See Brooke-Rose, "Historical Genres," 144–58; in the same number Todorov, "Origin of Genres," 159-70; and McKeon, *Origins of the English Novel*, introduction.

2. Burke is reported to have estimated that around 1790 the English reading public numbered some eighty thousand persons, though the thirty thousand copies of his *Reflections* sold in that year at 3 shillings, and the very much larger sales (around two hundred thousand) claimed a few years later for the cheap sixpenny edition of Tom Paine's *Rights of Man* suggest that this may have been an underestimate. In 1801 the first census revealed a total population in England of around 9 million (as contrasted with an estimate of 5.5 million in 1700), and this was to grow to 10.5 million by 1811. From 1785 on, this population growth was accompanied by a marked increase in the number of Sunday schools, with some corresponding increase in the already quite high level of literacy (though of course it should be remembered that, as in all ages, not all those who could read actually did so to any significant extent). See Altick, *English Common Reader*, chapters 2 and 3; and Schofield, quoted in Laslett, *World We Have Lost*, 232.

3. Some confirmation of this generic link can be noticed in the extent to which, from *The Parish Register* onwards, Crabbe gave almost all his characters both a Christian name and a surname, and chose them in each case from ones that were currently in use locally. In this he was following the practice of the eighteenth-century novelists who, after Defoe, had come increasingly to name their characters "in such a way as to suggest that they were to be regarded as particular individuals in the contemporary environment." See Watt, *Rise of the Novel*, 18–21; and Fowler, *Kinds of Literature*, 82–87.

4. Kroeber, *Romantic Narrative Art*, 3.

5. Sigworth took over this idea from J. W. Draper, who had claimed that, contrary to the generally held view that "satire and didacticism . . . extinguished the versified tale . . . a closer examination, especially of minor writers, showed that the eighteenth century had an unbroken tradition of such writings." But apart from naming a number of forgotten authors and poems, and classifying some of them into a few types described as "generally Neoclassical in tone," Draper provided little substantiation for his thesis, and a careful checking of the material in question will show that his generalizations were at once too dogmatic and too schematized. See Draper, "Metrical Tale," 147–82.

6. Elton, *Survey of English Literature*, 54.

7. Kroeber, *Romantic Narrative Art*, 118.

8. Paulson, *Hogarth's Graphic Works*, 1:169.

9. Elton, *Survey of English Literature*, 54.

10. See, for instance, the following, from the unsigned review in *Critical Review*, July 1810; "The character of Blaney, the old man with young vices, and the corrupt and frivolous Clelia, deserve to be repeatedly read for their great moral utility. The author has thought proper to apologise in his Preface for the portrait of Benbow: this was perfectly unnecessary, since it is perhaps the most useful character in the book." (Quoted in Pollard, *Crabbe*, 109.)

11. See for instance Kelly, *English Fiction of the Romantic Period*.

Chapter 10. Crabbe, "Realism," and Poetic Truth

1. Barthes, "L'effet du réel," 181–92.

2. See John Ruskin, *Modern Painters* (London, 1856).

3. See Stephen, *Hours in a Library*, vol. 2.

4. Edwards, "Crabbe's So-called Realism," 303–20; Hazlitt (1821) quoted in Pollard, *Crabbe*, 299; Wordsworth (1808), quoted in Pollard, *Crabbe*, 290.

5. For some of these sources, see Thomas, "Crabbe's *Borough*," 181–92.

6. Edwards, "Crabbe's So-called Realism," 305; Christopher Hill, *God's Englishman*, 271–72.

7. Letter to Mrs. Leadbeater, 1 December 1816, reproduced in Crabbe, *Life*, 119–22.

8. Letter from James Lecky to Mrs. Leadbeater, dated 21 November 1820, reporting a conversation he had had with Crabbe in October 1820 (quoted in Bareham, *George Crabbe*, 16).

9. McKeon, *Origins of the English Novel*, 2.

10. Watt, *Rise of the Novel*, 33.

11. McKeon, *Origins of the English Novel*, 2-4.

12. Thomas, "Crabbe's *Borough: The Process of Montage*."

13. It should perhaps be noted that the "inclosing" referred to in the Squire Asgill section of letter 16 of *The Borough* was not an enclosure of common land but consisted of planting clumps of trees round the perimeter of the estate. The relevant lines read:

> He never planted nor inclos'd—his Trees
> Grew like himself, untroubl'd and at ease:
> Bounds of all kinds he hated, and had felt
> Chok'd and imprison'd in a modern Belt,
> Which some rare Genius now has twin'd about
> The good old House, to keep old Neighbours out. . . .
> —*The Borough*, letter 16, 80–85

14. There was, for instance, an enclosure at Stathern in 1792 three years after Crabbe had ceased acting as curate there. More significantly, at West Allington, the small parish that he held jointly with Muston, there was an enclosure in 1793, the year after Crabbe had removed to Suffolk, leaving a curate in charge of his Leicestershire parishes; by 1813 this had the result of producing for him a considerable increase in the value of the West Allington living.

15. Laslett, *World We Have Lost*, 159.

16. Ibid., 178.

17. Snell, *Annals of the Labouring Poor*, 345.

18. See in particular Laslett, "The Wrong Way," 319–42.

19. Ibid., 321.

20. Jakobson, "On Realism in Art,".38–46.
21. Wimsatt and Brooks, *Literary Criticism*.
22. S. Richardson, postscript to *Clarissa*, Everyman edition (London: Dent, 1932): 4:562 and 564.

Chapter 11. Crabbe and Indeterminacy

1. Derrida, *Of Grammatology*, 158.
2. For further discussion, see Whitehead, "Boggling the Mind," 1–12; and Abrams, *Doing Things with Texts*, 297–332.
3. Derrida, *Of Grammatology*, 246.
4. Abrams, *Doing Things with Texts*, 314.
5. Miller, "Ethics of Reading," 19–41.
6. K. D. M. Snell reports the mean age at first marriage in the period 1800–1849 as 23.4 for women and 25.3 for men; he also estimates the average sum saved in the late eighteenth century between the two married as "probably about £50–60." Snell, *Annals of the Labouring Poor,* 345 and 348.
7. Though Anne K. Mellor has argued strongly for its presence in Byron and Keats, in her *English Romantic Irony* (1980).

Chapter 12. Crabbe and Ideology

1. Sales, *English Literature in History.*
2. See Meepham, "Theory of Ideology." Also relevant is the discussion in Lovell, *Pictures of Reality*, esp. chap. 3. For a useful recent discussion of differing conceptions of ideology, see Freadman and Miller, *Re-thinking Theory,* chap. 4.
3. Supporters of the New Historicism would perhaps see this omission as indicating the presence in the background of what Marjorie Levinson calls "repressed material"—another instance of the way in which "a poem will either center or marginalise what it represents, and certain matters salient to the work will be left out of its accounting altogether" (McGann, *Social Values and Poetic Acts,* 55). On this hypothesis Crabbe could be convicted of dismissing from consciousness an uncomfortable and distressing social problem. However, the omission can more appropriately be seen by the historically minded reader as yet a further manifestation of Crabbe's tendency to evoke in his portrayals the countryside of some decades earlier than the time of writing—in this case the decades prior to the agricultural employment crisis of the 1790s. Another minor example of this tendency can be noted in the matter of the "badgeman's blue" worn by Rupert in "Procrastination," tale 4 of *Tales* (1812). An act of 1697 had made compulsory for paupers the wearing of a badge bearing the letter *P* and the initials of their parish, and in Crabbe's native Aldeburgh an entry in the churchwarden's account book shows that in 1773 it was decided to enforce this requirement there. (See Thomas, "Crabbe's View of the Poor," 453–85.) It is not known how long the requirement was maintained by Aldeburgh, but in general, according to Oxley, the badges fell into disuse and had largely disappeared by the time the legislation was repealed in 1810. (See Oxley, *Poor Relief,* chap. 3.)
4. See Thomas, "Crabbe's View of the Poor," 460–63.
5. Even the "harmless idiot" with his hoard of "Silver Shells" (letter 18, lines 40–41) is clearly felt to be better off lodged with the former mistress of the Dame school than he would be in an institution.
6. See *The Parish Register*, pt. 1, lines 49–50; *The Borough*, letter 19, lines 229–31.

7. The poem reads,

> He poached the Wood and on the Warren snar'd;
> 'Twas his, at cards, each Novice to trepan,
> And call the Wants of Rogues the Rights of Man;

(lines 813–15)

8. The relevant paragraphs from the *Tatler* read as follows:

I remember a young gentleman of moderate understanding, but great vivacity, who by dipping into many authors of this nature [i.e., "modish French authors"] had got a little smattering of knowledge, just enough to make an atheist or freethinker, but not a philosopher or a man of sense. With these accomplishments, he went to visit his father in the country, who was a plain, rough, honest man, and wise though not learned. The son, who took all opportunities to show his learning, began to establish a new religion in the family, and to enlarge the narrowness of their country notions so well, that he had reduced the butler by his table-talk, and staggered his elder sister. The old gentleman began to be alarmed at the schisms that arose among his children, but did not yet believe his son's doctrine to be so pernicious as it really was, till one day talking of his setting-dog, the son said, he did not question but that Tray was as immortal as anyone of the family; and in the heat of the argument told h is father that for his own part he expected to die like a dog. Upon which the old man, starting up in a very great passion, cried out, "Then, sirrah, you shall live like one"; and taking his cane in his hand, cudgelled him out of his system. This had so good an effect upon him, that he took up from that day, fell to reading good books, and is now a Bencher of the Middle Temple.

I do not mention this cudgelling part of the story with a design to engage the secular arm in matters of this nature; but certainly, if it ever exerts itself in affairs of opinion and speculation, it ought to do it on such shallow and despicable pretenders to knowledge, who endeavour to give man dark and uncomfortable prospects of his being, and destroy those principles which are the support, happiness, and glory of all public societies as well as private persons.

9. McGann, *Beauty of Inflections*, 302.

Chapter 13. Biographical Speculations

1. See Watt, "Ironic Voice," 101.
2. *Life*, chap. 7, 155–56.
3. See Southey, *Selections from the Letters*, 2:90–91.
4. Crabbe, *Selected Letters and Journals*, 117–18.
5. A reference to Andrew Baxter (1686–1750), who had suggested in his *Enquiry into the Nature of the Human Soul* (1733) that dreams are caused by the action of spiritual beings. The allusion is taken up again in the phrase "Baxter's sprites" in the second stanza of the poem "The World of Dreams."
6. Abrams, *Milk of Paradise*, and Hayter, *Opium*.
7. Freud, *Collected Papers*, 4:174.

Afterword

1. Austen-Leigh, *Memoir of Jane Austen*, 89; Austen, *Letters*, 2:82.
2. Pollard, *Crabbe*, 15.
3. Gregor, "Last Augustan," 37–50.
4. See Speirs, *Poetry Towards Novel*, esp. 199.

Select Bibliography

Abrams, M. H. *Doing Things with Texts.* New York: W. W. Norton, 1989.

———. *The Milk of Paradise.* Cambridge, Mass: Harvard University Press, 1934.

———. *The Mirror and the Lamp.* Oxford: Oxford University Press, 1953.

———. *Natural Supernaturalism: Tradition and Revelation in Romantic Literature.* New York: W. W. Norton, 1971.

Ainger, A. *Crabbe.* London: Macmillan, 1903.

Altick, R. D. *The English Common Reader: A Social History of the Mass Reading Public, 1800–1900.* Chicago: University of Chicago Press, 1957.

Austen, Jane. *Letters.* Vol. 2. Edited by R. W. Chapman. London: Oxford University Press, 1932.

Austen-Leigh, J. E. *Memoir of Jane Austen.* Oxford: Clarendon Press, 1926.

Bareham, T. *George Crabbe.* London: Vision Press, 1977.

Bareham, T., and S. A. Gattrell. *A Bibliography of George Crabbe.* New Haven: Yale University Press, 1978.

Barthes, Roland. "L'effet du réel" (1968). Translated as "The Reality Effect." In *French Literary Theory Today,* edited by T. Todorov. Cambridge: Cambridge University Press, 1982.

Belanger, T. "Publishers and Writers in Eighteenth-Century England." In *Books and Their Readers in Eighteenth-Century England,* edited by I. Rivers. Leicester: Leicester University Press, 1982.

Broadley, A. M., and W. Jerrold. *The Romance of an Elderly Poet: A Hitherto Unknown Chapter in the Life of George Crabbe.* London: Paul, 1913.

Broman, Walter E. "Factors in Crabbe's Eminence in the Early Nineteenth Century." *Modern Philosophy* 51 (1953): 42–49.

Brooke-Rose, C. "Historical Genres/Theoretical Genres." *NLH* 8 (1976): 144–58.

Butler, Marilyn. *Jane Austen and the War of Ideas.* Oxford: Clarendon Press, 1975.

———. *Romantics, Rebels, and Reactionaries.* Oxford: Oxford University Press, 1981.

Chamberlain, Robert L. *George Crabbe.* New York: Twayne, 1965.

Chatman, S. *Story and Discourse: Narrative Structures in Fiction and Film.* Ithaca: Cornell University Press, 1978.

Crabbe, George. *Complete Poetical Works.* 3 vols. Edited by N. Dalrymple-Champneys and A. Pollard. Oxford: Clarendon Press, 1988.

—. *Selected Letters and Journals.* Edited by Thomas C. Faulkner. Oxford: Clarendon Press 1985.

—. *Poetical Works.* 8 vols. London: Murray, 1834.

—. *The Village.* Edited by Arthur Sales. London: University Tutorial Press, 1950.

Crabbe, George [Crabbe's son]. *The Life of the Rev. George Crabbe, LL.B., by his son the Rev. George Crabbe, A.M.* London: Murray, 1834.

Derrida, Jacques. *Of Grammatology.* Translated by G. Spivak. Baltimore: Johns Hopkins University Press, 1976.

Draper, J. W. "The Metrical Tale in Eighteenth-Century England." *PMLA* 52 (1937): 147–82.

Edwards, Gavin. "Crabbe's So-called Realism." *Essays in Criticism* 37, no. 4 (October 1987): 303–20.

Elton, O. *A Survey of English Literature, 1760–1832.* London: E. Arnold, 1912.

Erskine-Hill, H. *The Augustan Idea in English Literature.* London: E. Arnold, 1983.

—. "Augustans on Augustanism: England, 1655–1759." *Renaissance and Modern Studies* 2 (1967): 55–83.

—. *The Social Milieu of Alexander Pope.* New Haven: Yale University Press, 1975.

Forster, E. M. *Aspects of the Novel.* London: E. Arnold, 1927.

—. *Two Cheers for Democracy.* London: E. Arnold, 1951.

Fowler, A. *Kinds of Literature.* Cambridge: Harvard University Press, 1982.

Freadman, R., and S. Miller. *Re-thinking Theory: A Critique of Contemporary Literary Theory and an Alternative Account.* Cambridge: Cambridge University Press, 1992.

Freud, Sigmund. *Collected Papers.* Vol. 4. London: Hogarth Press, 1949.

Frye, Northrop. "Varieties of Sensibility." *Eighteen Century Studies* 24, no. 2 (1991): 157–72.

Gregor, Ian. "The Last Augustan." *The Dublin Review* 229 (1955): 37–50.

Haddakin, Lilian. *The Poetry of George Crabbe.* London: Chatto and Windus, 1955.

Hayter, Alethea. *Opium and the Romantic Imagination.* London: Faber, 1968.

Hazlitt, W. *Complete Works.* Edited by P. P. Howe. London: Dent, 1930–34.

Hill, Christopher. *God's Englishman.* London: Weidenfeld and Nicolson, 1970.

Huchon, René. *George Crabbe and His Times, 1754–1832: A Critical and Biographical Study.* Translated from the French by Frederick Clarke. London: Murray, 1907.

Hunter, R., and I. Macalpine, eds. *Three Hundred Years of Psychiatry, 1535–1860: A History Presented in Selected Texts.* London: Oxford University Press, 1963.

Jacobus, M. *Traditional and Experiment in Wordsworth's "Lyrical Ballads" (1798).* Oxford: Clarnedon Press, 1976.

Jaeger, M. *Before Victoria: Changing Standards of Behavior, 1787–1837.* London: Chatto and Windus, 1956.

Jacobson, Roman. "On Realism in Art." In *Readings in Russian Poetics,* edited by L. Matejka and K. Pomorska, 38–46. Cambridge, Mass.: M.I.T. Press, 1971.

Johnson, J. W. "The Meaning of 'Augustan'." *JHI* 19 (1958): 507–22.

Jones, Kathleen. *Law, Lunacy and Conscience, 1744–1845.* London: Routledge & Paul, 1955.

Kelly, Gary. *English Fiction and the Romantic Period, 1789–1830.* London: Longman, 1989.

Kroeber, Karl. *Romantic Narrative Art.* Madison: University of Wisconsin Press, 1960.

Laslett, P. *The World We Have Lost Further Explored*. London: Methuen, 1983.

―――. "The Wrong Way through the Telescope: A Note on Literary Evidence in Sociology and in Historical Sociology." *British Journal of Sociology* 27, no. 3 (September 1976): 319–42.

Leavis, F. R. *Revaluation*. London: Chatto & Windus, 1936.

Lovell, T. *Pictures of Reality: Aesthetics, Politics and Pleasure*. London: BFI (British Film Institute), 1963.

Mayo, R. "The Contemporaneity of the *Lyrical Ballads*." *PMLA* 69 (1964).

McGann, Jerome J. *The Beauty of Inflections*. Oxford: Clarendon Press, 1985.

―――. *The Romantic Ideology*. Chicago: University of Chicago Press, 1983.

―――. *Social Values and Poetic Acts: The Historical Judgment of Literary Works*. Cambridge: Harvard University Press, 1988.

McKeon, M. *The Origins of the English Novel, 1600–1740*. Baltimore: Johns Hopkins University Press, 1987.

Meehan, Michael. *Liberty and Poetics in Eighteenth-Century England*. Baltimore: Johns Hopkins University Press, 1986.

Meepham, J. "The Theory of Ideology in *Capital*." In *Issues in Marxist Philosophy*, vol. 3, edited by J. Meepham and D. H. Rabin. Hassocks: Harvester Press, 1979.

Mellor, Anne K. *English Romantic Irony*. Cambridge: Harvard University Press, 1980.

Miller, J. Hillis. "The Ethics of Reading." In *American Criticism in the Post-Structuralist Age*, edited by I. Konigsberg. Ann Arbor: University of Michigan Press, 1981.

Muir, Edwin. *The Structure of the Novel*. London: Hogarth Press, 1928.

New, Peter. *George Crabbe's Poetry*. London: Macmillan, 1976.

Oxley, G. W. *Poor Relief in England and Wales, 1601–1841*. Newton Abbot: David & Charles, 1974.

Paulson, R. *Hogarth's Graphic Works*. 2 vols. New Haven: Yale University Press, 1965.

Piper, H. W. *The Active Universe*. London: Athlone Press, 1962.

Pollard A. *Crabbe: The Critical Heritage*. London: Routledge & Kegan Paul, 1972.

Porter, Roy. *Mind-forg'd Manacles*. London: Athlone Press, 1987.

Rogers, Pat. *The Augustan Vision*. London: Weidenfeld & Nicolson, 1974.

Sales, Roger. *English Literature in History, 1780–1830: Pastoral and Politics*. London: Hutchinson, 1983.

Scott, Sir Walter. *Letters*. Edited by H. J. C. Grierson. London: Constable, 1937.

Sigworth, O. *Nature's Sternest Painter*. Tucson: University of Arizona Press, 1965.

Snell, K. D. M. *Annals of the Labouring Poor: Social Change and Agricultural England, 1660–1900*. Cambridge: Cambridge University Press, 1985.

Southey, Robert. *Selections from the Letters of Robert Southey*. Edited by J. W. Warter. London: Longman, 1856.

Speirs, John. "Crabbe as Master of the Verse Tale." *Oxford Review* 2 (1966).

―――. *Poetry Towards Novel*. London: Faber, 1971.

Stauffer, D. A. *The Art of Biography in Eighteenth-Century England*. Princeton: Princeton University Press, 1941.

Stephen, Leslie. *Hours in a Library.* 2 vols. London: Smith, Elder, 1876.

Taylor, Houghton W. "'Particular Character': An Early Phase of a Literary Revolution." *PMLA* 60 (1945): 161–74.

Thomas, W. K. "Crabbe's *Borough:* The Process of Montage." *University of Toronto Quarterly* 36, no. 2 (January 1967): 181–92.

———. "Crabbe's View of the Poor." *Revue de L'Université d'Ottawa* 36 (1966).

———. "George Crabbe: Not Quite the Sternest." *Studies in Romanticism* 7 (1966).

Todorov, T. "The Origin of Genres." *NLH* 8 (1976): 159–70.

Watt, Ian. "The Ironic Voice." In *The Augustan Age: Approaches to its Literature, Life and Thought,* edited by Ian Watt. Greenwich, Conn.: Fawcett Publications, 1968.

———. *The Rise of the Novel.* Berkeley: University of California Press, 1957.

———. "Two Historical Aspects of the Augustan Tradition." In *Studies in the Eighteenth Century,* edited by R. F. Brissenden, 67–88. Toronto: University of Toronto Press, 1968.

Weinbrot, Howard. *Augustus Caesar in "Augustan" England.* Princeton: Princeton University Press, 1979.

Whitehead, F. "Boggling the Mind: George Crabbe and Indeterminacy." *Cambridge Quarterly* 19 (1990): 1–12.

———. "George Crabbe's Verse-Tales." In *The New Pelican Guide to English Literature,* vol. 5: *From Blake to Byron,* edited by B. Ford. London: Penguin Books, 1982.

Wiles, R. M. "Middle-Class Literacy in Eighteenth-Century England: Fresh Evidence." In *Studies in the Eighteenth Century,* edited by R. F. Brissenden. Toronto: University of Toronto Press, 1968.

Wimsatt, W. K., and Cleanth Brooks. *Literary Criticism.* New York: Knopf, 1957.

Wordsworth, William. *Poetical Works of William Wordsworth.* Edited by E. de Selincourt and H. Darbishire, fragment 4, v. 343. Oxford: Clarendon Press, 1940–49.

———. *Wordsworth's Literary Criticism.* Edited by Nowell C. Smith and H. Mills. Bristol: Bristol Classical Press, 1980.

Index